Global Antitrust Economics
Current Issues in Antitrust and Law & Economics

Editors
Douglas H. Ginsburg
Joshua D. Wright

Assistant Editors
Nicolas Charbit
Elisa Ramundo
Duy D. Pham

60 Broad Street, Suite 3502, NY 10004
www.concurrences.com
contact@concurrences.com

Printed in the United States of America
First Printing, 2016

ISBN 978-1-939007-48-3

Publisher's Cataloging-in-Publication
(Provided by Quality Books, Inc.)

Global Antitrust Economics Conference

(2015 : Arlington, Va.)
Global antitrust economics : current issues in antitrust and law & economics / editors: Douglas H. Ginsburg, Joshua D. Wright ; associate editors: Nicolas Charbit, Elisa Ramundo, Duy D. Pham.
pages cm
Includes bibliographical references.
LCCN 2016932014
ISBN 978-1-939007-48-3 (hardcover)
ISBN 978-1-939007-49-0 (e-book)

1. Antitrust law (International law)--Congresses. 2. Antitrust law—Economic aspects--Congresses. 3. Conference papers and proceedings. I. Ginsburg, Douglas H., 1946- editor. II. Wright, Joshua D., editor. III. George Mason University. School of Law. Law and Economics Center, sponsoring body. IV. Institute of Competition Law (New York, N.Y.), sponsoring body. V. Title.

K3850.A6G56 2015 *343.07'21*

QBI16-257

Cover and book design: Yves Buliard, www.yvesbuliard.fr
Layout implementation: Darlene Swanson, www.van-garde.com

Concurrences Books

ANTITRUST IN EMERGING AND DEVELOPING COUNTRIES
Eleanor Fox - Harry First • 2016

CONSUMER CHOICE: THE EMERGENCE OF
A POWERFUL CONCEPT IN COMPETITION LAW
Paul Nihoul • 2016

COMPETITION CASE LAW DIGEST:
A SYNTHESIS OF EU AND NATIONAL LEADING CASES
Nicolas Charbit - Elisa Ramundo • December 2015

ANTITRUST IN EMERGING AND DEVELOPING COUNTRIES
Eleanor Fox - Harry First • October 2015

IAN S. FORRESTER QC LL.D. A SCOT WITHOUT BORDERS
LIBER AMICORUM — VOLUME II
Sir. David Edward, Jacquelyn MacLennon, Assimakis Komninos • December 2015

IAN S. FORRESTER QC LL.D. A SCOT WITHOUT BORDERS
LIBER AMICORUM — VOLUME I
Sir. David Edward, Jacquelyn MacLennon, Assimakis Komninos • September 2015

WILLIAM E. KOVACIC: AN ANTITRUST TRIBUTE
LIBER AMICORUM —VOLUME II
Nicolas Charbit - Elisa Ramundo • September 2014

WILLIAM E. KOVACIC: AN ANTITRUST TRIBUTE
LIBER AMICORUM —VOLUME I
Nicolas Charbit - Elisa Ramundo • January 2013

All books are published in print and electronic format.

Editors' Note

Douglas H. Ginsburg
Joshua D. Wright
Nicolas Charbit
Elisa Ramundo
Duy D. Pham

Concurrences Review in partnership with George Mason University School of Law, Law and Economics Center held The Global Antitrust Economics Conference in Arlington, Virginia on May 29, 2015. The conference featured keynote speech from Maureen Ohlhausen, Commissioner of the US Federal Trade Commission and five panels of prominent speakers that engaged in a heated debate about the different aspects of Antitrust Law and Economics.

Antitrust law has become increasingly important in recent years, especially as the number of antitrust related disputes increases. It becomes crucial to analyze how courts and agencies currently deal with these cases; how they assess the concepts of market definition and market power; how they evaluate coordination issues, such as information exchange and price signaling, and what conduct can be considered as violations of antitrust laws; how they determine remedies and settlements; and how they establish who should be punished in cases of antitrust violation (the violating firm, its agents or both). The Global Antitrust Economics Conference brought together lawyers, enforcers, economists, and academics to animate the discussion on those topics.

In this book, 13 prominent authors offer 11 contributions that tackle some of the most stimulating topics debated during this one-day event in Global Antitrust Economics. Thus, **Pierre-Yves Cremieux** and **Aaron Yeater**, while they underline that convergence in antitrust economics is recent and remarkable, they also point out the still existing conflicts in economic evidence presented by competition experts; **John Harkrider** explains his point of view according to which the US Federal Trade Commission and Department of Justice are both law enforcers and regulators, enforcing laws that are regulatory in nature, relying more on economists than eyewitnesses, reacting more to what may happen, than what has already occurred; **Keith Hylton** discusses why monetary fines, to be a more effective deterrent threat, should focus on the firm rather than on its agents; **Francine Lafontaine** offers an analysis of the use of economics in support of the competition mission at the US Federal Trade Commission; **Carlos Mena-Labarthe** discusses the Mexican experience to show how remedies and their negotiation are valuable tools for emerging competition authorities; **Maureen Ohlhausen** tackles the "Brother, May I?" problem or the challenge of competitor control over market entry; **William Page** tries to identify those signals that solicit cooperation to achieve noncompetitive equilibria, thus bringing about agreements under Section 1 of the Sherman Act; **Dan Rubinfeld** explains why, in his point of view, our current systems of private and public enforcement can be improved if more attention is given toward increasing individual incentives; **Loren Smith** and **Maria Stoyadinova** highlight the prominence of market definition in antitrust evaluation and litigation; **Gregory Werden** addresses the concept of the relevant market by highlighting that it is a device for separating active competitive forces that directly and immediately affect economic performance (e.g., prices) from forces that are passive or have indirect, delayed, or highly uncertain effects on economic performance; finally, **Lawrence White** shows why the US Merger Guidelines and its guidance on market definition continue to provide a robust and powerful analytical framework for defining markets for the purpose of merger analysis.

This volume guides readers through some of the most important and cutting-edge issues in global antitrust economics.

The editors would like to give their sincere thanks to the 13 authors for their hours of labor dedicated to this unique collection of articles.

Foreword

Douglas H. Ginsburg
Joshua D. Wright

During the Global Antitrust Economics conference that took place last May, we heard from panels on a variety of topics, including the use of economic evidence in antitrust cases, the role of market definition in modern antitrust analysis, the mechanisms through which competitors coordinate with each other, the process of negotiating settlements and remedies, and the relative merits of punishing corporations and individuals. Many panelists submitted papers for inclusion in this volume; in this Foreword we briefly describe each of their contributions.

Commissioner Maureen Ohlhausen of the US Federal Trade Commission led off the event with a trenchant analysis of the challenge to competition when incumbent firms have control over market entry. Like restrictions that require innovators to obtain permission from government gatekeepers before entering a market – which she likened to the childrens' game "Mother, May I?" – competitor-imposed restrictions upon entry may also undermine free-market principles and economic liberty, and may do so to an even greater extent. This particular problem, which Ohlhausen aptly coins the "Brother, May I?" problem, may manifest itself as a law or regulation, a decision of a financially-interested state board, or exclusionary conduct by a monopolist. The paper examines the problem through the lens of three recent cases: North Carolina State Board of Dental Examiners v. Federal Trade Commission (state licensing boards), Federal Trade Commission v. Phoebe Putney Health Systems, Inc. (certificate-of-need laws), and McWane, Inc. v. Federal Trade Commission (exclusionary conduct). In addition to its sound analysis, the paper contributes to antitrust scholarship a simple expression to describe a widespread problem that may take varied forms. We predict the term "Brother, May I?" will, in short order, be ubiquitous in the vernacular of the antitrust bar.

Pierre-Yves Cremieux of the Analysis Group in Boston proceeded from the observation that, though economists rarely disagree regarding fundamental principles, such as gains from trade or the importance of incentives, highly qualified economists appear on opposite sides of litigation in virtually every case. Use and Abuse: The Myth of Divided Antitrust Economics, which Cremieux co-authored with his colleague Aaron Yeater, posits that the reason for such divergent conclusions is not attributable to theoretical or methodological disagreement and only rarely is attributable to unprofessional arguments; rather, economists reasonably may make different underlying assumptions about the characteristics of the market in question. As an example, the authors explain that in the highly publicized LCD price-fixing case, one economist found a 20% overcharge while the other found none. The authors explain that this wide variation in overcharge estimates is attributable to the economists' disagreement over whether the Producer Price Index for microprocessors was an appropriate proxy for costs.

John Harkrider, a partner at Axinn, Veltrop & Harkrider in New York City, writes that the U.S. Department of Justice and Federal Trade Commission straddle a fine line between law enforcement and regulation. Harkrider defines the regulatory role as one that aims to address firms' future conduct, seeks remedies that require affirmative conduct, and involves interpretation of the agency's own rules, while a law enforcement role usually addresses conduct that has already occurred, seeks only cessation of the challenged conduct, and is governed by court decisions. Although the agencies insist that they are engaged in law enforcement simpliciter and forswear the title of regulator, Harkrider argues that many of their activities indeed seem to fit the regulatory role. For example, with respect to mergers, the agencies require pre-notification, assess future effects, often require affirmative commitments such as guarantees of nondiscriminatory access to facilities, and are governed not only by court decisions but by the Merger Guidelines, which the agencies wrote themselves. Because of their twin roles, Harkrider argues, the agencies must exercise their power carefully and transparently, and should solicit input from market participants regarding their rules and practices.

Francine Lafontaine, a professor at the University of Michigan and, at the time of the conference, Director of the Bureau of Economics at the Federal Trade Commission, offers heretofore unavailable insights into the Bureau's role in the agency. Lafontaine describes, for example, its participation in investigations and policy formation and its more general research and outreach objectives. The Bureau's economic analyses – both theoretical and empirical – allow the Bureau of Competition to make better informed enforcement decisions. Meanwhile, its outreach efforts take the form not only of public comments but also of informal discussions with lawmakers, participation in workshops, and contributions to US submissions to the OECD. The economists cannot do it alone, however; the economic analysis is "greatly enriched by the interaction and cooperation between the FTC's economists and attorneys during the course of the investigations, as they work together to gather relevant information, meet with parties, carry out investigational hearings, and so on."

A trio of submissions address the persistent role of market definition in antitrust litigation and agency analyses despite recent calls to reduce its influence. Greg Werden, Senior Economic Counsel at the Antitrust Division and a prolific author on antitrust economics, maintains in The Relevant Market Concept in Antitrust Law that, despite the advent of powerful economic tools that permit economists to examine competitive effects directly, the concept of the relevant market "is not the relic of a bygone era;" it properly remains the foundation for all modern competition analysis in antitrust cases. In support of his claim, Werden discusses the role of the relevant market in coordinated effects merger cases, in unilateral effects merger cases, and in Sherman Act conduct cases.

Lawrence White, a professor of economics at the Stern School of Business, New York University, likewise discusses the importance of defining a market. White explains that the first step in merger analysis should be to establish the boundaries of a market, and then to determine whether the proposed merger might allow the merging firms to exercise market power, as measured by the hypothetical monopolist or "SSNIP" test. White argues, however, that the SSNIP test is less useful when applied to unilateral effects cases and to monopolization cases.

Loren Smith, Senior Vice President of Compass Lexecon and former Federal Trade Commission staff economist, explores the difference between agency analysis and evaluation of mergers and analysis prepared for trial. Smith argues that agencies and practitioners place more emphasis on competitive effects until they prepare for trial, when the focus turns to market definition and other forms of evidence. In The Prominence of Market Definition in Antitrust Evaluation and Litigation, Mr. Smith describes the steps agencies take to analyze mergers, steps that often allow agency economists to avoid market definition altogether, as well as the shift in analytical focus when preparing to persuade a judge that the merger will substantially lessen competition.

The contributions by Professor Keith Hylton of the Boston University School of Law, Should Antitrust Fines Target Firms of Agents?, and by Professor Daniel Rubinfeld, of the New York University School of Law, Improving Antitrust Sanctions, deal with the issue of optimal deterrence of cartel behavior. In particular, they focus on the structure of antitrust sanctions most likely to deter cartels efficiently. A critical question for antitrust policy is whether sanctions for cartel behavior should be borne both by the individuals perpetrating the illegal conduct as well as by their corporate employers and if so, how exactly individuals should be sanctioned. In Antitrust Sanctions, a previously published article by the authors of this Foreword, we argued that the optimal mix of antitrust sanctions requires a significant shift in focus toward individuals, that ever-increasing corporate fines are unlikely to increase deterrence, and that competition agencies ought to embrace debarment as a useful tool to increase the efficiency of cartel sanctions. Each contribution addresses those proposals in the course of developing new economic arguments aimed at improving the efficiency of antitrust penalties for collusion.

Professor Hylton argues that monetary fines levied against firms are always the most efficient deterrent against price-fixing. Hylton's analysis challenges our call in Antitrust Sanctions for a shift in the allocation of overall "sanction capital" from the corporation to the individual. Hylton argues that if a firm has an incentive to fix prices, and only the firm's agents are punished, then the firm can always reward its agents enough to induce antitrust law violations. The key assumption of Hylton's analysis is that agency costs within the firm are sufficiently low that this form of contracting is efficient. In Hylton's model, because a firm can always contract with its agent to compensate it for the cost of any antitrust sanction imposed on the individual, the individual sanction cannot improve deterrence. Ultimately, he argues, rather than targeting agents, eliminating price-fixing incentives for firms remains the most efficient method for preventing violations of antitrust laws.

Professor Rubinfeld takes the opposite position. He argues that efficient cartel deterrence requires improving the incentives for individuals in the firm to avoid cartel behavior. Exploring different proposals to improve both public and private antitrust sanctions, Rubinfeld argues that the heterogeneity in the sensitivity of different cultures to different forms of sanctions requires competition regimes to think of criminal fines and private actions as playing complementary roles in deterring anticompetitive conduct—with private enforcement emphasizing compensation and public enforcement focused on penalizing anticompetitive behavior. Professor Rubinfeld also offers suggestions for improving both public and private enforcement in antitrust through appropriate and targeted prison sentences along with expanded and increased rewards for whistleblowers.

Enforcement agencies seek to reach effective settlements and implement sound remedies for both merger and non-merger antitrust cases. In Negotiation of Settlements and Remedies by Young Competition Agencies: The Mexican Experience, Carlos Mena-Labarthe, who heads the Investigative Authority in the Federal Economic Competition Commission of Mexico, explores the difficulties young competition agencies face when evaluating the effectiveness of remedies. Labarthe assesses the institutional concerns that young agencies must consider when implementing a settlement policy. Legitimacy, credibility, and deterrence are all factors that must be weighed on account of the agencies' limited experience in relation to other jurisdictions. More specifically, the author addresses the challenges faced by the Mexican authority, such as cultivating a comprehensive discourse for addressing competition concerns and setting consistent standards to generate predictability.

Identifying anticompetitive information exchanges and price signaling is necessary for effective antitrust enforcement. Panelists discussed price and behavior signaling as it relates to coordinated conduct. William Page, a Professor in the Levin College of Law at the University of Florida, provides a legal framework for distinguishing lawful from unlawful information exchanges in his paper, Signaling and Agreement under Section 1 of the Sherman Act. Professor Page concludes that prearranged signals are clearly unlawful. He argues that private exchanges between rivals should be viewed skeptically and that implicit signals and public comments made to the market should generally be lawful. By employing this framework, courts, practitioners, and agencies can navigate the differences between tacit and express collusion.

The Global Antitrust Economics conference provides a forum for antitrust economists, practitioners, regulators, and legal scholars to explore the most critical issues, both substantive and procedural, arising in competition law around the world. The papers submitted by panelists and selected for this volume are representative of the careful and insightful perspectives presented at the conference, the wide range of topics discussed, and the power of economic analysis in providing a common language to facilitate communication about issues facing competition agencies and courts around the world.

Table of Contents

Contributors

Pierre-Yves Cremieux
Analysis Group

John D. Harkrider
Axinn, Veltrop & Harkrider

Keith N. Hylton
Boston University School of Law

Francine Lafontaine
University of Michigan, Ross School of Business
Formerly US Federal Trade Commission

Carlos Mena-Labarthe
Federal Economic Competition Commission of Mexico

Maureen K. Ohlhausen
US Federal Trade Commission

William H. Page
University of Florida, Levin College of Law

Daniel L. Rubinfeld
University of California, Berkeley
New York University School of Law

Loren Smith
Compass Lexecon

Maria Stoyadinova
Compass Lexecon

Gregory J. Werden
US Department of Justice

Lawrence J. White
New York University, Stern School of Business

Aaron C. Yeater
Analysis Group

Use and Abuse: The Myth of Divided Antitrust Economics

PIERRE-YVES CREMIEUX

pierre.cremieux@analysisgroup.com

Managing Principal, Analysis Group

AARON C. YEATER

Aaron.yeater@analysisgroup.com

Vice President, Analysis Group

Abstract

The new pattern of global antitrust regulation established by government authorities shows that, despite much being made about economists' inability to agree on anything, convergence in antitrust economics is both recent and remarkable. Economists today near-unanimously believe that antitrust enforcement is beneficial to both consumers and economic growth and that it is a necessary component of any modern free-market economy. Despite this agreement, conflicting economic evidence presented by experts in competition disputes remains. While economists, lawyers, and triers of fact may interpret opposing positions as reflecting a misuse of economics, in the vast majority of instances, disagreement among experts reflects differing underlying beliefs about the interactions of firms and consumers, as well as differences in their understanding of what constitutes competition in the market at issue. This discussion explores a series of questions to consider—What do economists believe? What methods do economists rely on? Where do the differences lie?—to help focus on the root cause of common disagreements among economic experts in antitrust litigation. These questions are then considered in the context of litigation surrounding Best Buy in the matter of alleged cartel activity among thin-film-transistor liquid-crystal display ("TFT-LCD") manufacturers.

I. Introduction

The new pattern of global antitrust regulation established by government authorities shows that, despite much being made about economists' inability to agree on anything, convergence in antitrust economics is both recent and remarkable. Economists today near-unanimously believe that antitrust enforcement is beneficial to both consumers and economic growth and that it is a necessary component of any modern free-market economy. Testimony based on antitrust economics on topics including monopolization, horizontal agreements, and mergers reflect this uniform agreement among economists that competition is welfare enhancing.

The Act for the Prevention and Suppression of Combination formed in the Restraint of Trade, voted by the Canadian Parliament in May 1889, is widely seen as the first competition statute in the world. It was followed promptly by the well-known Sherman Act, approved by the US Congress on July 2, 1890, which still left more than 80 percent of the world economy devoid of antitrust regulation. It was only in 1957, with the signing of the Treaty of Rome, that more than 50 percent of world Gross Domestic Product ("GDP") was brought under an antitrust statute. The former Soviet republics enacted their own antitrust laws in the early 1990s, bringing nearly 70 percent of world GDP under antitrust scrutiny. With the enactment by China of its Anti-Monopoly Law on August 1, 2008, more than 95 percent of world GDP is now under antitrust scrutiny.

However, economists have not always agreed with this now-accepted belief. For example, in his 1932 book *Cartels, Concerns and Trusts*, the well-known (at the time) German economist Robert Liefmann stated that: "The possibilities of a rise in price resulting from monopolistic organization—and in particular from a merely contractual organization such as is a cartel—are generally greatly over-estimated.[1] The cartels are quite unable to influence the prices of consumers' goods, especially of goods in general use, to such an extent as might be expected having regard to the great number of monopolistic organization."[2] On the issue of consumer welfare, he states that: "In particular, we called attention to the greater stability shown by the coal syndicate's prices since 1900, and showed that this is generally more beneficial to the consumer than violent price fluctuations on the scale of earlier years."[3] Finally, on the role of the state, he explains that: "Once the value of cartels as a means of regulating economic life came to be realized, the State ceased merely to obstruct their development and to eliminate the resulting abuses; it frequently went so far as to *encourage them*" (emphasis in original).[4]

Similarly, on the industry side, cartels were considered beneficial to stability and a standard mode of operation potentially superior to competition. In a 1935 article from the French periodical *L'Illustration*, the director of the Toa cement factory in Japan was quoted as saying:

> By common agreement, we have reduced our production by 57%. The quantity we are allowed to produce is fixed every three months by our industrial union created 11 years ago. During the first five years, the period anticipated by the agreement that all industrialists had signed at the time, everything was fine. But during the second period, a certain number of industrialists wanted

1 Robert Liefmann, a German economist born in 1874, was an internationally recognized expert on "business associations and cartels," the field in which he obtained his Doctorate. He had toured the United States extensively in 1907, 17 years after the Sherman Act was enacted. Deported to the Gurs concentration/internment camp in France in 1940 for being Jewish, he died in 1941.

2 Robert Liefmann, Cartels, Concerns and Trusts 108 (1932).

3 *Id.* at 141.

4 *Id.* at 215.

> to get their freedom back and, because of the fall in price resulting from this renewed competition, we found ourselves in an inextricable situation. We then asked the government to intervene and force all the cement manufacturers to abide by the orders of the industrial union. The law voted in December 1934, therefore very recent, has finally reestablished this obligation.[5]

Despite the near-uniform agreement on the merits of antitrust enforcement today, conflicting views on what constitutes competition and appropriate economic evidence in competition disputes remain. While economists, lawyers, and triers of fact may interpret opposing positions as reflecting a misuse of economics, in the vast majority of instances, disagreement among experts reflects differing underlying beliefs about the interactions of firms and consumers, as well as differences in their understanding of competition in the market at issue. These may result from differing information or underlying assumptions provided by counsel or other experts. These differences translate into subtle methodological differences, some of which may affect the expert's conclusion dramatically. For counsel, judges, and jurors, appreciating where and how economists agree, as well as the roots of their remaining disagreement, is often difficult. In this discussion, we propose a series of questions to consider to help focus on the root cause of common disagreements among economic experts in antitrust litigation.

II. Question 1: Establishing Common Ground: What Do Economists Believe?

Economists tasked with evaluating market dynamics and firm behavior to assess allegations related to collusion and monopolization offer analysis to clarify whether collusive conduct or abusive monopolistic conduct best explains pricing and production decisions. They may provide expert insight into how a market would have evolved but-for particular behavior by a group of firms or a single dominant firm. While their conclusions may diverge, a first useful step is to establish what economists on opposing sides of a case agree on. As a general matter, the drivers of economic activity—human behavior, organizational activities, and market operations—are widely agreed upon by economists across the discipline. Indeed, the underlying principles that shape economic analysis seem as natural to the vast majority of economists as the laws of physics:

» We all agree that incentives matter.

» We agree that firms generally maximize their profits while consumers maximize their utility, although we may disagree on how profits and utility should be measured.

» We acknowledge, through our use of discount rates, the importance of immediacy (i.e., something today is better than something tomorrow).

» We recognize that opportunity costs are an important driver of economic behavior, in that every choice results in the loss of the alternative choice. This means that individuals and firms make decisions at the margin.

» We view trade, when entered into freely, as making both sides better off.

---

5 Emile Schreiber, *Enquête au pays du soleil levant*, L'Illustration, July 6, 1935, at 355-358.

III. Question 2: What Methods Do Economists Rely On?

Beyond our shared underlying understanding of economic reality, economists typically rely on very similar methods to identify anticompetitive behavior. They can be divided into two categories. First, we all rely on economic theory, which is nothing more than the mathematical or graphical expression of our underlying beliefs about economic interactions. Second, we generally rely on statistical analysis, which provides a powerful set of tools to analyze data and construct alternative ("but-for") scenarios. There is general agreement on the use of these tools. For example, on the theory side, our models typically recognize that because individuals make decisions at the margins, the concept of marginal cost as a determinant of price under competitive conditions is a good starting point for economic analysis. Similarly, we view the use of statistics to draw inferences about populations from a sample of observations as a good starting point. Notwithstanding disagreement about the application of statistical averages and the correct level of aggregation in the context of class-wide analysis, our set of statistical tools is common across experts, who generally rely on similar distributional assumptions and count on appropriate parameterization to ensure accurate results. We all rely on theory and/or econometrics (the application of statistics to economic data) as tools in antitrust litigation to evaluate a coherent set of issues, including:

» Market dynamics and organizational behavior;

» The role of collusive or unilateral conduct on pricing and production decisions; and

» The nature of any number of "but-for" worlds absent the behavior at issue.

IV. Question 3: Where Do the Differences Lie?

Despite this remarkable agreement around behavioral assumptions and methodologies, attorneys, judges, and juries are often confronted by dueling economic opinions that can result in polar-opposite conclusions. This is only rarely related to the application of "unprofessional" economic arguments. More often, it is the result of different views of what constitutes competition or subtle differences in the application of generally shared economic theories and statistical tools, the choice of data, or the consideration of external factors.

That the outcomes of these analyses can vary so drastically is a source of significant dismay by triers of fact and is a direct manifestation of minor discrepancies in economists' understanding of the basic building blocks of the economic world. These subtle differences of opinion about the nature of competition or the determinants of production or demand can have significant consequences because they result in differences in the interpretation of empirical facts or the specification of statistical modeling.

V. Case Example: TFT-LCD (Flat Panel) Antitrust Litigation

Consider the litigation surrounding Best Buy in the matter of alleged cartel activity among thin-film-transistor liquid-crystal display ("TFT-LCD") manufacturers.[6] This lawsuit stemmed from a long-running US investigation of a conspiracy to set artificially high prices for, and restrict the supply of, various sizes of TFT-LCD panels. The plaintiffs claimed that the defendants had engaged in price-fixing since 1998, resulting in overcharges to direct purchasers of TFT-LCD panels and to indirect purchasers of finished products containing those panels (such as televisions and computer monitors).

In this litigation, two top economic experts presented opposing models to measure the alleged overcharges. Both experts are affiliated with respected universities and are widely recognized as highly qualified in their fields, having published numerous articles on the subject in highly ranked scholarly journals and having received numerous awards. Yet, they reached remarkably different conclusions in their economic analyses, particularly with respect to how to measure input costs:

» The plaintiffs' expert modeled TFT-LCD panel prices as a function of several variables, including the price of microprocessors, which was used as a proxy for input costs, to demonstrate an overcharge of roughly 20 percent.

» The defendants' expert found that by altering the specification used by the plaintiffs' expert in a very minor way, namely by replacing the price of microprocessors with any number of alternative input price indexes, the overcharge was close to zero.

After a six-week trial and a day of deliberation, a California federal jury found the defendant Toshiba Corporation not liable for conspiracy to fix the prices of TFT-LCD panels. Defendant HannStar Display Corporation had previously acknowledged its participation in a conspiracy to fix the prices of certain TFT-LCD panels; however, the same jury awarded only $7.4 million in direct damages, based on figures calculated and presented by the testifying expert. The Best Buy plaintiffs had asked for $770 million in damages based on their economic experts' analysis and overcharge estimate.

VI. Assessing Opposing Economic Arguments in the TFT-LCD Case

Given the complexity and sophistication of the economic analyses on both sides, what is counsel—or a jury—to do in circumstances such as this? A typical response has been to raise the Daubert standard: Is the analysis scientifically rigorous? For economic experts, the standard is sometimes thought of as a determination of whether the work done meets academic levels of rigor. While this strategy sometimes works, I purposely selected an example where the statistical analyses were standard and differed only in subtle ways between the two parties. It has also become increasingly apparent that economic analyses published in scholarly journals without the submission of data and without the testing of alternative

---

6 *In re TFT-LCD (Flat Panel) Antitrust Litigation*, MDL No. 1827 (N.D. Cal. 2012).

specifications by referees cannot be as thoroughly examined as similar analyses presented in a litigation context where the opposing side has complete access to the underlying data and programs.[7]

Absent gross errors or the exclusion of one of the experts through a Daubert motion, what is the trier of fact to do? The TFT-LCD matter provides a concrete example of how to assess opposing economic arguments. Both experts proposed a statistical analysis to explain the price of TFT-LCD panels in order to isolate the effect of the conspiracy. Both agreed that various measures of costs and demand would be important determinants of prices with or without a conspiracy. In fact, they seemed to disagree principally on only one issue. Namely, they disagreed on whether the Producer Price Index ("PPI") for microprocessors is an appropriate proxy for costs.[8] The plaintiffs' expert included the PPI for microprocessors in his analysis and found an overcharge resulting in damages of more than $700 million for all purchases and more than $230 million for direct purchases alone. The defendants' expert took the identical model but replaced the PPI for microprocessors with any number of other PPIs for TFT-LCD panel inputs and showed that the overcharge became indistinguishable from zero, thereby suggesting *de minimis* damages. What is the jury to do in a situation like this? Ultimately, the right answer is a matter of belief rather than statistical modeling or theoretical equations.

"Is the PPI for microprocessors a good proxy for the cost of building TFT-LCD panels?"[9] This is a perfect example of a fundamental disagreement between economists that does not involve the use or misuse of the tools of economics but rather a matter of disagreement in underlying beliefs. The question may be relatively easy to grasp for the trier of fact. Jurors may agree with the plaintiffs' expert that the PPI for microprocessors is a necessary component of any good analysis of the determinants of TFT-LCD panel prices because, for example, they heard testimony that microprocessors represent a significant cost factor. Alternatively, they may believe that if substituting any number of alternative PPI into the analysis makes the overcharge go away, then the results are not robust and ultimately suspect since they may be the result of a fishing expedition. This, of course, would reflect a failure of methods as much as a disagreement between the experts.

Uncovering the fundamental disagreements in beliefs that underlie econometric or theoretical analyses are likely to be much more effective than trying to explain the relative merits of one statistical specification over another. Statistics and theory are only as good as the underlying assumptions, data, and phenomena that they translate. An alternative approach is to call in a third expert who can stress test the opinion of the two disagreeing experts based, for example, on the nature of the industry, the workings of the cartel, and the likelihood that it would result in successful price-fixing. Notably, a jury in Washington state reached a different conclusion regarding the same analyses when presented with a separate but similar litigation by the retailer Costco; that jury "split the difference" between the experts' opinions and awarded higher damages.

7 Based on recent instances of lapses in scholarly review, the academic standards that have served as a rubric in Daubert hearings may themselves become insufficient benchmarks of quality.

8 The defendants' expert analysis was completed in the context of the broader observation that the modelling of TFT-LCD panel prices more generally was much more difficult and likely to result in error than the plaintiffs' expert believed.

9 Although the issue is not relevant to this discussion, the plaintiffs' expert argued that the PPI for microprocessors was appropriate because it was a good proxy for demand, since monitors and computers are complements.

VII. Conclusion

Over the last few decades, economists have reached a degree of consensus in antitrust unprecedented in recent history. Nevertheless, economic experts working in good faith can and do reach vastly different conclusions when applying similar economic theory and econometrics to the same set of facts and data. In practice, this means that strongly conflicting opinions do not automatically indicate that economic evidence is being misused. Instead, it reflects more subtle tensions in economists' beliefs about human behavior, organizational activities, firm characteristics, and market dynamics, which all influence their development of models that describe their economic reality and that help define but-for worlds. Counsel play an important role by uncovering these underlying beliefs, understanding how they are translated into the economist's theoretical or empirical construct, and assisting the trier of fact in evaluating the relative merits of the two positions.

Betwixt and Between: The FTC and DOJ as Regulators and Law Enforcers

John D. Harkrider*

jharkrider@axinn.com

Partner, Axinn, Veltrop & Harkrider

Abstract

While the FTC and DOJ strongly contend that they are law enforcers and not regulators, it is not clear why they draw this distinction given that neither model is clearly superior. For example, while law enforcement might imply a more limited role for the government than the term regulation implies, it also has a number of negative connotations, including the agency as a prosecutor, bringing a case, instead of evaluating it, and the parties to a transaction as suspects, instead of petitioners, and the consent decree as a plea bargain, instead of good public policy. Moreover, while there is no clear definition of law enforcement and regulation there are least three characteristics that frequently distinguish the two different models: law enforcement involves conduct that has already occurred, while the act of regulation frequently involves conduct that is yet to occur; law enforcement usually requires the cessation of activity, while regulation frequently requires affirmative conduct; and regulation typically involves interpretation of agency rules, while law enforcement is mostly governed by court decisions and generally leaves a defendant with a clear path to judicial review. Seen this way, agency action under the Sherman Act closely resembles law enforcement. For example, enforcement against cartels and monopolists typically involves conduct that

* The author would like to thank Russell Steinthal, Rick Dagen, Morris Bloom, Michael Keeley, and Michael O'Mara for their input (and at times disagreement) with the views set forth in this article. In addition, the author would like to thank Sean Sullivan for his work in assembling the database of citations for mergers challenged by the DOJ and FTC.

has occurred and the remedy involves the cessation of the activity in question. In contrast, agency action on HSR Reportable transactions and under Section 5 of the FTC Act (especially if it does not also violate the Sherman Act) can be seen as regulatory. In both cases, legality is frequently determined by internal guidelines and policy views rather than legal precedent, remedies especially in vertical mergers are complex, with affirmative requirements, including firewalls, and in some cases, obligations to make certain products available with certain pricing benchmarks. In truth, the FTC and DOJ are both law enforcers and regulators, enforcing laws that are regulatory in nature, relying more on economists than eyewitnesses, more on what may happen, than what has already occurred. In the end, though, it does not matter what term is used to describe agency behavior, what matters is that the agency adopt clear and transparent rules that are fairly enforced, where the parties always have a right to go to court to challenge the government's decision.

I. Introduction

The US Department of Justice ("DOJ") and Federal Trade Commission ("FTC") have made it clear that they regard their primary role as law enforcers rather than regulators. But the truth is more nuanced, especially in the case of merger enforcement and patent abuse relating to Standard Essential Patents ("SEPs").

In both of these cases, the actions of the FTC and DOJ are virtually indistinguishable from entities such as the European Commission ("EC"), Brazil's Conselho Administrativo de Defesa Econômica and China's Ministry of Commerce, none of which shy away from the description of their function as regulatory. Indeed, it has become common for the DOJ and FTC to seek international convergence with these other regulators.

In truth, a case can be made that the FTC and DOJ lie somewhere in between law enforcers and regulators. This is not surprising given that these agencies are enforcing a law that is regulatory in nature; a law that looks at the impact of a practice on consumer welfare as opposed to individual victims; a law that relies upon econometricians and formal models more than eyewitnesses and evidence of intent. Furthermore, at least in the case of merger enforcement, it is a law that courts evaluate in the context of guidelines that the agencies themselves wrote.

And this gives the agencies incredible power, one that combines the power of both regulators (to approve or disapprove future events) and law enforcers (to investigate and prosecute violations of law). Because mergers touch so many parts of our economy, it is a power that imposes costs and benefits on almost all sectors of the economy. This is why it must be exercised carefully and transparently.

II. We Are not Regulators

In delivering remarks at the GCR Live 4th Annual Antitrust Law Leaders Forum, Assistant Attorney General William Baer stated:

> We must remember our mission. It is about effective law enforcement. I recoil at the suggestion that antitrust equates to regulation. That is not what we do. And it is not how we ought to think about what we do. Our work is to use our statutory authority to remove restraints on competition and prevent behavior or consolidation that risks limiting competition. We do not aspire to be

> regulators or to pick winners and losers. Instead antitrust enforcement, done right, focuses on removing impediments to competitive markets and protecting market structures that facilitate competition.[1]

The view that the antitrust agencies are engaged in law enforcement rather than regulation is not new. Justice Stephen Breyer wrote in *Regulation and its Reform*:

> [I]n principle the antitrust laws differ from classical regulation both in their aims and in the methods. The antitrust laws seek to create or maintain the *conditions* of a competitive marketplace rather than replicate the *results* of competition or correct for the defects of competitive markets. In doing so, they act negatively, through a few highly general provisions *prohibiting* certain forms of private conduct.[2]

It is significant, however, that the definition of regulation referred to by Breyer and Baer is largely outmoded. Few regulators see themselves as protecting the results of competition, as opposed to the process. The EC, for example, would shudder at the thought that they were picking winners and losers. Moreover, regulators in the United States, such as the Securities and Exchange Commission and the Federal Election Commission ("FEC"), do not think of themselves as picking winning stocks or candidates. Instead, they see their role as ensuring that stock and electoral markets act in a competitive manner, with consumers (and voters) being empowered to make informed choices to select their preferred alternative.

Others take the view that the US antitrust agencies are, in fact, regulators. For example, Judge Frank Easterbrook wrote that: "Many antitrust suits are regulatory. The Department of Justice used antitrust suits to establish district courts as regulatory agencies over industries which the Antitrust Division was persuaded that competition was 'unworkable,' but in which the political process had not acted."[3] Doug Melamed, Harry First, and others have all characterized antitrust as a form of regulation, though one that may have more of a "legalistic regulatory culture" as opposed to a "bureaucratic regulatory culture."[4]

To be fair, Baer is clearly correct that the Sherman Act imposes significant limitations on the power of the DOJ to impose certain remedies. The Sherman Act, for example, is focused on the improper acquisition or maintenance of market power but does not limit the pricing of lawfully obtained monopolies. This is very different than the EC, which has an abuse of dominance standard.

That said, courts have routinely described the FTC and DOJ as regulators, especially in the context of merger enforcement. For example, the Fifth Circuit wrote that "HSR's fundamental goal was to improve the efficiency of merger regulation."[5] Similarly, in the context of securities litigation following the DOJ's decision to block (but not litigate) WorldCom's proposed acquisition of Sprint, the court wrote: "Considering the size of the proposed merger and the state of competition within the telecommunications industry, regulators from the Federal Communications Commission ("FCC"), the DOJ Antitrust Division, and the

---

1 William Baer, Asst. Att'y Gen., Remarks at the GCR Live 4th Annual Antitrust Law Leaders Forum (Feb. 6, 2015), available at http://www.justice.gov/opa/speech/assistant-attorney-general-bill-baer-delivers-remarks-global-competition-review-fourth.

2 Stephen Breyer, Regulation and Its Reform 156 (1982).

3 Frank Easterbrook, *The Limits of Antitrust*, 63 Tex. L. Rev. 1, 35 n.72 (1984) (citations omitted).

4 Harry First, *Is Antitrust "Law"?*, 10 Antitrust 9 (Fall 1995); A. Douglas Melamed, *Antitrust: The New Regulation*, 10 Antitrust 13 (Fall 1995); A. Douglas Melamed, *Antitrust as Law Enforcement*, 27 Antitrust 76 (Fall 2012).

5 *Mattox v. F.T.C.*, 752 F.2d 116, 122 (5th Cir. 1985).

EC were interested in the proposed merger."[6] Similarly, the Southern District of New York held that there was no immediate threat of irreparable harm related to Apollo's attempted hostile takeover of Vantico Holdings because "[a]n acquisition by Resolution of Vantico in an auction process would require approval by antitrust regulators in the United States, particularly the Federal Trade Commission ("FTC") and in Europe."[7] Other courts have noted that the FTC has "regulatory authority" to "investigate mergers"[8] and that the FTC "has authority to regulate tender offers" under the antitrust laws.[9]

III. The History of the Agencies

The Sherman Act was not intended to be enforced by a regulatory agency.[10] Indeed, Senator Sherman made clear that he believed that the Sherman Act should be enforced by the courts as opposed to by an agency, writing because "it is difficult to define in legal language the precise line between lawful and unlawful combination. This must be left for the courts to determine in each particular case."[11]

For the first few years after the Antitrust Division was formed in 1933, its principal mandate was to police the regulatory and protectionist codes under the National Industrial Recovery Act. But that changed in 1937 when Thurmond Arnold became the head of the Antitrust Division. Arnold characterized antitrust as the "cop on the beat" and expressly characterized the mission of the Antitrust Division as a prosecutor, albeit one that was not hostile to business.[12]

Congress created the FTC in 1914 during the Wilson Administration. It is an independent agency of the United States, similar to the Federal Communications Commission, the Federal Energy Regulatory Commission ("FERC"), and the FEC. Unlike the DOJ, it was not originally permitted to bring actions in court in its own name, although it ultimately obtained that ability.

In contrast to the DOJ, the FTC was intended to be an expert regulatory body that could provide guidance to the business community and could address the risk that the antitrust laws would not be enforced by the courts.[13] It was entrusted with rulemaking authority, the ability to use subpoenas to study and report on industries, and entrusted with an administrative court.

Like the DOJ, the FTC characterizes itself as a law enforcement agency. For example, on its website, the FTC writes that: "The Commission's main responsibility is as a law enforcer." This view was also expressed by former Commissioner Tom Rosch, who stated: "First, and above all, the Commission is a

---

6 *In re Sprint Corp. Securities Litigation*, 232 F. Supp. 1193, 1202-1203 (D. Kansas 2002). *See also In re TFT-LCD (Flat Panel) Antitrust Litigation*, 586 F. Supp.2d 1109, 1119 (N.D. Ca. 2008) ("the plaintiffs were unaware of their claims and discovered them only as a result of investigations by the Department of Justice (DOJ) and other antitrust regulators"); *Cableamerica Corp. v. Federal Trade Commission*, 795 F. Supp. 1082, 1092 (N.D. Ala. 1992) ("the FTC is properly exercising its regulatory authority in investigating the merger"); *Macfadden Holdings, Inc. v. JB Acquisition Corp.*, 641 F. Supp. 454 (S.D.N.Y. 1986) ("The Court adopts this definition because the FTC has authority to regulate tender offers under the antitrust laws.").

7 *Vantico Holdings S.A. v. Apollo Management, LP*, 247 F. Supp.2d 437, 445 (S.D.N.Y. 2003).

8 *Cableamerica*, 795 F. Supp. at 1092 ("the FTC is properly exercising its regulatory authority in investigating the merger").

9 *Macfadden Holdings*, 641 F. Supp. at 464 n. 6 ("The Court adopts this definition because the FTC has authority to regulate tender offers under the antitrust laws.").

10 Spencer Weber Waller, *The Changing Nature of Antitrust Enforcement*, 77 Ore. L.R. 1383, 1387 (1998).

11 *Id.* at 1388.

12 Thurman W. Arnold, The Bottlenecks of Business 97, 134-35, 191, 272-73 (1940).

13 Earl Kintner, The Legislative History of the Federal Antitrust Laws and Related Statutes, 3703 (1978).

law enforcement agency charged with protecting competition and consumers."[14] As Dan Crane explains: "insofar as its antitrust mission is concerned, the FTC has essentially the status of a law enforcer and not a norm creator."[15]

IV. The FTC and DOJ as Merger Regulators

There is no clear definition of the distinction between law enforcement and regulation, perhaps because it is not clear that the distinction has legal significance in most cases. But taking a step back, it seems like law enforcement can be distinguished from regulation along three dimensions:

» Law enforcement agencies are primarily concerned with actions that have already occurred, while regulators are empowered not only to review past events but to review future events as well. For example, FERC reviews tariffs that have not yet gone into effect (though they also review whether the approved rates are actually followed).

» Second, the output of law enforcement is simple: a judicial determination of guilt or innocence and, if appropriate, a fine, a prison term, a probationary period, an agreement not to continue the practice, etc. In contrast, the output of regulation is usually very complex: pages and pages of detailed affirmative obligations relating to future conduct.

» Third, courts turn to case law to determine whether a law was violated; regulators instead look to not just statutes and case law, but frequently also regulations that they themselves promulgated, as do courts in evaluating the appropriateness of the agency's action.

Against these three dimensions, the FTC and DOJ's pre-merger notification and review process seems regulatory in nature.

First, the FTC and DOJ examine the impact of an act that has yet to occur, namely, the acquisition of stock or assets subject to the Clayton Act. Certainly it is unusual for a law enforcement agency to require pre-notification of future conduct that may or may not violate the law. Nor is it usual for a law enforcement agency to require a suspect under investigation to incur millions of dollars in costs to submit information relating to that future offense, including documents relating to the parties' intent in taking that future action.

Those who view the FTC and DOJ as law enforcers even in the context of pre-merger notification may correctly point out that they do not technically "approve" a merger under the HSR Act, but rather simply let the pre-merger notification period expire, and always retain the right to sue if the conduct violates the Clayton Act. But this distinction is largely formalistic in that the HSR Act legally prevents the parties from merging until the expiration of the applicable waiting period. So the FTC and DOJ "approve" the right to close the deal (though they reserve the right to challenge the transaction in the future). And whether it is approval, or simply a failure to act that allows for the parties to merge, the essential distinction between future and past conduct remains.

---

14 J. Thomas Rosch, Commissioner, Fed. Trade Comm'n, *The Federal Trade Commission as a Law Enforcement Agency*, Lecture at the University of Virginia (Apr. 23, 2012), *available at* https://www.ftc.gov/sites/default/files/documents/public_statements/federal-trade-commission-law-enforcement-agency/120423uvalecture.pdf.

15 Daniel Crane, *Technocracy*, 86 Tex. L. Rev. 1159, 1206 (2008).

Second, consent decrees are hardly simple. To the contrary, at least in the context of vertical mergers, consent decrees provide dozens of pages of detailed obligations regarding, among other things, nondiscriminatory access,[16] the internal use of confidential information,[17] and, at least in one case, an obligation to price current and future products using benchmarks identified in the decree.[18]

Third, perhaps the most significant deviation of the Premerger Notification regime from traditional law enforcement is the fact that courts evaluate the legality of mergers in accordance with guidelines established by the agencies themselves. Specifically, the agencies have four times written merger guidelines, many of them significantly different than past iterations. While these guidelines are not technically binding on the courts, they have effectively become the merger law of the land, cited and followed almost without question in more than 55 different mergers over the past few decades.

Those who support a view of pre-merger notification as a form of law enforcement undoubtedly will argue that the merger guidelines are not binding on the courts. That's true. But given that the merger guidelines have been cited more times since the passage of the HSR Act than *Brown Shoe*,[19] *Philadelphia National Bank*,[20] and *Baker Hughes*[21] combined, it seems difficult to dispute that they are not the backbone of judicial merger analysis.[22]

Number of Citations in Merger Cases Since 1976

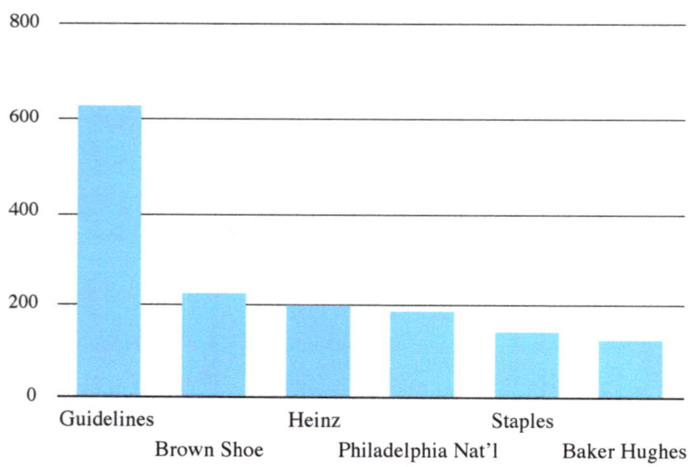

16 *See, e.g.*, Final Judgment, *U.S. v. Google, Inc.*, No. 1:11-cv-00688 (D.D.C. Oct. 5, 2011), *available at* http://www.justice.gov/atr/case-document/final-judgment-99; Decision and Order, *In the Matter of AOL, Inc.*, Fed. Trade Comm'n, Dkt. No. C-3989 (Apr. 18, 2001), *available at* https://www.ftc.gov/sites/default/ files/documents/cases/2001/04/aoltwdo.pdf.

17 Decision and Order, *In the Matter of PepsiCo., Inc.*, Fed. Trade Comm'n, Dkt. No. C-4301 (Sep. 28, 2010), *available at* https://www.ftc.gov/sites/default/files/documents/cases/2010/09/100928pepscodo.pdf; Final Judgment, *U.S. v. Tickemaster, Entertainment, Inc.*, No. 1:10-cv-00139 (D.D.C. Jul. 30, 2010), *available at* http://www.justice.gov/atr/case-document/final-judgment-180.

18 *U.S. v. Google*, *supra* note 16.

19 *Brown Shoe Co., Inc. v. U.S.*, 370 U.S. 294 (1962).

20 *U.S. v. Philadelphia National Bank*, 374 U.S. 321 (1963).

21 *U.S. v. Baker Hughes Inc.*, 908 F.2d 981 (D.C. Cir. 1990).

22 This counts every citation to the relevant authority in merger cases brought by the DOJ or FTC since 1976. Others may argue that the U.S. antitrust agencies have promulgated other guidelines, such as the FTC and DOJ's Statements of Antitrust Enforcement Policy in Health Care. U.S. Dep't. of Justice & Fed. Trade Comm'n, Statements of Antitrust Enforcement Policy in Health Care (1996), *available at* https://www.ftc.gov/sites/default/files/attachments/competition-policy-guidance/statements_of_antitrust_enforcement_policy_in_health_care_august_1996.pdf. But these guidelines have only been cited in only seven cases, and in only one did they form the backbone of the decision. *See Cason-Merenda v. Detroit Medical Center*, 862 F. Supp.2d 603 (E.D. Mi. 2012).

It is hard to find an example in law enforcement where courts judge lawfulness according to guidelines as opposed to case law. As one commentator noted: "For example, a number of federal statutes impose criminal liability without requiring proof of a specific dollar amount of loss. For any number of reasons, the government may choose as a matter of prosecutorial discretion not to prosecute violations that do not cause financial harm of a substantial nature. However, it is highly unlikely that a defendant would be able to use the government's policy, even if embodied in written guidelines, to successfully defend himself in a prosecution which otherwise met the requirements of the statute."[23]

Thus, it is difficult to reconcile the Premerger Notification regime with any traditional type of law enforcement. As some practitioners have commented, the premerger notification rules of the HSR Act are "the most important factor in the replacement of merger control through litigation with a comprehensive scheme of merger regulation."[24]

V. The FTC as a Regulator of Standard Essential Patents

Standard Essential Patents ("SEPs") are those patents that have been declared as essential to an industry standard. In many cases, the standard has been set by a standard setting body that requires its members to license their patents that are essential to the standard on Fair, Reasonable, and Non-Discriminatory ("FRAND") terms.

For years there has been concern as to whether the rates charged for SEPs were not, in fact, FRAND. This is because SEP holders typically demand a percentage of the end device even though the patent in question only read on functionality that represented a small percentage of the value of the device. For example, firms like Qualcomm charge 5% of the value of the smartphone even though their patents relate largely to the voice functionality of the phone, which represents only a small percentage of the value of a smartphone to a typical user.

The FTC and DOJ reached the conclusion that firms were able to charge rates that were supra FRAND because they were able to threaten injunctions if a firm did not license their SEPs. Their theory was that the threat of an injunction would cause firms that had refused to pay the FRAND rate to pay virtually all of their profits to avoid having their smartphones enjoined.

The problem was that the rules of standard setting organizations did not expressly prohibit the granting of injunctions. Indeed, SEP holders had routinely been able to seek injunctions or exclusion orders on their SEPs.

---

23 Waller, *supra* note 10, at 1407 n. 112.

24 Joe Sims & Deborah P. Herman, *A Case Study in the Law of Unintended Consequences Applied to Antitrust Legislation*, 65 Antitrust L.J. 865, 865 (1997).

The FTC had been concerned about abuses in the standard setting context for years, but had never prevented a firm from seeking an injunction on an SEP. To the contrary, the FTC had expressly granted Rambus—a defendant in an FTC standard setting case—the ability to seek injunctions on properly declared SEPs.[25]

That changed in 2012 when the FTC issued a complaint against Bosch on a merger that had little to do with standard setting.[26] But because Bosch was obtaining a few SEPs as a part of its merger, the FTC insisted that Bosch agree not to seek injunctions on these SEPs.[27] Either because Bosch did not care about getting injunctions, or because it feared not being able to close the deal without including this provision in the consent decree, or for some other reason, Bosch agreed.

The FTC then brought an action against Motorola Mobility, claiming that it had violated Section 5 by seeking injunctions against Apple and Microsoft, both of whom had categorically refused to pay Motorola its requested rate of 2.25% of the end device. Significantly, the backbone of the FTC's complaint was that Motorola Mobility "used these threats of exclusion orders and injunctions to enhance its bargaining leverage against willing licensees and demand licensing terms that tended to exceed the FRAND range."[28] This statement could only be made if the FTC determined that the rate that Motorola had offered Apple—which was 2.25% of the end device—was not fair and reasonable.

Motorola ultimately accepted a consent decree that provided pages of detailed obligations on Motorola in terms of the offer they must make, the time they must wait, and the process they must follow in seeking an injunction.[29] In effect, the FTC rewrote the Rules of Civil Procedure for seeking an injunction on SEPs.

The effect of these two decisions was to radically reduce the value of SEPs because there was no longer an ability of an SEP holder to seek an injunction for infringement, thus forcing the SEP holder to bring potentially hundreds of individual infringement actions for damages. While this may have been the appropriate competition result as the existing rates for SEPs were hardly FRAND, it would be difficult to describe this as law enforcement, especially as it invariably involved a judgment as to whether a particular rate was fair and reasonable.

Importantly, however, the reversal in the FTC's position as to the lawfulness of seeking injunctions on SEPs was not published for public comment prior to adoption in *Motorola Mobility*. The FTC did not transparently invite in market participants from sectors other than telecommunications, many of which had SEPs. And the entire investigation and change in industry rules occurred in less than seven months.

---

25 Opinion, *In the Matter of Rambus Inc.*, Fed. Trade Comm'n, Dkt. No. 9302 (Apr. 27, 2007), *available at* https://www.ftc.gov/sites/default/files/documents/cases/2007/04/070427commopinionpetreconsideration_pv.pdf (Complaint Counsel and Amici "argue that treble damages and injunctive relief are inconsistent with the fundamental purpose of JEDEC. . . . The argument of Complaint Counsel and Amici are not persuasive . . . [In the but-for world] Rambus would have been able to seek injunctions against those who infringed without seeking licenses . . . it is not our intent to leave Rambus without access to any remedies of infringement that would have been available to it under applicable law.").

26 Complaint, *In the Matter of Bosch*, Fed. Trade Comm'n, Dkt. No. C-4377 (Nov. 26, 2012), *available at* https://www.ftc.gov/sites/default/files/documents/cases/2012/11/121126boschcmpt.pdf.

27 Decision and Order, *In the Matter of Bosch*, Fed. Trade Comm'n, Dkt. No. C-4377 (Apr. 24, 2013), *available at* https://www.ftc.gov/sites/default/files/documents/cases/2013/04/130424robertboschdo.pdf.

28 Complaint, *In the Matter of Motorola Mobility LLC*, Fed. Trade Comm'n, No. 1210120, at 5 (Jan. 3, 2013), *available at* https://www.ftc.gov/sites/default/files/documents/cases/2013/01/ 130103googlemotorolacmpt.pdf.

29 Decision and Order, *In the Matter of Motorola Mobility LLC*, Fed. Trade Comm'n, No. 1210120 (Jul. 24, 2013), *available at* https://www.ftc.gov/enforcement/cases-proceedings/1210120/motorola-mobility-llc-google-inc-matter.

VI. The DOJ as Telecommunications Regulator

Similarly, the DOJ has historically played an essentially regulatory function with respect to telecommunications. Through a series of agreements with AT&T, starting first with the Kingsbury Letter, then the 1956 Consent Decree, then the 1984 Modified Final Judgment, and then finally its enforcement of Section 271 of the 1996 Telecommunications Act, the DOJ has performed a regulatory as opposed to law enforcement function.

DOJ regulation of telecommunications started in 1913, when Nathan Kingsbury, the Vice President of AT&T, sent a letter to the DOJ that acknowledged the DOJ's agreement not to pursue its monopolization suit against AT&T, provided that AT&T sell off its interest in Western Union and refrain from acquiring any company that was operated in competition with the Bell System if the Interstate Commerce Commission objected.[30] In exchange, AT&T agreed that independent companies could interconnect with the Bell System, provided that the subscriber paid the normal toll charge in addition to a connection charge of ten cents to AT&T.[31]

In 1949, the DOJ sued AT&T and its subsidiary Western Electric for violating the Sherman Act by attempting to monopolize the market for telephone equipment. AT&T lobbied the Department of Defense ("DOD") throughout the Korean War to get the DOJ to drop the suit without success. After the war ended, AT&T continued its lobbying efforts, meeting directly with the DOJ and the DOD. At one meeting, Attorney General Herbert Brownell said that he believed that "a way ought to be found to get rid of the case," and that AT&T "could readily find practices that [it] might agree to have enjoined with no real injury to [its] business."[32]

As explained later by Judge Harold Greene: "Shortly after this meeting, AT&T again urged the Defense Department 'to intercede with the Justice Department to have the case settled on a basis that would not require divorcement of Western.'[33] To that end, Secretary of Defense Charles E. Wilson had a letter hand-carried to Attorney General Brownell urging him to end the litigation without divesting Western Electric. The rationale stated for this position was that the severance of Western Electric would "effectively disintegrate the coordinated organization which is fundamental to the successful carrying forward of these critical defense projects," and would "be contrary to the vital interests of the Nation."[34] However, the Wilson letter was actually prepared by AT&T.

The case was settled in 1956, under a decree that did not require AT&T to divest Western Electric, but restricted AT&T from selling equipment other than what was needed for the operating of its phone system. The decree allowed AT&T to divest itself of its equipment business, provided that such sale was "at a fair price and on reasonable terms."[35] Significantly, the decree prevented AT&T from entering into the computer

---

30 By 1924, the Interstate Commerce Commission had approved AT&T's acquisition of 223 of the 234 independent telephone companies.

31 Letter from N.C. Kingsbury, Vice President, AT&T, to U.S. Att'y Gen. (Dec. 19, 1913), *available at* http://vcxc.org/documents/KC1.pdf.

32 *U.S. v. AT&T*, 552 F.Supp.131, 137 (D.D.C. 1982) (citation and quotation omitted).

33 *Id.*

34 *Id.*

35 Albert B. Iardella, Western Electric and the Bell System 107-15 (1964), *available at* http://www.westernelectric.com/history/WEandBellSystemBook.pdf.

business and, foreshadowing the DOJ's later concerns over patents, required AT&T to give a royalty free license to its intellectual property. These two provisions relating to intellectual property gave rise to Bell Labs' UNIX OS, the first open source operating system.

In 1982, the DOJ and AT&T entered into a Modification of Final Judgment, which released AT&T from the 1956 decree, and breaking up AT&T into seven different Regional Bell Operating Companies ("RBOCs"), all of which were prohibited from selling equipment or offering long distance service.

In 1996, Congress passed the Telecommunications Act of 1996. Section 271 of the 1996 Act prevented the RBOCs from offering long-distance services unless they satisfied the specified conditions of Paragraph 271(c), which included, among other things, evidence of another facilities based competitor and evidence that the RBOC was providing that competitor with non-discriminatory access to components or services they would need to compete with the RBOC (e.g., unbundled network elements and services like directory assistance, 911, operator call completion services, etc.). Although the FCC was nominally in charge of Section 271 applications, the 1996 Act provided that the FCC must give "substantial weight" to the DOJ's assessment as to whether the RBOC met the requirements of Section 271.

It is difficult to view the DOJ's history with AT&T as anything other than regulatory. The settlements the DOJ entered into with AT&T were almost entirely forward looking, imposing interconnection and pricing requirements that seem foreign to law enforcement. They also required royalty free licensing of validly obtained patents, in the hopes that this would lower the barriers to entry into computing markets.

Moreover, anybody who worked at the Telecommunications Task Force after entry of the Modification of Final Judgment can attest, the job of determining whether an RBOC had met the 14 requirements of the 1996 Telecommunications Act was regulatory in its most tedious sense.

VII. The FTC and DOJ as Prosecutors

It is well recognized that prosecutors are aggressive litigators. There are times where the FTC and DOJ follow the same tact, using procedural advantages in order to force parties to abandon a transaction.

One place this occurs is in a telecommunications merger where the DOJ files a complaint to enjoin a transaction where the FCC has also declined an application by one company to transfer control of its licenses to another company. In such a case, the DOJ's policy seems to be to issue a complaint, and then steadfastly refuse to litigate the merger in court along the defendant's timetable, knowing that the parties cannot close given the FCC refusal to approve. This was true in Echostar/DirectTV, WorldCom/Sprint, and more recently AT&T/T-Mobile, all of which were abandoned by the parties because they were unable to litigate the matter in a timely fashion.[36] While timing is a consideration in all transactions, it is telling that the DOJ has never litigated a telecommunications deal where the FCC opposed the transaction.

Another place where the agencies have purposefully refrained from filing a complaint in district court is in the context of hostile tender offers. In such a case, the FTC may not file in district court, knowing that a target's board is not going to approve a merger until the antitrust issues are resolved. This occurred in 2013 when the FTC brought a Part III proceeding instead of filing in district court to block Omnicare's

---

36 While some may argue that without FCC approval of the transfer of the license, there is no value in getting a judicial determination that the transaction does not violate Section 7. But the parties in these transactions clearly see a value in a speedy judicial determination. *See, e.g.*, Edmund Sanders, *EchoStar Races to Save DirecTV Deal*, L.A. Times, Nov. 6, 2002, *available at* http://articles.latimes.com/2002/nov/06/business/fi-echo6.

proposed acquisition of PharMerica. Because no hostile tender offer can survive for the time that a Part III proceeding takes, the parties were forced to abandon the transaction. Ironically, this policy seems at variance with the Williams Act, which is intended to allow for an efficient market for corporate control. As the US Supreme Court wrote in *Edgar v. Mite Corp*:

> Congress reemphasized the consequences of delay when it enacted the Hart-Scott-Rodino Antitrust Improvements Act of 1976 [because] . . . it is clear that this short waiting period [the 10-day period for proration provided for by § 14(d)(6) of the Securities Exchange Act, which applies only after a tender offer is commenced] was founded on congressional concern that a longer delay might unduly favor the target firm's incumbent management, and permit them to frustrate many pro-competitive cash tenders. This ten-day waiting period thus underscores the basic purpose of the Williams Act—to maintain a neutral policy towards cash tender offers, by avoiding lengthy delays that might discourage their chances for success.[37]

This is not to say that the FTC's refusal to litigate the matter in district court in a compressed time schedule is unlawful, unethical, or somehow inappropriate if we regard them as a law enforcement body. Certainly, prosecutors routinely engage in tactics designed to obtain desired outcomes. But there is a difference between efforts by a prosecutor to obtain leverage to obtain a settlement that represents a compromise between the parties as routinely occurs in plea bargains and an effort by a prosecutor to inflict the maximum penalty permitted under law (here preventing the parties from merging under any circumstances) through a pocket veto.

VIII. Conclusion

It is clear that the FTC and DOJ are not like most regulators. They do not, for example, regularly interact with all market participants within a specific industry as FERC does with energy companies. Instead, they interact in an ad hoc and episodic manner, which minimizes the risk of rent-seeking behavior.

The FTC and DOJ also are unlike most law enforcers. When conducting a merger review, agency staff do not act like prosecutors (at least until the decision to file a complaint is made). In the investigation phase, the staff are evaluating evidence and trying their best to make the right decision in the particular case, much as a regulator would do (though one must acknowledge that at some point they cross the line to prosecutor). Indeed, it is precisely that the FTC and DOJ appear like regulators that parties are more transparent with them than would typically exist with a law enforcement body.

Yet because the FTC and DOJ have the power of both law enforcement and regulator, they have an obligation to exercise that power carefully. When they are creating new rules and norms the way a regulator might, they should carefully consider the costs and benefits on all impacted markets. And doing so, they should listen to as many industry participants as possible to hear their views as to the impact of the new rule.

In the merger context, the agencies have an obligation to enforce the law carefully because in many cases they wrote it; and because they have tremendous power to achieve a complete victory by simply not bringing a case when the parties cannot close the deal until the antitrust issues are resolved. This is not

37 457 U.S. 624, 638 (1982) (quoting H.R. Rep. No. 94-1373, at 12 (1976), U.S. Code Cong. & Admin. News, at 2572, 2644).

to suggest that they do not exercise their power carefully; but it is to suggest that just because they have a procedural advantage does not mean they should always exercise it.

And that is significant because the agencies tell the parties little in the HSR process because of confidentiality concerns. The parties do not know the identity of companies that are complaining against them and do not know what those companies are saying. They cannot explain why those views are wrong or motivated by rent-seeking. The parties can rely upon the agencies, of course, to evaluate the credibility of the complaints; but if the agencies are law enforcers, we should recognize that they are not only evaluating a case, they are building it.

Importantly, the agencies bend over backwards to be transparent where they can. They conduct workshops, publish data and guidelines, and often publish closing letters. Yet, the FTC and DOJ do not *always* publish closing letters when clearing a case; and they certainly do not publish interim reports of their investigation as the EC does with 6.1.C. Reports and Statements of Objections, which means the parties themselves are frequently not fully aware of the evidence against them (which can be excruciating when being forced to abandon a multi-billion dollar merger and pay a potentially billion dollar reverse break fee).

But it is only in court that the parties can see the case against them. Yet the FTC and DOJ in tender offer and telecommunications mergers, respectively, do not allow the parties their day in court, meaning the parties never have an opportunity to learn about the true strength of the case against them. Thus, some may wonder as to the legitimacy of the government's decision to sue: what was the rationale, the law, the facts? Some of this is in the complaint, but only from the government's point of view. A lack of transparency as to the strength of the government's case may undermine the legitimacy of its decision to block the case even when that action is completely legitimate.

Whatever we call them, there is no question that the FTC and DOJ represent the government's very best. Their staff are incredibly knowledgeable and hardworking. Their reasoning (while not transparent) is always rigorous. And even where regulatory best practices are not followed, as in the case of SEPs, the result was completely correct. But given their enormous power and the scale of the mergers and lives their decisions impact, it does not seem unfair to respectfully request more transparency. Nor does it seem unreasonable to seek a commitment not to kill deals through pocket vetoes, especially in the case of hostile tender offers because their use seems directly contradictory to the purpose of having a shortened second waiting period for tender offers.

Should Antitrust Fines Target Firms or Agents?

Keith N. Hylton

knhylton@bu.edu

William Fairfield Warren Distinguished Professor, Boston University
Professor of Law, Boston University School of Law

Abstract

Probably the main difference between the US and the EU antitrust enforcement regimes is that the US tends to rely more on penalties against agents to deter violations while the EU tends to rely on penalties against firms. A policy of using monetary fines against firms, as the EU does, probably would be more efficient than the existing US punishment system. In a recent paper published in the *Iowa Law Review*, I examined the economics of punishing agents versus firms. In this short piece I provide a simpler and shorter presentation of my argument, not using the mathematical equations that I used in the Iowa publication. The basic message is that the firm can provide its own governance structure for agents. If the firm does not want to commit a particular crime, it can design its reward structure for agents to remove the incentives for them to commit the crime. Alternatively, if the firm prefers to commit a particular crime, it can almost always design its reward structure to induce agents to commit the crime. An effective deterrent threat will therefore have to focus on the firm.

I. Introduction

Probably the main difference between the US and the EU antitrust enforcement regimes is that the United States tends to rely more on penalties against agents to deter violations while the EU tends to rely on penalties against firms. In the United States, an antitrust violation can result in a fine against the firm and a prison sentence for the agents who carried out the anticompetitive actions. In the EU, a fine against the firm is the sole punishment in the vast majority of cases.[1]

A policy of using monetary fines against firms probably would be more efficient than the existing US punishment system.[2] Monetary fines could be imposed with relatively little cost to society. Prison sentences, by contrast, are costly to society because they require the forfeiture of the convicted agent's labor and taxation of the productive sector of society to pay for the agent's upkeep in prison.

Discussions on revising the Criminal Sentencing Guidelines have brought the question of optimality in punishment to the fore recently.[3] DC Circuit Judge Douglas Ginsburg and former Commissioner of the Federal Trade Commission Joshua Wright have proposed a shift toward greater punishment for the agent, by debarring convicted agents from work in their industries.[4] Connor and Lande would raise the penalties imposed on firms,[5] marshalling evidence that penalties in the United States are too low to provide optimal deterrence against cartels.[6]

In a recent paper published in the *Iowa Law Review*,[7] I examined the economics of punishing agents versus firms.[8] I set out both positive and normative analyses. The normative analysis demonstrated that whenever the firm has an incentive under existing penalties to engage in some illegal act that may result in relatively modest punishment for its agents, it can almost always induce its agents to carry out the illegal act. The positive part of the analysis provided an explanation for observed patterns in punishment, such as the plea agreements firms negotiate with the Department of Justice defining which employees are subject to criminal punishment and, in particular, the observed tendency to impose prison sentences on mid-level employees.

My analysis can be applied to many areas of the law but applies especially to price fixing, with its combination of firm-targeted and relatively modest agent-targeted penalties. Almost any plausible effort to use penalties against agents to deter price fixing can be undone by the firm's own system of rewards for agents. Similarly, the firm can almost always eliminate the agent's incentive to price fix whenever it

1 Douglas H. Ginsburg & Joshua D. Wright, *Antitrust Sanctions*, 6 Competition Pol'y Int'l 3, 17-19 (2010).

2 Gary S. Becker, *Crime and Punishment: An Economic Approach*, 76 J. Pol. Econ. 169, 193-99 (1968).

3 In June 2014, the United States Sentencing Commission issued a notice in the Federal Register that it is conducting a study of antitrust offenses, including examination of fine provisions governing bid-rigging, price fixing, and market allocation agreements. *See* Melissa R. Ginsberg & Deirdre A. McEvoy, *Criminal Antitrust Fines: Trends And Recent Developments*, Mondaq, Aug. 6, 2015, http://www.mondaq.com/unitedstates/x/333024/Cartels+Monopolies/Criminal+Antitrust+Fines+Trends+and+Recent+Developments. For public comments in response to the notice, *see* Public Comment from July 29, 2014, http://www.ussc.gov/amendment-process/public-comment/public-comment-july-29-2014 (last visited Nov. 12, 2015).

4 *See* Ginsburg & Wright, *supra* note 1.

5 John M. Connor & Robert H. Lande, *Cartels as Rational Business Strategy: Crime Pays*, 34 Cardozo L. Rev. 427, 435-442 (2012).

6 *Id.*

7 Keith N. Hylton, *Deterrence and Antitrust Punishment: Firms Versus Agents*, 100 Iowa L. Rev. 2069 (2015). This paper offers a simpler and more focused discussion of the same issues, borrowing heavily from my article.

8 Daniel Sokol, *Policing the Firm*, 89 Notre Dame L. Rev. 785 (2014); Bruce H. Kobayashi, *Antitrust, Agency, and Amnesty: An Economic Analysis of the Criminal Enforcement of the Antitrust Laws Against Corporations*, 69 Geo. Wash. L. Rev. 715, 735-737 (2001) (discussing agency costs of cartel enforcement); Giancarlo Spagnolo, *Managerial Incentives and Collusive Behavior*, 49 Eur. Econ. Rev. 1501, 1515–16 (2005) (discussing how incentives of managers to smooth income may enhance cartel stability).

does not have an incentive to fix prices (that is, the firm-level expected penalty is greater than the profit from price fixing). This implies that penalties against the firm sufficient to eliminate the incentive to fix prices are necessary to deter price fixing.

In this short piece I will provide a simpler and shorter presentation of my argument, not using the mathematical equations that I used in the *Iowa Law Review* publication. The law review paper presents a simple and stylized model of the interaction between firm and agent incentives and, although the model is simple, it is still overly complicated for the standard law review. Here I want to focus on the intuition behind the stylized model.

The basic message is that the firm can provide its own governance structure for agents. If the firm does not want to commit a particular crime, it can design its reward structure for agents to remove the incentives for them to commit the crime. Alternatively, if the firm prefers to commit a particular crime, it can almost always design its reward structure to induce agents to commit the crime. An effective deterrent threat will therefore have to focus on the firm.

II. Firm versus Agent Incentives

In this part I will offer a brief and general presentation of the incentive divergence problem that this paper examines. Suppose there is one agent and one firm. A firm cannot commit a crime without the assistance of the agent.

Whenever the gain to the firm from the crime is greater than the expected penalty (i.e., the probability of firm punishment multiplied by the fine imposed on the firm), the firm will commit the crime.

In deciding whether to commit the crime, the agent will compare his utility in the state in which he does not commit the crime to his utility in the state in which he does commit the crime. If his expected utility is lower in the state in which he commits the crime, he will not commit the crime, and vice versa. This generates four incentive scenarios to consider:

	Expected utility from compliance greater than expected utility from commission	Expected utility from compliance less than expected utility from commission
Gain to firm from crime less than expected penalty	Both Firm and Agent comply	Firm complies Agent commits
Gain to firm from crime greater than expected penalty	Firm commits Agent complies	Both Firm and Agent commit

Source: Keith N. Hylton, *Deterrence and Antitrust Punishment: Firms Versus Agents*, 100 Iowa L. Rev. 2069 (2015).

In the first cell, both agent and firm prefer to comply with the law because the firm's gain from the crime is less than the expected penalty and the agent's expected utility from the crime is less than his expected utility from commission.

In the second cell, we observe a conflict: the agent prefers to commit the crime while the firm prefers to comply with the law. This scenario might arise if the agent expects a net gain from committing the crime and does not expect the firm to respond by eliminating the gain to the agent. There are several reasons why this might occur: (1) the firm may be unable to identify and punish the agent who has caused it to suffer a penalty; (2) the cost of identifying and punishing the responsible agent may exceed the deterrence gain the firm might get; or (3) the firm cannot credibly commit to impose a penalty that would deter the agent.

In the other conflict scenario, the firm prefers to commit the crime but the agent prefers to comply. In this case, the firm could rearrange its compensation structure to give the agent an incentive to commit the crime. If the agent prefers not to commit the crime because the expected penalty exceeds any gain he might receive, the firm can increase the agent's wage conditional on committing the crime. Hence the scenario in which the firm prefers to commit the crime, but the agent does not, can easily be transformed into the scenario in which both firm and agent commit the crime.

It is this second conflict scenario which is the focus of this paper. If, under ordinary circumstances, a firm can easily alter the agent's incentive to induce him to commit a crime, then law enforcement will need to focus on the incentives of the firm rather than those of the agent.

III. Agent Underdeterrence Problem

Now let's consider the features of real-world antitrust enforcement. The expected penalty to the agent for price fixing is the likely prison term imposed under the Sherman Act, discounted by the probability that the agent will be detected and prosecuted. The average prison sentence for defendants convicted of fixing prices is now 25 months—or roughly two years.[9] Thus, the penalty that the agent expects to receive, if he is detected and prosecuted, is the loss of wage income for two years. The expected gain to the agent for price fixing is the reward given by his firm (or by another firm that hires the agent) for the additional profit the agent secures for the firm through price fixing. If the firm does not reward the agent, then the agent's expected gain from price fixing is negative, since he takes the risk that he will be imprisoned and gets nothing in return.

This is just a standard gamble. The agent can engage in price fixing and take the risk of being caught and losing his salary for the period of imprisonment. On the other hand, if he is not caught, he gains the reward the firm gives directly or indirectly for price fixing—again, the reward may be just a bonus for increasing profits. Suppose the probability of getting caught is 10 percent, the agent's salary (I will use the term "wage" at times) is \$100,000, and the reward (bonus for increasing profits) is \$30,000. This implies that the wage loss from a two-year prison sentence is \$200,000. Thus, the agent will compare (.9)(\$30,000) – (.1)(\$200,000) = \$27,000 - \$20,000 = \$7,000. In this case, the agent would have an incentive to fix prices since his net reward (\$7,000) is positive after taking the punishment into account.

9 Antitrust Division 2013 Criminal Enforcement Update, http://www.justice.gov/atr/public/division-update/2013/criminal-program.html (last visited Nov. 12, 2015).

Looking at the agent's incentive a bit more generally, note that the current-period bonus is one third of the agent's salary. The gamble the agent faces boils down to a comparison of the odds of detection, 1/10, to the ratio of the bonus percentage to the years in prison. If the latter ratio exceeds the former, the agent will have an incentive to fix prices. Thus, if the firm wants to guarantee that the agent will have an incentive to fix prices, it just has to make sure that the ratio of the current-period bonus percentage to the number of years in prison is greater than the odds of detection. In this example, the odds of detection are set by the government's enforcement policy at 1/10. Under the assumptions of the example, the ratio of the current-period bonus percentage to the years in prison is simply the ratio of 1/3 to 2. Since the ratio of 1/3 to 2 exceeds the detection odds, the agent has an incentive to fix prices. Note that the bonus percentage could fall to 25 percent and the agent's incentive to fix prices would still be positive. However, if the bonus percentage falls to 20 percent, the agent's incentive to fix prices would no longer be positive.

One can analogize the firm to a gambling house in this presentation. Given a set of fees and rewards for a lottery, a gambling house can alter the punter's odds of winning to ensure that the house's expected profit is positive. In the law enforcement game, the government moves first and determines the odds of detection. The firm moves second, using the information on the odds of detection and penalties. If the firm has an incentive to fix prices given the government's detection odds and penalties, then it can easily modify agent rewards so that the agent is likely to profit from committing the crime.

There is more to consider in this simple survey of incentives. Suppose the firm offers the agent a bonus in later years of employment as another reward for price fixing. To simplify this analysis, I will assume that the firm offers, as an additional reward for price fixing, a 10 percent bonus for 10 years which begins after the punishment period of two years. The agent receives this bonus whether or not he is caught by the antitrust authorities. Now the employee compares (.9)($30,000) – (.1)($200,000) + $100,000 = $107,000, which makes price fixing even more attractive to the agent.

I could change the assumptions in various ways to make the incentive for the agent stronger or weaker. But this example should be sufficient to suggest that it is not difficult, under the current penalty system, for a firm to structure incentives so that the agent will find it personally rewarding to engage in price fixing. In general, the firm always has two tools at its disposal, current-period rewards and deferred compensation. By using these tools skillfully, the firm can exert a great deal of control over the agent's incentive to follow the law.

IV. Increasing the Sentence

Of course, one response to the agent under-deterrence problem identified in the previous part is to increase the length of the sentence imposed on the agent. If the sentence is increased sufficiently, the agent's incentive to engage in price fixing can be eliminated.

Let us change the assumptions of my example. Again, suppose the probability of getting caught is 10 percent, the agent's wage is $100,000, and the reward is $30,000. Now let the prison sentence be four years. This implies that the wage loss from a four-year prison sentence is $400,000. Thus, assuming the employer continues to offer the same bonus during the first year and does not offer a bonus for the later years, the agent will compare (.9)($30,000) – (.1)($400,000) = $27,000 - $40,000 = -$13,000. Now the agent will not have an incentive to fix prices after taking punishment into account.

If the firm would prefer the agent to fix prices, the firm could respond to the longer prison sentence by increasing the bonus to the agent for increasing profits, or by offering a bonus in later years. Suppose the bonus for increasing profits is raised to $60,000. Now the net reward to the agent, taking prison into account, is (.9)($60,000) – (.1)($400,000) = $54,000 - $40,000 = $14,000 and, as a result, the agent will have an incentive to fix prices after taking punishment into account.

As in the previous example, I could easily change the numerical assumptions to make price fixing more or less attractive to the agent. However, the point of this exercise remains valid: it is not difficult for the firm to structure incentives so that the net reward from price fixing is positive for the agent, and this is so even if the average prison sentence length is doubled.

One possible answer to this problem is to just keep increasing the sentence to the point where it is unlikely that the firm can undo the deterrence effect of the threatened sentence. While increasing the sentence is a possible solution, there are constraints. The numerical examples considered here suggest that for any plausible increase in the sentence, the firm can probably undo its deterrence effect by increasing the reward to the agent for increasing profits, or by steepening the wage profile. The sentence length would have to be increased by a large amount in order to prevent the firm from undoing its deterrence effect. However, increasing the sentence by a factor of five, say from an average of 2 years in prison for price fixing to an average of 10 years, would be difficult to get courts to accept, after having sentenced within a certain range for many years. Certainly defendants would challenge such sentences as disproportionate, given the nature of the harm caused by price fixing. It would be difficult to defend against proportionality challenges a sentence scheme that puts price fixers in prison for as long, or longer, than most violent criminal offenders. The average prison sentence for murder is 149 months (or around 12 years) and the average prison sentence for kidnapping is 104 months (or around 9 years).[10] Increasing the sentence for price fixing to 10 years would result in price fixers serving longer sentences than many murderers.

Increasing the sentence drastically is unlikely to be a solution to the problem of firms being able to undo the deterrent effect of punishment for price fixing. It is too easy for the firm to undo the deterrence effect for reasonable sentence enhancement levels, and to prevent the firm from undoing the effect would require the sort of increase in sentences for price fixing that would invite challenges based on fairness and proportionality in criminal punishment.

V. Debarment

Ginsburg and Wright propose debarment as a solution to the agent under-deterrence problem.[11] Under the debarment approach, the agent would be barred from returning to work in his industry in the post-punishment period.

Being debarred from returning to the industry, the agent will suffer a loss to the extent that his within industry wage in the post-punishment period exceeds his wage level working outside of the industry. It is plausible that this loss would be substantial because the agent's within industry wage will reflect the value of his experience in the industry—that is, the market value of the agent's industry-specific human capital. The debarment incentive changes the agent's incentives primarily by reducing the value of the promise of a post-punishment reward from the firm (or the industry).

---

10 Lawrence A. Greenfeld, *Prison Sentences and Time Served for Violence*, Bureau of Statistics: Selected Findings, April 1995, *available at* http://bjs.gov/content/pub/pdf/PSATSFV.PDF.

11 *See* Ginsburg & Wright, *supra* note 1.

If the agent is detected, debarment means that he loses his wages over the time of imprisonment and also loses the wage differential he would receive compared to his out-of-industry wage after his time of imprisonment. If the differential is zero, or very small, debarment will not alter the agent's incentives any more than the standard punishment. Suppose the agent's differential is substantial, such as $30,000 per year. Again, I will consider a post-punishment period of 10 years. If the agent is detected he loses $200,000 + $300,000 = $500,000 under the debarment plan. If the agent is not detected, he receives his current-period bonus of $30,000 and the deferred bonus of $100,000, for a total of $130,000. Thus, the agent will find the net reward for price fixing is (.9)($130,000) – (.1)($500,000) = $117,000 - $50,000 = $67,000, which implies that the agent will find it attractive to fix prices even taking the risk of debarment into account.

If the firm does not offer a post-punishment bonus, the effect of debarment is much greater. In that case, the net reward for price fixing is (.9)($30,000) – (.1)($500,000) = $27,000 - $50,000 = -$23,000, which implies that the agent would be deterred from price fixing. If there were no debarment threat, the net reward would be (.9)($30,000) – (.1)($200,000) = $27,000 - $20,000 = $7,000. So it is clear that debarment alters incentives in a way that makes price fixing less attractive to the agent.

Debarment raises the stakes but does not completely eliminate the incentive for the agent to fix prices. Again, I could alter the numerical assumptions to make debarment a greater or lesser threat to the agent. However, the basic message remains: the firm can easily undo the deterrence effect of punishment, even if the punishment includes debarment.

I have assumed that the firm does not compensate the agent, if he is detected and punished, during the punishment phase. However, if the firm compensates the agent while he is under punishment,[12] and in addition provides a reward if he escapes punishment, the deterrent effect of debarment can be largely eliminated.

VI. Some Positive Implications

The discussion so far reveals the ease with which a firm that has an incentive to price fix can induce its agents to carry out the acts of price fixing. This may provide an explanation for the many cases of price fixing brought by enforcement agencies in the United States even though the penalties imposed on agents are severe. The incentives within the firm may have undone the effects of the Sherman Act's punishment provisions aimed at agents.

Firms will never admit openly that they have structured incentives to induce agents to fix prices. But economic analysis focuses on actual incentives and results, rather than what firms say they are doing. Any firm that greatly rewards agents for increasing profits, without inquiring into how those profits were generated, has in effect created a reward for price fixing.

This framework also offers an explanation for some of the puzzling features noted about prison sentences. Most prison sentences in antitrust are imposed on mid-level employees, well below the top-level of management.[13] Carve-out agreements, which are negotiated plea deals by the firms in which they specify certain employees for prosecution, tend to sacrifice mid-level employees of the firm.[14] What explains this pattern?

---

12 Connor & Lande, *supra* note 5, at 440-41 n. 54 (noting reports that some companies continue to pay convicted agents while they are in prison).

13 *Id.* at 440-441.

14 *Id.*

Return to the incentive analysis of the preceding part. First, the set of potential agents suitable for prosecution will tend to be either mid-level or senior. Junior employees will seldom be in a position to arrange or direct a price fixing agreement with rival firms. A mid-level agent, unlike a senior agent, can be rewarded by the firm after he completes his (typically two-year) sentence. With the prospect of such a reward in view, the threat of prosecution against mid-level employees can easily be undone by the compensation policies of the firm. Thus, the US sentencing data probably reflect the rational economic response of firms that have incentives to engage in price fixing to the enforcement policies of the Justice Department. The firms can induce mid-level employees to break the law and carve them out for later prosecution in plea deals. To the extent such a strategy reduces the expected sanction against the firm, it could tip the incentives of some firms in favor of price fixing. In other words, if in the absence of a carve-out strategy the firm would not have an incentive to fix prices, the option of a carve-out strategy, coupled with a reduced sanction on the firm, might change the firm's incentives toward preferring price fixing.

VII. Conclusion

The Sherman Act imposes penalties both on the firm and on the agent and therefore generates the possibility of a conflict in which the agent may have an incentive to violate the statute while the firm does not, or vice-versa. The message of this paper is that the conflict scenario in which the firm has an incentive to violate the statute and the agent does not is much more worrisome than the reverse scenario. The firm has sufficient tools at its disposal to discourage the agent from violating the statute when the firm prefers to comply with it. However, if the firm has an incentive to violate the statute, it can almost always induce its agent to violate the statute. This implies that the preferable approach to deterrence is to treat the deterrence at the firm level as a higher priority concern than deterrence at the agent level.

On the Use of Economics in Support of the Competition Mission at the FTC

FRANCINE LAFONTAINE

laf@umich.edu

Senior Associate Dean for Faculty and Research &
William Davidson Professor of Business Economics and Public Policy
Ross School of Business, University of Michigan;
Former Director, Bureau of Economics, US Federal Trade Commission

Abstract

The Bureau of Economics ("BE") at the Federal Trade Commission ("FTC") supports both the consumer protection and maintaining competition missions of the Commission. In this paper, I describe in particular the activities of the BE in support of the antitrust or maintaining competition mission of the agency. In the process, I discuss some of the ways in which the work of economists is managed within the agency, and incorporated into the decision processes at the Commission. I begin by addressing the role of economists in what constitutes the bulk of the agency's work product, namely investigations and policy enforcement. I then comment on the role of research and outreach, to which the BE dedicates important amounts of resources. This allows me to further discuss the research role of economists at the Commission more broadly, and describe how the research performed by BE economists not only informs the Commission generally, but also plays a major role in the enforcement and advocacy and other outreach activities of the Commission.

I. Introduction

The Bureau of Economics ("BE") at the Federal Trade Commission ("FTC") supports both the consumer protection and antitrust missions of the Commission. BE staff consist of roughly 80 PhD economists, another 20 or so research analysts (who typically have undergraduate or masters degrees in economics), four or five financial analysts, and support staff. BE plays three major roles in support of both missions at the FTC. Its primary function is to work with Commission attorneys on competition and consumer protection enforcement matters, and, in particular, to provide economic analyses—both theoretical and empirical analyses—to better inform enforcement decisions. Second, the economists in BE are actively engaged in research that sheds light on agency-relevant issues. Third, BE staff are involved in the advocacy and outreach work performed at the FTC. In this domain, BE economists frequently share their expertise, jointly with other FTC staff, not only in the form of formal comments,[1] but also via informal discussions with Congressional staff, state legislators, and regulators and representatives of other agencies. On both the national and the international fronts, BE staff and management participate in numerous workshops and related activities.[2] In terms of international affairs, BE staff contribute substantially to US submissions to the OECD[3] and also work alongside legal staff at the FTC in collaboration with colleagues from around the world in the International Competition Network.[4]

In the remainder of this paper, I describe in greater detail the activities of the BE as they relate to the maintaining competition mission of the FTC. The foregoing is based largely on remarks I prepared for the May 2015 Global Antitrust Economics Conference organized jointly by the Concurrences Journal and the George Mason University School of Law's Law and Economics Center, where I was asked, as BE Bureau Director at the time, to speak on a panel on the "Use and Abuse of Economic Evidence in Antitrust Cases."

II. BE and the FTC's Maintaining Competition Mission: Enforcement

About two-thirds of BE staff operate in one of its two antitrust divisions. The Bureau's antitrust divisions support the FTC's Maintaining Competition Mission by: (1) identifying and taking actions to address anticompetitive mergers and practices that harm consumers; (2) engaging in effective research and stakeholder outreach to promote competition, advance its understanding, and create awareness of its benefits to consumers; and (3) collaborating with domestic and international partners to preserve and promote competition.

---

1 For numerous examples of advocacy comments, *see* https://www.ftc.gov/policy/advocacy/advocacy-filings.

2 For example, in the last several months, BE staff have interacted with economists and other staff at competition agencies around the world, and with practitioners from various countries as well, on several occasions. Earlier this year, a BE economist made a presentation about the research we have done on ex-post merger evaluations at an OECD Workshop on the Ex-Post Evaluation of Competition Authorities' Enforcement Decisions. Also, in the last few weeks, two economists spoke at international conferences: one attended the OECD Latin American Competition Forum on September 16-18 to speak about competition in the retail grocery industry. The other spoke at the 8th Annual Eastern European Competition Workshop held in Bucharest, Romania, on September 10-11. Moreover, another BE staff member concluded his four-month detail at the Competition and Markets Authority at the end of September. Similarly, the BE front office often engages with practitioners, economists, and other staff at other competition agencies. In the last several months, for example, the BE director has participated in workshops in Belgium, France, and Australia in addition to a number of workshops and conferences here in the USA.

3 *See* https://www.ftc.gov/policy/reports/us-submissions-oecd-other-international-competition-fora.

4 *See* http://www.internationalcompetitionnetwork.org/.

In terms of enforcement, the bulk of the effort at the FTC—and thus the bulk of the economists' efforts as well—is dedicated to the assessment of potentially anticompetitive, often horizontal, mergers. For example, in fiscal year 2014, 1,663 mergers and acquisitions were reported to the US Department of Justice ("DOJ") and the FTC, up from 1,326 in fiscal year 2013.[5] Only a small percentage of these result in the antitrust authorities undertaking an extended review. Though timing issues and the duration of cases make calculations of percentages problematic, it is instructive to know that in total, in fiscal year 2014, the FTC issued only 30 Second Requests, and the DOJ 21. Moreover, the FTC brought only 17 merger enforcement actions in that same year.[6] Of these, the majority (13) were consent orders that permitted the merger to proceed subject to certain conditions, another three were transactions that were abandoned or restructured during the investigations, and one resulted in a complaint in federal court to enjoin the transaction. The FTC also brought eight non-merger antitrust enforcement actions in fiscal year 2014, six of which were resolved with consent agreements.[7]

The major role of BE staff in these investigations is to analyze the likely effects of the merger or practice on competition in order to advise the Commission on whether or not, from an economic perspective, the merger or practice should be challenged. Such analyses often are quite complex. Moreover, the exercise generally is predictive, and the future is always uncertain. Economists rely on theory, in particular analyses of the incentives of various parties, and of changes in these incentives going forward, as well as data and empirical methodologies to develop their understanding of the likely competitive effects of the merger or practice so as to inform their recommendations. Of course, data are never as complete as one might want, and models, by definition, are approximations. In addition, particularly in merger cases reportable under the Hart-Scott-Rodino Act, staff must work under the time constraints imposed by the review process. Nonetheless, in my view, staff economists produce very high quality work product that FTC Commissioners truly can rely upon as they strive to understand the market and the implications of the merger or conduct in question.

While attorneys sometimes equate economics to statistics, it is important to understand that economic analysis is not just about data and statistics. Economists rely heavily on theory to interpret the patterns in the data, and, when possible, to inform the type of assumptions they rely on in the development of their empirical models and statistical analyses. In some matters, staff have little data to rely on—either because the past is not a good representation of the future (e.g., in potential competition cases) or the firms' data are simply not reliable or useful for the question to be analyzed. In those cases, the BE analysis tends to be mostly theoretical, such as in the Verisk/Eagleview matter discussed in this year's *Review of Industrial Organization* paper.[8] Of course, when data are available, statistics are a useful tool as they allow us to describe and organize the information available from companies and other sources, and measure various objects of interest. Still, economic theory plays a critical role even in data intensive cases, as it drives the specifications used and the interpretation of data patterns.

---

5 Fed. Trade Comm'n & U.S. Dep't of Justice, Hart-Scott-Rodino Annual Report: Fiscal Year 2014 (2015), *available at* https://www.ftc.gov/system/files/documents/reports/federal-trade-commission-bureau-competition-department-justice-antitrust-division-hart-scott-rodino.s.c.18a-hart-scott-rodino-antitrust-improvements-act-1976/150813hsr_report.pdf.

6 *See id.* at 5. Again, timing issues make direct comparisons of these numbers to the number of Second Requests problematic, so one should not infer a probability of enforcement action to Second Request based on these. Indeed, experience suggests that such a probability is greater than the 50% suggested by the figures above.

7 For merger and non-merger enforcement statistics for each year starting in 1996, *see* https://www.ftc.gov/competition-enforcement-database.

8 *See* Balan, David J., DeGraba, Patrick, Lafontaine, Francine, McAlvanah, Patrick, Raval, Devesh, and David Schmidt. 2015. "Economics at the FTC: Fraud, Mergers and Exclusion," 47 Review of Industrial Organization, 4 (Dec. 2015) pp. 371-398 *available at* http://link.springer.com/article/10.1007/s11151-015-9488-6. Also see Section 3 for more on the yearly special issue of this journal focusing on antitrust and regulatory economics.

An important benefit that the Commission derives from the economic modeling of competitive effects performed by economists and, where data of sufficient quality are available, the empirical estimation of the size of those effects, is that the structure of the analysis makes explicit the assumptions used in the model. Because they are predictive, analyses of competitive effects, whether legal or economic, must rely on various assumptions. Formal modeling approaches have the advantage that, by their nature, they require that one make assumptions explicit. Decision makers then are in a position to gauge their degree of comfort with the assumptions given other information obtained in the course of the investigation. Moreover, the sensitivity of predictions regarding competitive effects can be tested by altering the model's assumptions. This in turn yields information as to which assumptions are most critical to the assessment and to the estimated magnitudes of effects. This modeling and robustness testing process thus provides critical information that aids the FTC Commissioners in their decision making.

At the FTC, the work of the BE staff economists on competition matters reaches the Commissioners in the form of a memorandum describing the economic analyses and results that form the basis for the economists' recommendation in the matter, sent alongside the memorandum and recommendation prepared by the staff of the Bureau of Competition ("BC") and/or by one of the regional offices.[9] Not surprisingly, the economic analysis and recommendation are greatly enriched by the interaction and cooperation between the FTC's economists and attorneys during the course of the investigations, as they work together to gather relevant information, meet with parties, carry out investigational hearings, and so on. Similarly, the BC staff analyses and recommendation greatly benefit from the insights generated by the interactions of the legal staff with the economists throughout the investigation. In part because of this cooperation, which allows both staff attorneys and economists to consider all the evidence as well as the arguments that they all view as critical to a given case, staff of both Bureaus arrive at the same conclusion regarding the merits of a case in the vast majority of cases. Nonetheless, there are circumstances where the perspectives and recommendations remain different.[10] In those cases, the Commissioners are made aware of the differences through the normal set of briefings that are held for each matter, as well as the staff memoranda and recommendations, and, in many cases, memoranda and recommendations issued by Bureau management (i.e., BC and BE front offices).

In addition to working alongside the legal staff throughout the process, staff economists are supported by a structure that ensures ongoing interactions with BE managers as well, all of whom have substantial antitrust experience. The end result is the type of high quality work product that in my view could well withstand a peer review process such as the one imposed by academic journals for publication purposes. Indeed, the work is subjected to a robust review process internally. For example, it is typical for a single staff economist to be assigned to a case. For cases that involve more empirical work, two or three staff economists may work together on a case. Staff work under the direct and ongoing supervision of a manager who is himself or herself an experienced antitrust PhD economist. In addition, as cases move towards a full phase investigation, the BE front office, namely the Bureau Director and Deputy Director for Antitrust, become more involved in discussions about the case, and in the details of arguments and analyses. The end result is a staff memorandum that contains a thoughtful and thorough economic analysis of the merger or practice, with detailed supporting evidence. Moreover, as would be the case with published papers, the memorandum will provide a clear articulation of limitations and potentially

---

9 Some of the regional offices at the FTC bring antitrust cases, but the vast majority of cases are handled by BC staff. Given this, in the remainder of this paper, I use BC staff as shorthand to refer to both.

10 The extent of differences in the views of economists and attorneys on various matters, when they occur, can be fairly minor, or focused on a very specific issue without leading to different recommendations. In a small subset of cases, they are great enough to lead to different overall recommendations on a case. But this is particularly rare.

open questions. Once the staff memorandum is sent to the offices of the Commissioners, the work is further reviewed by the Commissioners and their staffs. The Commissioners and their staffs also will have been briefed and met with the parties involved in the matter in question, and they may raise additional questions about various aspects of the analyses.[11] Finally, especially in more complex cases, the BE front office may choose to provide further support for the staff recommendation via a short memorandum of its own, which may highlight or emphasize particular aspects of the case. In rare cases, the BE front office may weigh the evidence differently or incorporate other factors and, as a result, arrive at a different recommendation than BE staff. While unlikely, the fact that this can occur again encourages BE staff to conduct a very thorough economic analysis and explain that analysis clearly in their memorandum.

III. Research, Outreach, and Transparency

At various times during my term as Director of the Bureau of Economics at the FTC, I have been asked to explain the type of analyses used in specific cases, or have received requests that such analyses be made more transparent to parties. In my experience, much transparency is achieved through two main mechanisms.

First, staff do discuss methodology and results generally with parties involved in investigations or with their economists. Of course, how much detail they can provide is limited by data confidentiality issues and related considerations. Nonetheless, much information is made available to the parties or their economists.

Second, through its research and outreach activities, the BE often provides rather detailed information about issues that arise in specific cases and the approaches taken by staff to analyze data and other facts presented to them in the course of investigations. In particular, each year the Bureau Director and coauthors (who are staff involved in specific matters) write a paper discussing recent economic issues at the FTC. These papers, published in the *Review of Industrial Organization* ("RIO") in its yearly special issue entitled "Antitrust and Regulatory Update" (which includes contributions from the US Department of Justice's Antitrust Division, the Federal Communications Commission, and the European Commission's Directorate General for Competition), are available on the FTC website.[12]

This year, the FTC's contribution to the special issue includes a discussion of two consumer protection topics, followed by an account of two competition-related investigations. The first of the competition topics included in this year's RIO paper is a discussion of the Verisk/EagleView merger investigation. Verisk makes and markets software to insurance companies to help them prepare property insurance claims estimates. One of the inputs this software relies on is an estimate of the size and shape of the roof of the insured building. EagleView developed and marketed software to estimate a roof's size and shape using overhead photographs, which allows these estimates to be obtained without having to send an individual to perform a physical inspection. These products were complements, but Verisk also had developed software to estimate roof sizes from photographs in direct competition with EagleView. In the

11 At present, each of the Commissioners' offices at the FTC has a BE staff economist serving as an economic advisor on a part-time basis.

12 *See* https://www.ftc.gov/policy/reports/policy-reports/economics-research/economics-ftc.

paper, we describe the economic analysis of that horizontal competition between the companies, and address the vertical issues that arose due to the complementary nature of the companies' primary products.

The second competition policy investigation described in this year's RIO paper is the FTC's case against the North Carolina Board of Dentistry. This case made it to the US Supreme Court based on an important question regarding the legal requirements for actions of state governments to be exempt from federal antitrust enforcement. This issue was decided in the FTC's favor in February of this year. However, a determination that an action is not exempt from the antitrust laws still leaves open the question of whether the action is in violation of those laws. The FTC alleged that the dental board had violated Section 5 of the Federal Trade Commission Act by issuing cease and desist letters to non-dentist providers of teeth whitening services. In the paper, we discuss the type of economic analysis that is relevant to the question of whether that action constitutes anticompetitive exclusionary conduct.

The series of RIO papers published in years past have covered a number of topics relevant to the FTC's competition mission. The papers have covered topics as varied as office supply retailer mergers (in the 2014 paper), quality effects in hospital mergers (also in 2014), physician practices mergers (in the 2013 paper), the economics of standard essential patents (also in 2013), drug manufacturer mergers (in the 2012 paper), as well as a detailed account of the way we approach hospital mergers (in the 2011 paper).[13] The 2011 paper also includes an analysis of the effect of authorized generic drugs on consumers and competition, which was the subject of an August 2011 FTC report.[14]

IV. The Role of BE Research beyond Transparency

The 2011 FTC report on authorized generic drugs mentioned above is an example of research conducted by BE as part of large Commission studies, many of which involve staff from both BE and the legal Bureaus. Other examples of such large studies in support of the FTC's competition mission are two ongoing studies, one on patent assertion entities,[15] and a recently announced study of remedies in FTC merger cases.[16] In addition, BE staff work on more focused economics research projects that are often published in academic journals and/or released in the BE Working Paper series.[17] BE staff also engage with the larger economics community by presenting their research at academic conferences, putting together an active seminar series, and, with the Office of Policy and Planning, organizing workshops on specific topics of interest to the FTC. Finally, they organize and host the annual FTC Microeconomics Conference, the eight of which was held in November of 2015 in Washington, DC. Paper sessions, panel discussions, and keynote addresses covered a variety of topics, including potential uses of user-generated data in policy analysis, economic analysis and the Comcast Time Warner Cable merger proposal, hetero-

13 The 2009 paper also contains a discussion of merger retrospectives, with a focus on hospital mergers.

14 *See* Fed. Trade Comm'n, Authorized Generic Drugs: Short-Term Effects and Long-Term Impacts (2011), *available at* https://www.ftc.gov/reports/authorized-generic-drugs-short-term-effects-long-term-impact-report-federal-trade-commission.

15 *See* Press Release, Fed. Trade Comm'n, FTC Seeks to Examine Patent Assertion Entities and Their Impact on Innovation, Competition (Sept. 27, 2013), *available at* https://www.ftc.gov/news-events/press-releases/2013/09/ftc-seeks-examine-patent-assertion-entities-their-impact.

16 *See* Press Release, Fed. Trade Comm'n, FTC Proposes to Study Merger Remedies (Jan. 9, 2015), *available at* https://www.ftc.gov/news-events/press-releases/2015/01/ftc-proposes-study-merger-remedies.

17 *See* https://www.ftc.gov/policy/reports/policy-reports/economics-research/working-papers.

geneous consumer preferences and public policy, and negotiations within and between firms.[18] The previous FTC Microeconomics Conference was held in in October 2014, and focused on topics such as the impact of big data on consumers and firms, merger remedies, peer-to-peer internet markets, and narrow healthcare networks.[19] In addition to contributing to knowledge that is directly relevant to the FTC's twin missions, and allowing staff to improve or hone their research skills, all these activities also allow BE staff to maintain their visibility among the scholarly community, thereby facilitating their interactions with the external economic experts that the FTC often relies on when matters proceed towards litigation.

BE staff engage in research in part because they are interested in it for its own sake: individuals who pursue a PhD tend to value the idea of doing research, and the opportunity to do so is an important factor in the capacity of the BE to hire and retain the type of high-quality staff members that can support its twin missions. Research is also valued by staff as it affords them the opportunity to increase their understanding of various industries and the regulations that affect them (e.g., hospitals and the various state laws that affect mergers in this industry, pharma and the Hatch-Waxman Act, etc.), as well as the opportunity to continuously update their skill sets. Finally, research is a crucial input into both enforcement and advocacy, as strong contributions to these activities require BE staff to remain current with literature on all sorts of agency-relevant topics.

V. Conclusion

In this paper, I have described the various ways in which the BE supports the competition mission of the FTC. In doing so, I also have discussed how the BE is organized and how it functions within the FTC, in particular as it relates to analyzing competition matters. Moreover, I have emphasized the important role that research plays for BE economists and for the Bureau in supporting enforcement actions as well as the advocacy and other competition-related outreach activities of the FTC.

Given that the primary role of BE economists is to advise the Commission on investigations and other matters that are largely non-public, some of the creative and thorough analyses performed by BE economists will only be observed by those of us who work at the Commission. While the public at large undoubtedly benefits from well-informed policy makers, they cannot directly observe these contributions given the confidentiality issues involved. As a result, research papers are the main way in which BE staff economists are able to disseminate the general information they obtain and the lessons learned through their enforcement work. I therefore encourage those interested in better understanding the approaches and analyses that BE economists conduct in support of the FTC's missions to consult the working papers and publications of the staff economists regularly.

18 *See* https://www.ftc.gov/system/files/documents/public_events/633601/agenda2015_1.pdf for a complete agenda.

19 For details, *see* https://www.ftc.gov/news-events/events-calendar/2014/10/seventh-annual-federal-trade-commission-microeconomics.

Negotiation of Settlements and Remedies by Young Competition Agencies: The Mexican Experience

CARLOS MENA-LABARTHE*

cmena@cofece.mx

Head, Investigative Authority
Federal Economic Competition Commission of Mexico

Abstract

Young competition agencies face many challenges in order to create a sound competition policy. This paper discusses how remedies and their negotiation are valuable tools for emerging competition authorities. Along these lines, the paper will try to address the many facets that the settlement and negotiation of remedies entail. In the case of young competition agencies, their limited experience in these matters poses difficulties in setting criteria and evaluating the effectiveness of the remedial measures imposed or accepted. Furthermore, agencies will usually have to weigh vital institutional concerns, such as legitimacy, credibility, and deterrence, when implementing a settlement policy. The Mexican competition regime is relatively new compared to other jurisdictions. This paper will take advantage of the authority's experience to illustrate the arguments contained within. The development of thorough analyses of the possible solutions to address competition concerns and the importance of setting standards in order to generate predictability and certainty are some of the challenges the Mexican authority has faced. Moreover, the design and negotiation of remedies for the new market investigation procedure will also be discussed. Finally, the paper will conclude by outlining some recommendations for young agencies when developing a remedies and settlements policy.

---

* This paper does not reflect the position of the Federal Economic Competition Commission of Mexico. I wish to thank Laura Méndez for her research assistance.

I. Introduction

This paper will approach the remedies topic from the perspective of a young agency trying to expose the main concerns and constraints that jurisdictions with similar characteristics face in their efforts to build an effective remedies' policy.

In Mexico, the creation of a competition agency first happened in 1993 when the first competition law entered into force. Of course, the competition law has already suffered several amendments, not to mention the "major surgery" it recently went through with a Constitutional amendment for competition and the enactment of a new law.[1] However, as opposed to the many experienced agencies in developed jurisdictions such as in Europe or the United States, the Mexican competition policy is one that is still at a young stage.

Remedies and settlements are areas where the lack of experience can be most notable and complicated for the agencies, as well as for the firms operating in such jurisdictions. When compared with other competition issues, literature devoted to remedies falls short from enough, and this is not a trivial problem. Moreover, the existence of fast-changing markets, new technologies, and regulated industries has resulted in complexities that make the design and implementation of remedies a highly controversial topic. Even so, it is undeniable that settlements enable authorities to maintain and restore competition, while at the same time minimizing costs.

Both tools play an important role in competition policy: that is, to enhance welfare. In order to come from the same theoretical basis, it is important to understand the concept of remedies. Despite there not being a universal definition of remedies in competition law, as it has been recognized as a concept with multiple meanings, we could define them as those measures used to restore and preserve competition. Among other classifications of remedies, we can find: (i) coercive and non-coercive remedies; (ii) substitutionary and specific remedies; and (iii) remedies according to their functions: coercion, restitution, compensation, etc.[2]

Even though remedial measures are not necessarily punitive, if they are used to complement fines, they may acquire a punitive nature.[3] Remedies resulting from abuse of dominance cases can be settled in most jurisdictions, which means that they can be negotiated between the settling firm and the competition authorities before a decision is reached. Moreover, in the context of mergers, remedies can be negotiated through what is commonly referred to as "commitments" procedures.

Settlements can also be achieved in cartel cases in most advanced jurisdictions. In Mexico, this is not the case and I certainly consider it a disadvantage of our system.

The absence of general formulas for the selection of remedies and the necessity to consider each situation on a case-by-case basis makes the selection of remedies a difficult task. Above all, envisaging the remedies' potential impact in the market would normally require some technical knowledge about the given industry and related industries. This assessment would have to be conducted within the context of limited resources for agencies.

---

1 Constitución Política de los Estados Unidos Mexicanos [C.P.], *as amended*, Diario Oficial de la Federación [DO], 5 de Febrero de 1917; Ley Federal de Competencia Económica [LFCE] [Federal Law on Economic Competition], *as amended*, Diario Oficial de la Federación [DO], 24 de Diciembre de 1992.

2 Ioannis Lianos & Damien Geradin, Handbook On European Competition Law: Enforcement and Procedure 373 (2013).

3 *See* UNCTAD, Appropriate sanctions and remedies 3-5 (2010), *available at* http://unctad.org/en/Docs/tdrbpconf7d5_en.pdf.

Moreover, deciding when to impose a remedy as a sanction along with a fine, and when to settle a case, is not a simple issue for competition agencies. Especially for young agencies, it is important to demonstrate that enforcement is credible in order to generate deterrence. In this regard, sometimes imposing huge fines is more useful to achieving the agency's objectives. Over the long-term, such fines will increase the incentives for the wrongdoers to settle cases, thus placing the agencies in a better bargaining position.

In Mexico, the negotiation of remedies in competition law remains an unexplored topic. Despite the relatively recent merger and non-merger cases where remedies were settled, there are still no specialized studies on their impact and effectiveness. Nonetheless, due to the new powers granted to the Federal Commission of Economic Competition (hereinafter "COFECE", by its acronym in Spanish, or "Commission"), remedies will become a central issue in competition policy, especially considering the introduction of new investigative powers to eliminate barriers to competition and to regulate essential inputs.

The aim of this paper is to analyze the important considerations that the negotiation of remedies imply for young agencies. Additionally, the experience in the design and implementation of negotiated remedies under the Mexican competition law will be discussed. Finally, some conclusions regarding the challenges of selecting and implementing remedies in the short-term in Mexico will be drawn.

II. Remedies and Settlements

1. Imposing Fines or Settling Remedies

Deciding in which cases are fines a better solution than settlements is one of the most important decisions that agencies should make. In some cases, the decision will be made based on the authorities' policy, say for instance, general deterrence, especially when there are clear-cut and serious infringements. In some cases, there might be a need to establish judicial precedence to generate certainty and settling cases would impede this. Moreover, settlements might preclude the possibility to claim civil damages. Finally, even when the authorities might be open to the possibility of settling a case, their decisions will depend on the proposals being offered by the firms and their sufficiency or insufficiency to addressing competition concerns.

In all cases, creating the right incentives for competition enforcement is key. If competition law infringements are not adequately investigated and sanctioned, the incentives for disobedience increase considerably,[4] as opposed to deterrence. In this regard, for young agencies, settlements and fines are complementary tools for achieving the effective enforcement of competition law; the relationship between settlements and fines is symbiotic. The imposition of strong sanctions, which include fines and/or punitive remedies, especially in high-impact cases, will send a message to the market: anticompetitive practices are not permissible and will be discovered and punished. Moreover, such cases will generate incentives for the wrongdoers to settle because of the fear of sanctions. In consequence, the higher the possibility of being strongly sanctioned, the higher the likelihood of negotiations and settlements. Also, the credibility of the agency's enforcement will place the agency in a better position for negotiating settlements.

---

4 *See generally* Gary Becker, *Crime and Punishment: An Economic Approach*, 76 J. Poli. Econ. 169, *available at* www.ppge.ufrgs.br/giacomo/arquivos/ead/becker-1968.pdf.

There have been discussions about establishing criteria to determine the admission of settlements. In general terms, it appears reasonable to consider that settlements are to be accepted when the benefits of an early termination of the violation and the cost savings outweigh the loss of deterrence.[5] As we will analyze later on in this paper, many legal, factual, and economic considerations will play an important role in such an evaluation.

Another important consideration that should be taken into account is that some jurisdictions provide settlements for both cartel and abuse of dominance cases. Nonetheless, it is important to point out that settling cartel cases is a highly controversial topic, due to the nature and purpose of prohibiting cartels, the graveness of the infringements, and the cartels' direct negative effect on consumer welfare. In consequence, if young agencies have the power to negotiate the termination of cartel investigations, they should be cautious to ensure they do not appear weak on prosecuting cartels. Under the Mexican competition law, settlements are only available in unlawful merger and abuse of dominance cases, referred to as "relative monopolistic practices," as well as for the new procedures to eliminate barriers to competition and to regulate essential facilities. In cartel cases, the only procedure available to avoid a sanction for wrongdoers is the Leniency Program, which allows wrongdoers to apply for leniency either before or during the investigation.

Finally, because of the complementariness of their character as competition law and policy instruments, sanctions and remedies reinforce each other. Firms will only have incentives to settle non-merger cases if the consequences of not cooperating appear costly and credible.

2. The Benefits of Negotiating and Settling Remedies

Authorities, markets, as well as firms may all benefit from remedies' negotiations. In general, negotiating and settling remedies helps to avoid unnecessary burdens for the authorities and firms involved. Their involvement in the remedies' design process fosters better-focused outcomes. This is particularly true taking into account that the specialization of the agency staff in every market is nearly impossible, thus the negotiation process allows authorities to have a better understanding of the market in question and allows for a better allocation of resources.

Furthermore, for competition purposes, the negotiation contributes to avoiding potential side effects and to diminishing the latent risks of hampering innovation and imposing costly remedies that might affect competition in the investigated and related markets. Furthermore, settlements reduce the uncertainty of judicial review for the agencies and firms. In addition, for firms, specifically in the case of mergers, commitments (conditions) allow the transactions to be approved and, in doing so, the merger-specific efficiencies can take place in the market.[6]

Negotiations for settlements are important to reduce the risk of damaging efficiencies, and/or raising costs, as well as inhibiting innovation. Lastly, settlements are important because they reduce the risk of imposing wrong remedial measures that will damage market efficiency, which would negatively affect both, producers and consumers.

---

5 *See generally* Francisco Marcos, *Diminishing Enforcement: Negative Effects for Deterrence of Mistaken Settlements and Misguided Competition Promotion and Advocacy* (Instituto de Empresa Business School Working Paper No. AJ8-187-I, 2012), *available at* http://papers.ssrn.com/sol3/papers.cfm?abstract_id=2153894.

6 American Antitrust Institute, *Merger Remedies: General Principles and Approaches*, American Antitrust Working Paper, (July 6, 2015, 10:59 am) http://papers.ssrn.com/sol3/papers.cfm?abstract_id=1103601.

In abuse of dominance cases, settlements provide some procedural flexibility to agencies in investigating potential violations and disposing of cases. Considering the limited resources of agencies and the complexity of cases, settlements are a tool that allow agencies to prioritize their needs and obtain greater benefits from their assets by resolving more cases in shorter timeframes and devoting resources to those cases that need special attention.

Nevertheless, it is important to stress that even when settlements help to reduce costs and focus scarce resources, authorities should refrain from taking advantage of settlements as a way to avoid in-depth analysis of the cases. This is important because in order to design remedies oriented to get the best outcomes for efficient functioning markets, authorities should have previously identified clearly the competition concerns. Otherwise, the remedies could distort efficient markets, among other side effects. On the other hand, a deep understanding of the competition concerns will be essential for the authorities to deciding whether to accept a settlement.

Likewise, in order to implement a successful settlement policy, young agencies should consider creating detailed, transparent, and public rules regarding the conditions and procedures required to negotiate settlements. Otherwise, there are risks that the settlement policy will appear as unfair or extremely discretionary. In accordance with this advice, the COFECE is about to issue for public consultation its guidelines for the early termination of abuse of dominance and unlawful merger procedures. Publishing guidelines also helps to create awareness of the possibility of settlements and provides guidance on proposing the best remedial measures.

Additionally, settlements help firms avoid huge fines. In Mexico, the fines can reach up to 8 percent of a firm's annual turnover for an abuse of dominance case. In recidivism cases, the COFECE can even order the divestiture of assets, social parts, or stock shares. Moreover, firms can be sanctioned by disqualifying senior officials who participated in any abuse of dominance for up to 5 years. Moreover, settlements help wrongdoers to avoid other costs arising from long-lasting investigations, such as monetary expenses, interferences with a high ranking official's duties, reputational losses, and uncertainty.

Finally, when weighing the benefits of settlements against sanctions, institutional arrangements and developments are crucial elements to have in mind. For instance, how much deterrence the competition authority should pursue in order to consolidate its legitimacy or credibility.

3. Weighing the Alternatives

There is no unique classification of remedies, either for merger or non-merger cases. So far, the most simple and common classification of remedies is confined to a division between structural and behavioral. As for a more detailed categorization of remedies, we could use prohibitory remedies, affirmative conduct remedies, disgorgement, and structural remedies.[7] For the purposes of this paper, both prohibitory and affirmative remedies will be categorized as behavioral.

Every remedy has its own advantages and disadvantages, and each of them raise some problems when crafting or implementing them. Tailoring remedies becomes a complicated endeavor since some presume that structural remedies can be intrusive and behavioral remedies might be deemed broad and costly. As

7 *Id.*

a rule, in abuse of dominance cases, behavioral remedies are preferred over structural ones and, in horizontal mergers, structural remedies are considered more appropriate to solve the competition concerns.

In this section, I will draw some differences between structural and behavioral remedies that will help to identify both pros and cons for each type of remedial measure. At the end, I will demonstrate that there is no generic formula to select remedies—in most situations the decision should be made on a case-by-case basis.

a. Structural Remedies

According to experience in most jurisdictions, structural remedies usually aim to change the structure of the markets in order to modify the incentives of dominant firms.[8] Structural remedies may involve divesting companies into two or more separate entities, either vertically or horizontally, divesting operations or machinery, licensing intellectual property rights to enable the entrance of competitors, etc. Divestitures will usually seek to address the lack of rivalry that arises from barriers to the entrance of a new competitor or from the strengthening of a market participant.[9]

Under Mexican competition law, structural remedies are available for both merger and non-merger cases, including abuse of dominance and market investigation cases (market investigations will be further discussed later on). However, in abuse of dominance cases, divestitures are only available as a punitive remedy when there is recidivism. Of course, this does not impede a firm from offering a divestiture in a settlement to terminate an investigation. In unlawful mergers cases, divestiture is also available. Additionally, under the new market investigation procedure, divestiture is provided as a last resort.

This kind of remedy has several benefits, including the definitive character of the remedy,[10] its straightforward application, its immediate effect, and the reduced monitoring costs when compared to behavioral remedies. In addition, the clear interpretation of structural remedies provides more certainty for both firms and agencies.

Nonetheless, structural remedies should be chosen carefully because their misplaced application, given their non-reversible character, might result in serious negative effects, such as potential disruption to client relationships and production facilities. Moreover, they could generate collusive effects by making the markets more symmetric.[11] Additionally, this kind of remedy is likely to modify incentives to invest in R&D if the firms believe that their assets will have to be shared with their rivals.[12] Consequently, the imposition of structural remedies might hamper innovation. Moreover, specifically in merger cases, they might even impede important benefits that could result from the transaction.

---

8 *See generally* OECD, Policy Roundtables: Remedies and Sanctions in Abuse of Dominance Cases (2006), *available at* http://www.oecd.org/competition/abuse/38623413.pdf.

9 *See* UK Competition Commission, Guidelines for market investigations: Their role, procedures, assessment and remedies 79 (2013), *available at* https://www.gov.uk/government/uploads/system/uploads/attachment_data/file/284390/cc3_revised.pdf.

10 *See* Frank P. Maier-Rigaud, *Behavioural versus Structural Remedies in EU Competition Law* 3-6 (2014), *available at* http://papers.ssrn.com/sol3/papers.cfm?abstract_id=2457594.

11 *See* Massimo Motta et al., *Merger Remedies in the European Union: An Overview*, Paper presented at the Symposium on "Guidelines for Merger Remedies – Prospects and Principles," Ecole des Mines, Paris 8 (January 17-18, 2002), *available at* ftp://ftp.igier.unibocconi.it/homepages/polo/RemediesMPV10.pdf.

12 *See* OECD, *supra* note 8.

b. Behavioral Remedies

In contrast, behavioral remedies, also known as "conduct remedies," aim to restore the pre-infringement level of competition in the market by requiring competitors to stop engaging in anticompetitive conduct. Cease and desist orders are a prohibitory remedy, while mandatory remedies, such as firewalls, are an example of affirmative conduct remedies. However, behavioral remedies only partially tackle the anti-competitive problems because firms can still try to neutralize or evade the remedy.[13]

Behavioral remedies are generally less intrusive but they can still produce significant benefits since they avoid causing strong disruptions in a market and allow for a flexible approach as they can be revised over the time. On the other hand, behavioral remedies also have some negative traits, especially since they are often difficult to design and generally involve high monitoring costs.[14] Moreover, it may be difficult to determine the proper duration for a behavioral remedy, and revising the remedy in order to adapt it to changing circumstances may become a permanent task.

4. Choosing the Appropriate Remedy

As mentioned above, to select or accept the appropriate remedy, agencies should take into account the interaction of a range of legal, factual, and economic considerations. Thus, this choice will depend on a case-by-case analysis.

Accordingly, a thorough study of the possible remedies becomes crucial in order not to make the market and, especially, consumers worse-off. To begin with, in all cases, remedies should address the competition concerns and competition agencies should avoid at all times acting in a regulatory role. Thus, it is vital that when assessing the suitability of a remedy, agencies should consider principles such as proportionality, necessity, and legal certainty in order to guarantee that the remedy will be limited to addressing the specific competition concerns without exceeding that goal. I have to admit that sometimes the competition concerns may go beyond the specific investigation and it is more convenient to address those problems in one remedy rather than to have less comprehensive remedies in various investigations.

In addition, competition agencies should be mindful of a remedy's effectiveness and the burden it would pose for both the firms and the agency. Hence, in order to choose a remedy, authorities should have performed an appropriate market-test analysis to identify the infringement and its market effects.[15] Additionally, it is advisable for agencies to contact third parties, in particular suppliers, customers, and competitors, to reach a better understanding of the competitive structure of the market by obtaining useful information and data.[16] In abuse of dominance cases, access to data might be limited because of confidentiality restrictions established in law. Nonetheless, there will always be the possibility to exchange non-confidential information with stakeholders.

---

13 *Id.*

14 Penelope Papandropoulos & Alessandro Tajana, *The Merger Remedies Study —In Divestiture We Trust*, 27 Eur. Competition L. Rev. 443, *available at* http://ecp.crai.com/ecp/assets/Papandropoulos_and_Tajana.pdf ("Against the argument that monitoring them is costly, it has been argued that they do not necessarily deal with pricing (which would require constant monitoring), but there may already be regulatory monitoring in place and if the market is in favor (customers for example), monitoring can be more easily shared with market participants.").

15 *See* Frederic Jenny, *Worst Decision of the EU Court of Justice: The* Alrosa *Judgment in Context and the Future of Commitment Decisions*, 38 Fordham Int'l L.J. 701 (2015), *available at* http://fordhamilj.org/files/2015/05/FILJ_Jenny_WorstDecisionoftheEUCourtofJustice.pdf.

16 *See* OECD, *supra* note 8.

Additionally, agencies should conduct their market tests using both empirical and economic techniques to predict expected effects. The presence of an economic perspective in these tasks will generate predictability, objectivity, and reliability in an agency's decisions.[17]

Furthermore, competition authorities' judgment should be very sharp in order to decide on the ideal timing for an effective negotiation of remedies. In this regard, it is important to keep in mind that the opportunity for settlement will depend on the specific case. However, early settlements could lessen deterrence and impede the authority from clearly identifying the competition concerns.

The now extinct Mexican Federal Competition Commission ("CFC") in the *Sabritas* case dealt with this issue. Following a complaint by its competitor, Sabritas, a snack company that was part of the Pepsico Group, was investigated for the establishment of conditioned sales. The defendant offered remedies to settle the case at the beginning of the investigation. However, the CFC thought that the investigation was still at too early a stage to properly understand the issues and the market. Consequently, the Commission decided to reject the settlement proposal given that the competitive concerns were still not clear at that time. Once the CFC carried out a deeper analysis of the case, it was finally settled.

In some cases, each country's legal framework will establish time constraints. For instance, in abuse of dominance and unlawful merger cases, under the Mexican competition law, firms are allowed to offer proposals only before the issuance of a statement of objections. This means that the defendants should be offering remedies even before the investigation stage has concluded. This limits the time for firms to offer remedies, as well as for the authority to identify the competition issues.

Designing and choosing remedies pose great challenges for competition agencies, as they must engage in a prospective analysis in order to predict the possible consequences arising from the adoption of the remedy. This can be extremely difficult, for instance, in fast-moving markets such as the high-tech sector where it is extremely important to take into account innovation, otherwise important efficiencies could be eliminated or inhibited.

Specifically, during investigations involving intellectual property, designing remedies can become an extremely difficult task. In consequence, competition authorities should acquire independent expert advice to assist in designing structural remedies in order to achieve a balance between preserving incentives for innovation and addressing competitive harm.[18] Moreover, we must keep in mind that the remedies should be updated as they will often have a shorter period of effectiveness than in traditional industries.

Getting it wrong in intellectual property markets can be very costly for market efficiency, as it might affect the buyer's ability to develop, produce, use, distribute, and sell products. This may be the result of imposing a license or partial transfer of a patent or industrial design, which could reduce the ability of the buyer to innovate and compete in the long-run.[19] Sometimes cooperating with other regulators and government departments can help in this regard.

Specifically, in abuse of dominance cases, where companies are constantly innovating, creating spillovers, and exploiting technologies, authorities should be cautious to avoid generating a negative impact on the innovation in the industry. Therefore, in cases where innovation in technology markets is at stake, it is

---

17 *See generally* William E. Kovacic & Carl Shapiro, *Antitrust Policy: A Century of Economic and Legal Thinking*, 14 J. Econ. Persp. 43 (2000), *available at* http://faculty.haas.berkeley.edu/shapiro/century.pdf.

18 *See* UK Competition Commission, Merger Remedies: Competition Commission Guidelines, *available at* https://www.gov.uk/government/uploads/system/uploads/attachment_data/file/284415/cc8.pdf.

19 *See* ICN, Merger Remedies Review Project 10-11 (2005), *available at* http://www.internationalcompetitionnetwork.org/uploads/library/doc323.pdf.

preferable to establish behavioral remedies in fair, reasonable, and non-discriminatory terms among competitors, rather than structural remedies such as the divesting of patents.

5. Evaluating and Generating Predictability

The existence of *ex post* remedies evaluations has proven to be very useful in analyzing the effectiveness of remedial measures. These evaluations include *Merger Remedies Study*[20] published by the European Union and the study by the U.S. Federal Trade Commission ("FTC") published in 1999, *A Study of the Commission's Divestiture Process*.[21] Both studies aimed to evaluate the benefits of the implementation of settlements in previous cases, as well as to identify areas where further improvements could be done. Very recently, the United Kingdom's Competition and Markets Authority ("CMA") announced its intention to carry out a review of 13 sets of remedies that were put in place more than a decade ago.[22] The FTC is also doing a new study on the effectiveness of its orders in merger cases where it required a divestiture or other remedy. The study should provide information on whether the orders met the FTC's remedial goals.[23]

Remedies studies have demonstrated that wrong remedial measures might be related to mistakes in the implementation more than the design. For instance, an inadequate scope of the divested business, issues of interim preservation, or an inadequate selection of the new buyers.[24] As a result, some divested businesses can no longer operate alone after a short period of time, causing the absence of proper competitors in the market. On the other hand, some remedies are so specific that they can be unpractical and generate higher risks of circumvention.[25] In this regard, the development of mechanisms for reviewing the effectiveness of imposed remedies is an important task for young agencies.

Since every young agency needs to go through a learning process that will provide them with more expertise and information to decide future cases, Kovacic and Shapiro have suggested that each competition agency should prepare a full statistical profile of its enforcement activity over time.[26] This type of analysis will provide a better understanding of trends in enforcement activity while allowing agencies to evaluate the effectiveness of previous settlements and to identify areas where further improvements could be done.

In this regard, *ex post* evaluations have allowed agencies to identify some elements that may have affected the effectiveness of past remedies in order to improve the resolution of future cases. Even if this task can be harder for new agencies that lack a body of cases, it is important for them to begin adopting this international best practice. It would also be a good idea for the Organisation for Economic Co-operation

---

20 European Commission, Merger Remedies Study (2005), *available at* http://ec.europa.eu/competition/mergers/legislation/remedies_study.pdf.

21 U.S. Fed. Trade Comm'n, A Study of the Commission's Divestiture Process (1999), *available at* https://www.ftc.gov/sites/default/files/attachments/merger-review/divestiture.pdf.

22 Press Release, UK Competition and Markets Authority, CMA launches reviews of old market remedies (July 14, 2015), *available at* https://www.gov.uk/government/news/cma-launches-reviews-of-old-market-remedies.

23 Press Release, U.S. Fed. Trade Comm'n, FTC Proposes to Study Merger Remedies (Jan. 9, 2015), *available at* https://www.ftc.gov/news-events/press-releases/2015/01/ftc-proposes-study-merger-remedies.

24 *See generally* European Commission, *supra* note 20.

25 *See* Alexander Italianer, Directorate General for Competition, European Commission, *Legal certainty, proportionality, effectiveness: the Commission's practice on remedies*, Presented at the Charles River Associates Annual Conference 3 (Dec. 5, 2012), *available at* http://ec.europa.eu/competition/speeches/text/sp2012_07_en.pdf.

26 *See* Kovacic & Shapiro, *supra* note 17.

and Development or the International Competition Network ("ICN") to perform these studies on various jurisdictions.

Finally, the existence of standards and criteria regarding settlements would be helpful for both agencies and firms because the required analysis will have to be made on a case-by-case basis. However, a standardized approach regarding procedural issues, such as uniform consent agreements and divestiture periods, would provide greater legal certainty and uniformity, which should be guiding principles in all remedies cases.

III. Settling and Negotiating Remedies under the Mexican Competition Law

1. Remedies in Merger Cases

In spite of their complexity, there are some general presumptions regarding remedies in merger cases. With horizontal mergers, structural remedies are traditionally preferred over behavioral ones. In vertical mergers, the presumption is the opposite and there has been a preference for behavioral remedies over structural ones.[27]

Nonetheless, there are horizontal merger cases where structural remedies would not be the most suitable choice. The 2005 ICN report on merger remedies recognizes some of them: (a) when the divestiture is not feasible or it is subject to high and unacceptable risks such as the absence of suitable buyers; (b) when the competitive concerns are possibly of limited duration because of fast-changing technologies or other factors; and (c) when the benefits derived by the merger are substantial, and they would be destroyed by a divestiture.[28]

The Mexican Federal Law on Economic Competition ("FLEC") establishes several remedial options that the competition authority may accept during the merger investigation:

i. Carrying out or abstaining from a specific action;

ii. Divesting specific assets, rights, partnership interest, or stock in favor of third parties;

iii. Modifying or eliminating terms or conditions;

iv. Committing to implement actions that are intended to encourage the participation of competitors in the market, such as providing access or selling them goods or services; or

v. Other measures aimed at preventing the merger from hindering, damaging or impeding competition.[29]

According to the COFECE's mergers experience, structural remedies have been primarily accepted in horizontal transactions where there is high market concentration that will raise the likelihood of coordinated

27 *See* OECD, *supra* note 8.

28 *See* ICN, *supra* note 19 at 12.

29 LFCE art. 91.

and non-coordinated effects. When this risk is added to the existence of barriers to entry and the absence of efficiencies that compensate for the anticompetitive harm, the Commission has opted for structural remedies.

Moreover, in most of the cases, the Commission has accepted a partial divestiture of assets, seeking to affect only those segments of the market where anticompetitive conduct may emerge. In this way, the Commission has found structural remedies to be an instrument that may prevent in a proportional and focused way anticompetitive harms that may arise from horizontal mergers, thus avoiding damage to any merger efficiencies.

During the last 10 years, the Commission has conditioned approval subject to structural remedies in four merger cases with horizontal overlaps: *Continental/Veyance Technologies*; *Novartis/Alcon*; *Nestlé/Pfizer*; and *Pfizer/Wyeth*. Other mergers were conditioned with behavioral remedies, such as the elimination of exclusive agreements, waiver of preferential rights, or elimination of non-compete clauses.

When accepting merger remedies in complex cases, such as multimarket companies or pharmaceuticals, the Commission has considered the divestiture of specific assets. For instance, in the *Novartis/Alcon* merger,[30] the Commission analyzed a global transaction where Novartis acquired Alcon. The Commission believed that the merger had negative effects on competition in the market for multiple-action anti-allergy drugs. The Commission also believed that the parties overlapped in the commercialization of some ophthalmic pharmaceutical products. In consequence, the parties offered to divest the overlapping products so the merger would be cleared.

The Commission has also imposed structural remedies in other unlawful mergers. In the *PTU* case,[31] for example, the authority investigated an unlawful merger between retail store chains to create a food allowance vouchers scheme, which was used to force their suppliers to only accept the vouchers issued by the company Prestaciones Universales ("PU"). In this case, the Commission believed that the creation of such a scheme enabled the companies to fix prices and to restrict the acceptance of other food allowance vouchers. Consequently, the Commission fined the retail store chains and ordered the total divestiture of PU in favor of third parties who were not linked with the sanctioned firms. A 30-day timeframe was granted to present the plan under which the divestiture was to take place.

In the Commission's experience, structural remedies have posed some difficulties. The following problems have been encountered with the design of this kind of remedy:

i. The divested assets might not be attractive for potential buyers or might not result in viable competitors;

ii. The possibility that the wrong buyers might be chosen;

iii. Partial divestitures might not be as effective as the divestiture of stand-alone business; and

iv. The assets could be degraded by the seller to avoid the creation of strong rivals.

To address some of these risks, the Commission has required some specific measures for the implementation of structural remedies. The establishment of limitation periods, as well as conditions on selling to the highest bidder after a limitation period has expired, has helped to diminish the risk of asset deteriora-

30 File CNT-017-2010, Federal Official Gazette (2010).

31 Administrative Appeal RA-46-2000, File DE-27-99, Federal Official Gazette (2010).

tion. In the *Continental/Veyance* merger,[32] for instance, the COFECE established a 30-day period for divesting the assets of Continental AG and Cartye CIM Agent. It was also required that if they failed to complete the sale within this timeframe, the business would be sold to the highest bidder during the following 30 days.

The *Nestlé/Pfizer* merger[33] is another good example of the COFECE's efforts to avoid the risks of a structural remedy. In this case, the Commission only accepted the divestiture of the parties' milk-based infant formula business if it included the manufacturing facilities, an exclusive license over intellectual property rights, sales teams and other important personnel in order to guarantee the viability of the business on a stand-alone basis.

As has been stated, structural remedies are preferred in most horizontal merger cases. However, there have been some exceptions where behavioral remedies have been accepted to address competition concerns. For instance, when Grupo Televisa requested the CFC to approve the acquisition of several cable companies, the Commission believed that there were competition issues regarding the access to content that could strengthen Grupo Televisa's market position in regional Pay TV markets. As a consequence, Grupo Televisa committed to providing any independent cable company non-discriminatory access to its signals (must-offer) and to broadcast the signals produced and transmitted by any independent stations (must-carry) so the transaction could be approved.

Moreover, in the merger of *Televisa/Iusacell*,[34] the Commission originally blocked the transaction because it was believed to generate anticompetitive effects in several markets such as television content and advertising in restricted and open television. However, during an administrative appeal, the parties negotiated remedies designed to guarantee that Televisa would separate the open signals from the restricted, which were at the time only sold jointly. Apart from that, Grupo Salinas (which was in control of the TV Azteca television networks and Iusacell) committed to sell its open television content on a non-discriminatory basis and without tying it to other content. Both companies also committed not to incorporate senior officers from one another's board of directors in order to avoid collusion. Finally, a mechanism was established so that Total Play (a firm offering related services in open and restricted television and mobile communications) would remain with Grupo Salinas.

In merger cases, authorities should not be afraid to block a deal entirely if the commitments do not resolve the competition concerns. In rare cases, the Commission has found that there were no available, either structural or behavioral, remedies for some horizontal mergers and thus has decided to block the transaction. This occurred in the proposed mergers between the main airlines in Mexico, *Mexicana/Aeroméxico* (in 2000 and 2007).[35] In both occasions, the Commission denied the combination between the competitors as it would negatively affect competition, noting that the take-off and landing slots allocation regime was a significant barrier to entry for new competitors. In 2007, the Commission believed that the remedies proposed by Mexicana did not compensate for the possible harm to competition that could result from the merger and, consequently, the merger was not authorized.

---

32 File CNT-084-2014, Federal Official Gazette (2014).

33 File CNT-035-2012, Federal Official Gazette (2012).

34 File CNT-031-2011, Federal Official Gazette (2012).

35 File CNT-25-95, Federal Official Gazette (1999); File CNT-101-2007, Federal Official Gazette (2007).

In the same regard, recently the Commission denied the *Sherwin Williams Company/Comex* merger arguing that it would strengthen the parties' market power and that the proposed remedies would not eliminate the competition concerns.

In some cases, the best solution might be a combination of both behavioral and structural remedies. For instance, in the *Mexichem/CYDSA* merger,[36] the Commission found that a merger between competitors in the market for polyvinyl chloride ("PVC") pipes represented risks to competition, as it would lead to the integration of the only two domestic producers of the main raw material used in the industry. In addition to the divestiture of assets, the Commission requested the merged company to refrain from claiming unfair trade practices and from affecting the supply of inputs to competitors. Additionally, it should not acquire PVC pipe factories, condition in any way the sales of PVC resins or deny their supply, or discriminate against those clients that would acquire imports.

2. Remedies in Abuse of Dominance Cases

Behavioral remedies are normally preferred in abuse of dominance cases. The flexibility and reversibility of these remedies make them appropriate tools for dealing with dynamic markets where the inappropriate imposition of structural relief may cause significant unexpected costs.

In abuse of dominance cases, the FLEC does not establish an exhaustive list of possible remedies. When settling, the Commission's approach has been that abuse of dominance cases should preferably be addressed with behavioral remedies. Up till now, all the abuse of dominance cases involving settlements have been resolved with behavioral measures including cease and desist orders and prohibitive and affirmative obligations. Examples of the obligations include granting low interconnection rates,[37] ensuring transparency,[38] implementing compliance programs,[39] creating call centers to report abusive conduct,[40] limiting the scope of exclusive dealing, untying services, and allowing access to essential services.[41]

For instance, in the *Beers* case,[42] the Commission investigated the existence of exclusivity agreements in the Mexican beer industry following a complaint filed by Miller and other breweries. In order to settle the case, market leaders Cuauhtémoc Moctezuma and Modelo offered a range of behavioral commitments that were approved by the CFC. The commitments included the limitation of the scope and duration of supply agreements (limiting the exclusivity deals to no more than 25% of their respective points of sale, which must be lowered to 20% by 2018), as well as opening unrestricted access to craft beers in restaurants, and other reporting duties.

In another famous case, *Telcel*,[43] the Commission had already imposed a fine of about US$759 million for Telcel's use of margin squeezing in the fixed loop telecommunications market. However, during the

36 File CNT-088-2009, Federal Official Gazette (2011).

37 File DE-037-2006, Federal Official Gazette (2006).

38 *Id.*

39 File DE-148-2008, Federal Official Gazette (2008).

40 *Id.*

41 File DE-030-2011, Federal Official Gazette (2011).

42 File DE-012-2010, Federal Official Gazette (2010).

43 File DE-037-2006, Federal Official Gazette (2006).

administrative appeal process, the CFC agreed to remit the fine as Telcel agreed to lower the interconnection rates for its competitors.

In a more recent case, *Avocados*,[44] the Commission investigated a tying arrangement due to a complaint filed by two companies. The investigated supplier conditioned its services under the requirement of obtaining a different one, thus preventing Hass avocado exports to the United States for any packers that were not affiliated to an association. The COFECE accepted the behavioral commitments proposed by the association. The commitments include untying services and allowing access to non-affiliated members to the certification process. The Commission considered the commitments suitable to eliminate and correct the anticompetitive behavior and to restore competition in the market for Hass avocado exportation to the United States.

IV. Challenges on the Horizon under the New Mexican Competition Law

Along with the traditional competition tools, there are other sort of investigations that involve regulatory and competition features, such as market investigations. Accordingly, in Mexico, the FLEC provides for market investigations in order to increase the COFECE's effectiveness and to enable it to tackle structural problems. This new procedure allows for the elimination of barriers to competition and the determination of essential inputs under Article 94 of the FLEC. Moreover, the procedure ensures that the COFECE is able to solve any structural problems that may exist in markets, while also protecting due process and ensuring that the resolutions will improve efficiency.

This procedure may begin either *ex-officio* or per the request of the Executive Branch. Then, during the investigation stage, the COFECE's Investigative Authority will look for the existence of barriers to competition or essential inputs within a designated timeframe, anywhere between 30 and 120 days.[45] Upon conclusion of the investigation, the Investigative Authority may either issue a Preliminary Opinion—in cases where there are issues to correct because there is no effective competition in the investigated market—and order corrective measures or propose the closure of the file to the Plenum. The corrective measures should eliminate competition concerns in the least costly and restrictive way possible for the firms in the investigated market.

Notably, with this procedure, the involved firms are allowed to propose to the Commission suitable and economically feasible measures to eliminate the competition problems identified.

Moreover, in order to ensure that innovation is not affected, the FLEC establishes a duty on the Commission to apply an "efficiency test" before imposing any kind of remedies. For such a test, the affected firms will have the opportunity during the investigation to demonstrate that the barriers to competition and/or the essential inputs are generating efficiency gains and have a positive impact on competition, which overweigh their possible anticompetitive effects. Among the efficiency gains, firms could argue those resulting from innovation in production, distribution, and commercialization of goods and services.

44 File DE-030-2011, Federal Official Gazette (2011).

45 This deadline may be extended twice. *See* LFCE art. 94.

As is the case for procedures regarding abuse of dominance and mergers, the remedies in market investigations should be selected and crafted carefully to ensure that efficiency is preserved in the market, having special consideration for innovation. However, this new procedure was conceived to be interventionist and, in consequence, the remedial measures that can be imposed might appear more of a "regulatory" nature.

According to the FLEC, the remedies may consist of recommendations to public authorities, orders to eliminate barriers to competition, issuance of guidelines to regulate essential inputs, and divestitures necessary to eliminate anticompetitive effects. It is important to highlight that, given the disruptive nature of divestitures, the FLEC establishes that divestitures shall be imposed only under circumstances where other corrective measures are insufficient to solve the identified competition problems.

The very nature of market investigations entails a challenging approach to remedies since the competition agencies granted with this kind of power are forced to exercise self-control over the imposition or negotiation of competition and regulatory measures.

The Commission has to remain open to dialogue and communication with firms, other regulators and other stakeholders. Since the Commission is not a sector regulator, there are technical issues, such as the existence of sunk costs, economies of scale, network externalities, or other determinants in the behavior of firms, which are difficult to understand during the investigation without the support of other government agencies or third parties.

Resulting from the establishment of this new procedure, the first market investigation was published in the Federal Official Gazette on February 16, 2015 regarding an *ex-officio* investigation into the market for the provision of air transport services that use the International Airport of Mexico City for landing and/or take off. In the forthcoming years, the Commission will have to set the criteria and standards for analyzing remedial proposals made by the parties and to clarify how the settlement process may be different from the settlement processes for abuse of dominance and merger cases.

V. Conclusions

Designing remedies involves necessarily a learning process for young competition agencies.[46] As we have discussed, remedies are useful tools for authorities to restore competition and to prevent harm to the competitive process. However, selecting and tailoring remedies is a difficult task that usually requires a good understanding of the markets involved in order to avoid imposing unnecessary burdens or making binding remedies that might generate negative effects, such as by hampering innovation.

Regarding settlements, legitimacy and credibility are values that young agencies should strengthen to reinforce their bargaining positions, as well as to enhance the likelihood of settlement. In this regard, agencies should look for a balance between imposing fines and sanctions and settling cases.

Mechanisms to provide certainty over the settlement procedures and the selection of remedies are useful for both authorities and firms. The establishment of guidelines and criteria facilitates certainty for authorities and encourages settlements. Additionally, guidelines help to establish the foundation for the development of long-term competition policy objectives.

---

46 *See* Spencer Weber Waller, *The Past, Present, and Future of Monopolization Remedies*, 76 Antitrust L.J. 11, (2008), *available at* http://papers.ssrn.com/sol3/papers.cfm?abstract_id=1146604&download=yes.

In the following years, the quest for adequate remedies and settlements will become a challenge for the COFECE and I believe this will be the case for many young agencies. This is especially true due to the nature of fast-moving economies and emerging and global markets.

The recent trends regarding deregulated markets and new competition tools that have been developed to tackle anticompetitive market structures impose another challenge for competition authorities. The new market investigation procedure under the FLEC will require the Commission to overhaul its current remedies policy.

Additionally, cooperation among agencies is important, especially in the presence of early remedies proposals given by parties, for instance, in a global merger. In these cases, where parties offer commitments in many jurisdictions, it is necessary to foster effective coordination between different competition authorities to avoid conflicting resolutions regarding remedies.

Finally, we can outline some recommendations for competition agencies to assist in the development of their remedies and settlements policies:

i. Agencies should engage in a deep analysis of the legal framework governing these tools in order to understand their scope, weaknesses, and potential.

ii. Agencies should adopt international best practices in accordance with their own goals and legal frameworks.

iii. Agencies should develop strategies for imposing remedies and accepting settlements, taking into consideration the different nature and objectives of the procedures involved (e.g., merger and non-merger).

iv. Agencies should establish methods for selecting remedies and proposing settlements that consider principles such as necessity, proportionality, and certainty.

v. Agencies should evaluate their policies periodically.

vi. Lastly, agencies should keep in mind that procedure is important. Both agencies and firms should try to be open, transparent and honest and to engage in dialogue to achieve the best results.

Brother, May I?: The Challenge of Competitor Control over Market Entry

Maureen K. Ohlhausen[*]

mohlhausen@ftc.gov

Commissioner, US Federal Trade Commission

Abstract

Those concerned with restrictions on innovative technologies and business models often decry the stultifying effects of a "Mother, May I?" approach, whereby the innovator needs government permission to enter a market. These are worthy concerns that regulators ought to take seriously. This speech focuses on a related issue, which I call the "Brother, May I?" problem or the challenge of competitor control over market entry. This problem arises when would-be entrants are effectively required to obtain permission from incumbent competitors to enter or expand within a particular market. Whether it is due to a law or regulation, the decision of a financially-interested state board, or conduct by a monopolist looking to maintain its market power, new entrants to a market generally should not have to get their competitors' permission to compete. That such permission is effectively required in an increasing number of situations is inconsistent with the free-market principles that ought to guide our economic policies. Three recent appellate victories by the Federal Trade Commission—in *North Carolina Dental*, *Phoebe Putney*, and *McWane*—all in some way involved the need to seek the permission of competitors to enter a market, and this speech addresses each case in turn.

---

* The views expressed in these remarks are my own and do not necessarily reflect the views of the Federal Trade Commission or any other Commissioner. I would like to thank Gregory Luib for his invaluable contributions to this speech.

I. Introduction

Good morning. Thank you, Judge Ginsburg and the folks at *Concurrences* and the George Mason University School of Law, for inviting me to speak. As always, I am delighted to return to my *alma mater*.

Those concerned with restrictions on innovative technologies and business models often decry the stultifying effects of a "Mother, May I?" approach to regulation, where the innovator needs government permission to enter a market. These are worthy concerns and, in recognition of them, I have repeatedly counseled what I call regulatory humility, advising regulators to wait to see if consumer harm occurs before enacting new legal obligations.[1]

My remarks today will focus on a related issue, which I call the "Brother, May I?" problem or the challenge of competitor control over market entry. This problem arises when would-be entrants are effectively required to obtain permission from incumbent competitors to enter or expand within a particular market. Whether it is due to a law or regulation, the decision of a financially-interested state board, or conduct by a monopolist looking to maintain its market power, new entrants to a market generally should not have to get their competitors' permission to compete. That such permission is effectively required in an increasing number of situations is inconsistent with the free-market principles that ought to guide our economic policies.

Public choice theory of course recognizes the problem of an industry capturing its regulators. The "Brother, May I?" scenario may be even more troubling as it is effectively "regulatory replacement" rather than capture, with competitors acting directly as a regulator. That such situations may arise likely would not have surprised James Buchanan and Gordon Tullock, the two co-founders of public choice theory, who spent significant parts of their careers on the George Mason faculty and who each, unfortunately, passed away during the past few years. Their presence is undoubtedly missed here.

Before I get too far, let me provide some context for my remarks. I believe strongly in the concepts of a free-market economy and economic liberty for individuals. Those fundamental principles influenced my decision to attend law school at George Mason, and they have since guided my views as a policy maker at the Federal Trade Commission ("FTC"). I also view sound antitrust enforcement—that is, enforcement efforts aimed at protecting consumer welfare, while minimizing burdens on otherwise efficient conduct—as a necessary part of a well-functioning free market. Competition is the first line of defense for consumers. Thus, targeted antitrust enforcement is good for the market because it makes other regulation less necessary.[2]

In addition, given my time as Director of the FTC's Office of Policy Planning, I have been a strong voice in support of competition advocacy. Such advocacy is necessary in many instances to combat proposed regulatory barriers to entry supported by incumbent interests. Thus, my long history with competition advocacy also shapes my views on these issues.

---

1 *See, e.g.*, Maureen K. Ohlhausen, Comm'r, Fed. Trade Comm'n, *Regulatory Humility in Practice*, Remarks before the American Enterprise Institute (Apr. 1, 2015), *available at* https://www.ftc.gov/system/files/documents/public_statements/635811/150401aeihumilitypractice.pdf; Maureen K. Ohlhausen, *The Procrustean Problem with Prescriptive Regulation*, 23 CommLaw Conspectus 1 (2014), *available at* https://www.ftc.gov/system/files/documents/public_statements/606381/141222commlaw.pdf.

2 *See, e.g.*, Timothy J. Muris, *Looking Forward: The Federal Trade Commission and the Future Development of U.S. Competition Policy*, 2003 Colum. Bus. L. Rev. 359, 364 (2003) ("Effective antitrust enforcement may preclude direct, command-and-control regulation of sectors of the economy, avoiding the significant inefficiencies such regulation entails.").

Finally, I would like to clarify that I am not here to advocate for requiring firms to assist their competitors. The courts, in *Trinko*[3] and other cases, have appropriately limited the general duty of firms to help their competitors compete. Similarly, I have argued against reliance on the essential facilities doctrine—particularly in the intellectual property area—by foreign antitrust agencies.[4] What I will argue here is that firms should not have to obtain their competitors' permission to compete and that the FTC's enforcement and advocacy efforts should seek to eliminate such anticompetitive market distortions. Interestingly, three recent victories by the FTC in the courts—*North Carolina Dental*, *Phoebe Putney*, and *McWane*—all in some way involved the need to seek the permission of competitors to enter a market, and I will address each case in turn.

II. *North Carolina Dental* and State Licensing Boards

One of the clearest examples of the "Brother, May I?" challenge arises in the state licensing of professionals. Here, my—and the Commission's—concern has been the artificial and unjustified barriers to entry erected by some state licensing boards, including, in particular, those composed of active participants in the very markets they regulate. This issue came to a head in the Commission's successful Sherman Act Section 1 case against the North Carolina Board of Dental Examiners (the "Board").

In that case, the FTC filed an administrative complaint, alleging that the Board—through its dentist-members—was "colluding to exclude non-dentists from competing with dentists in the provision of teeth whitening services."[5] After deciding that whitening teeth constitutes the practice of dentistry, the Board issued letters to non-dentist providers, stating they were illegally practicing dentistry without a license and ordering them to cease and desist.[6] As everyone in this audience is aware, our case ended up at the Supreme Court, which ruled in the Commission's favor earlier this year, holding that "a state board on which a controlling number of decisionmakers are active market participants in the occupation the board regulates must satisfy *Midcal*'s active supervision requirement in order to invoke state-action antitrust immunity."[7]

A few key aspects of the Court's opinion stand out. First, the Court reiterated the crucial role that antitrust plays in our economy, noting that "[f]ederal antitrust law is a central safeguard for the Nation's free market

---

3 *See* Verizon Commc'ns Inc. v. Law Offices of Curtis V. Trinko, LLP, 540 U.S. 398 (2004).

4 *See, e.g.*, Maureen K. Ohlhausen, Comm'r, Fed. Trade Comm'n, Testimony before the U.S.-China Economic and Security Review Commission 5-6 (Jan. 28, 2015), *available at* https://www.ftc.gov/system/files/documents/public_statements/621411/150128chinatestimony.pdf.

5 *In re* N.C. Bd. of Dental Exam'rs, Dkt. No. 9343, Complaint, at 1 (June 17, 2010), *available at* https://www.ftc.gov/sites/default/files/documents/cases/2010/06/100617dentalexamcmpt.pdf. The Board consists of six licensed dentists, one licensed hygienist, and one "consumer member," who is neither a dentist nor a hygienist. *Id.* ¶ 2.

6 *Id.* ¶ 20. The Board also issued letters to several third parties with interests in shopping malls, stating that teeth whitening services offered at mall kiosks are illegal. *Id.* ¶ 22.

7 N.C. State Bd. of Dental Exam'rs v. FTC, 135 S. Ct. 1101, 1114 (2015). Justice Kennedy wrote the opinion for the Court and was joined by Chief Justice Roberts and Justices Ginsburg, Breyer, Sotomayor, and Kagan. Justice Alito, with Justices Scalia and Thomas joining, dissented. Among other things, the dissent argued that *Parker* immunizes state agencies, the Board is a state agency, "and that is the end of the matter." *Id.* at 1117-18 (Alito, J., dissenting). The dissent further noted that the regulation of the practice of medicine and dentistry has fallen "squarely within the States' sovereign police power" since before the Sherman Act was passed in 1890. *Id.* at 1119. Thus, the state statutes that created, and conferred regulatory authority on, the Board "represent precisely the kind of state regulation that the *Parker* exemption was meant to immunize." *Id.*

structures."[8] Second, the Court focused on the important issue of political accountability, explaining that immunity for state agencies "requires more than a mere facade of state involvement, for it is necessary in light of *Parker* [*v. Brown*]'s rationale to ensure the States accept political accountability for anticompetitive conduct they permit and control."[9] Third, in addressing the states' concern about their licensing boards incurring antitrust liability and damages, the Court observed that states can ensure *Parker* immunity is available to agencies by adopting clear policies to displace competition, and, if those agencies are controlled by market participants, by providing active supervision.[10] Finally, the Court made clear that the critical inquiry is "whether the State's review mechanisms provide 'realistic assurance' that a nonsovereign actor's anticompetitive conduct 'promotes state policy, rather than merely the party's individual interests.'"[11]

The *North Carolina Dental* decision was a crucial victory for competition and consumers. Under our federal system, individual states can do a lot to meddle with the free market; that is their choice to make. However, states need to be politically accountable for whatever market distortions they impose on consumers.[12] Of course, with a nod to George Stigler's insights from the 1970s, the North Carolina Dental Board's conduct can be easily explained as rent-seeking behavior by incumbents to fend off a new source of competition.[13] Where there is a benefit concentrated in the hands of a relatively small number of incumbent providers, in this case dentists, and the competitive harm is dispersed across all consumers of health care services, public choice theory predicts such incumbent exploitation of state licensing laws and regulations.[14] The adverse competitive results of such behavior are manifest.[15] Now, some have described this type of situation as an example of regulatory capture.[16] But, it is more than regulatory capture; it is the regulated replacing and acting as the regulators.

Looking at *North Carolina Dental* and our other recent Supreme Court win in *Phoebe Putney*, which I will discuss shortly, the state action area is one of the best examples of the Commission using its unique institutional features to guide the courts and others in the development of competition law toward better outcomes for competition and consumers. Looking ahead, the Commission should continue to focus both its enforcement and competition advocacy efforts on anticompetitive licensing activities within the states.

---

8 *Id.* at 1109.

9 *Id.* at 1111. *See also id.* ("*Parker* immunity requires that the anticompetitive conduct of nonsovereign actors, especially those authorized by the State to regulate their own profession, result from procedures that suffice to make it the State's own.").

10 *See id.* at 1115-16.

11 *Id.* (quoting Patrick v. Burget, 486 U.S. 94, 100-101 (1988)).

12 *See, e.g.*, FTC v. Ticor Title Ins. Co., 504 U.S. 621, 636 (1992) ("Federalism serves to assign political responsibility, not to obscure it. Neither federalism nor political responsibility is well served by a rule that essential national policies are displaced by state regulations intended to achieve more limited ends.").

13 *See, e.g.*, George J. Stigler, *The Theory of Economic Regulation*, 2 Bell J. Econ. Mgmt. Sci. 3, 5 (1971) ("We propose the general hypothesis: every industry or occupation that has enough political power to utilize the state will seek to control entry.").

14 *See, e.g.*, Steven Menashi & Douglas H. Ginsburg, *Rational Basis with Economic Bite*, 8 N.Y.U. J.L. & Liberty 1055, 1087-88 (2014) ("By now, '[a]ll reasonably sophisticated persons know that a well-knit special interest group is likely to prevail over an amorphous 'public' whose members are dispersed and, as individuals, are not in sharp conflict with the organized interest.' The occupational licensing laws recently invalidated under rational basis review are just this type of special-interest legislation.") (quoting Walter Gellhorn, *The Abuse of Occupational Licensing*, 44 U. Chi. L. Rev. 6, 16 (1976)); Timothy Sandefur, *A Public Convenience and Necessity and Other Conspiracies Against Trade: A Case Study from the Missouri Moving Industry*, 24 Geo. Mason U. C.R. L.J. 159, 176 (2014) ("Public choice theory predicts that where the government can redistribute wealth or opportunities between private groups, those groups will invest their resources in obtaining favorable legislation that will benefit them or handicap their rivals. Entry restrictions like occupational licenses or CON laws are made-to-order examples.").

15 *See, e.g.*, Daniel J. Gilman & Julie Fairman, *Antitrust and the Future of Nursing: Federal Competition Policy and the Scope of Practice*, 24 Health Matrix 143, 165 (2014) ("[L]icensure may be used by incumbent professionals to insulate themselves from competition. By restricting the entry of competitors, licensure can restrict supply, which can increase the income of incumbents (at consumer expense) or decrease the pressure on incumbents to improve non-price aspects of their services, such as quality or convenience.") (footnote omitted).

16 *See, e.g.*, Herbert Hovenkamp, *Rediscovering Capture: Antitrust Federalism and the* North Carolina Dental *Case*, CPI Antitrust Chronicle (Apr. 2015).

Nonetheless, I believe we ought to give the states some breathing room to respond to the changed legal landscape that they now face. As I have discussed elsewhere,[17] the states would appear to have several viable options for avoiding both antitrust liability for, and excessive oversight of, their conduct. These options should not be terribly onerous to implement and should help states retain individuals with sufficient relevant expertise on their regulatory boards. Nonetheless, it will take the states some time to evaluate and modify, if necessary, their licensing boards. In the meantime, as Chairwoman Edith Ramirez mentioned at the American Bar Association Spring Meeting, the Commission has begun an effort to provide guidance to states seeking to satisfy the active supervision prong of the state action doctrine. I have had discussions with representatives from state attorneys general offices, and I hope to continue that dialogue over the next several months.

Now, the economic libertarian in me is hopeful that the states, while assessing the sufficiency of their supervision over licensing decisions, will also reevaluate some of the excessive occupational licensing requirements they have adopted over the years. As the states reconsider the composition and oversight of their regulatory boards, I would recommend that they also take a very hard look at their occupational licensing regimes to see if they are on balance helping or harming their citizens. Among the professions subject to state licensure requirements today are florists, interior designers, tour guides, barbers, hair braiders, and even "shampoo specialists."[18] In fact, roughly 30 percent of US workers are now required to obtain a license to pursue their occupation.[19] Multiple studies have found that prices increase—by as much as 33 percent—as a result of occupational licensing.[20] That might be tolerable if those price increases reflected improved quality; however, "economic studies have demonstrated far more cases where occupational licensing has reduced employment and increased prices and wages of licensed workers than where it has improved the quality and safety of services."[21] Overall, the drag on the economy of excessive occupational licensing is counted in hundreds of billions of dollars annually.[22] Moreover, the increased costs of excessive occupational licensing falls most heavily on those least able to afford them.[23]

A particular concern I have is that the "Brother, May I?" aspect of occupational licensing can create unnecessary barriers to entry for entrepreneurs seeking to take their first step on the economic ladder. This is particularly true for occupations that draw individuals who are just beginning a professional career. Licensing requirements, which often include educational components, can prevent lower-income workers,

---

17 *See* Maureen K. Ohlhausen, Comm'r, Fed. Trade Comm'n, *Reflections on the Supreme Court's* North Carolina Dental *Decision and the FTC's Campaign to Rein in State Action Immunity*, Remarks before the Heritage Foundation 14-16 (Mar. 31, 2015), *available at* https://www.ftc.gov/system/files/documents/public_statements/634091/150403hertiagedental.pdf.

18 *See* Stephanie Simon, *A License to Shampoo: Jobs Needing State Approval Rise*, Wall St. J. (Feb. 7, 2011), http://www.wsj.com/articles/SB10001424052748703445904576118030935929752; Melissa S. Kearney et al., *Nearly 30 Percent of Workers in the U.S. Need a License to Perform Their Job: It Is Time to Examine Occupational Licensing Practices*, Brookings Institution Up-Front Blog (Jan. 27, 2015 11:00 AM), http://www.brookings.edu/blogs/up-front/posts/2015/01/26-time-to-examine-occupational-licensing-practices-kearney-hershbein-boddy. For a comprehensive review of state licensing requirements, *see* Institute for Justice, License to Work: A National Study of Burdens from Occupational Licensing (May 2012), *available at* https://www.ij.org/licensetowork.

19 *See* Morris M. Kleiner & Alan B. Krueger, *Analyzing the Extent and Influence of Occupational Licensing on the Labor Market*, 31 J. Lab. Econ. 173, 175-76 (2013) (findings based on 2008 survey conducted as part of Princeton Data Improvement Initiative).

20 *See, e.g.*, Morris M. Kleiner, *Reforming Occupational Licensing Policies* 17-22 (The Hamilton Project, Discussion Paper 2015-01, 2015) [hereinafter Kleiner, *Reforming Occupational Licensing*], *available at* http://www.hamiltonproject.org/files/downloads_and_links/reforming_occupational_licensing_morris_kleiner_final.pdf (collecting studies).

21 *Id.* at 6. *See also id.* at 12-13 (collecting studies); Aaron Edlin & Rebecca Haw, *Cartels by Another Name: Should Licensed Occupations Face Antitrust Scrutiny?*, 162 U. Pa. L. Rev. 1093, 1111-12 (2014) ("The work of Kleiner and his contemporaries reveals a consensus in the academy: a licensing restriction can only be justified where it leads to better quality professional services—and for many restrictions, proof of that enhanced quality is lacking.").

22 *See* Kleiner, *Reforming Occupational Licensing*, *supra* note 20, at 6.

23 *See, e.g.*, *id.* at 16 ("The net effects [of licensing] can be regressive, as lower-income consumers—who now have to pay higher prices and may have less access to services ranging from haircuts to dental exams—pay more to the regulated practitioners, some of whom are well compensated.").

who may not be able to pay for additional education, from entering certain fields—even at the lowest rungs of the economic ladder. Competition and competitive markets, supplemented by sound antitrust enforcement where necessary—not excessive licensing—will promote entrepreneurship in this country and provide the best platform for the least advantaged in our economy to prosper.

III. *Phoebe Putney* and Certificate-of-Need Laws

Another example of needing to obtain permission from one's competitors to enter the market is found in certificate-of-need, or CON, laws that remain on the books in over two-thirds of the states.[24] Under these laws, would-be suppliers of a host of health care services, from acute care hospitals to nursing homes to rehabilitation centers, must seek approval from a state entity to enter the market. The real issue in a typical certificate-of-need determination is not, however, one of ensuring patient safety or the proper qualifications of the applicant—there are other laws and regulations that typically address those issues more directly—but rather the "need" for a new entrant in the market at issue, as determined by the state entity.[25] As I will discuss, CON laws have outlived their intended use and now effectively serve primarily, if not solely, to assist incumbents in fending off competition from new entrants. The Commission and the public were reminded of the anticompetitive effects of those laws most recently in the *Phoebe Putney* matter.

There, the FTC challenged a merger involving a local hospital authority in Albany, Georgia. The transaction was viewed by nearly everyone, including the Eleventh Circuit,[26] as a virtual merger to monopoly. As is well known at this point, the Commission litigated this case all the way to the Supreme Court, which ultimately sided with the agency in its unanimous 2013 decision.[27] To be immune from the antitrust laws under the state action doctrine, private and other non-sovereign entities must demonstrate that the state "clearly articulated and affirmatively expressed" a policy displacing competition and thus allowing the otherwise anticompetitive conduct at issue.[28] The Court held that a general grant of corporate powers to a sub-state entity, such as a hospital authority, is insufficient by itself to satisfy the clear articulation prong of *Midcal*.[29] The challenged transaction, thus, was not immune from antitrust scrutiny, and the case was remanded for further proceedings.

---

24 *See* National Conference of State Legislatures, Certificate of Need: State Health Laws and Programs, http://www.ncsl.org/research/health/con-certificate-of-need-state-laws.aspx (last visited Dec. 2, 2015) (indicating that 36 states retain some type of CON program as of 2014).

25 *See, e.g.*, Sandefur, *supra* note 14, at 160 ("Unlike occupational licensing laws, CON requirements do not purport to determine whether a person is educated, trained, or skilled before going into business. Instead, they are expressly aimed at preventing competition against established companies, regardless of quality or skill."). *See also* Roy Cordato, *Certificate-of-Need Laws: It's Time for Repeal* 27 (John Locke Found., Nathaniel Macon Research Paper No. 1, 2005), *available at* http://www.johnlocke.org/acrobat/policyReports/con_laws-macon_no.1.pdf ("Economist Friedrich Hayek in his Nobel Laureate lecture, 'The Pretense of Knowledge,' argued that central planners, like those charged with determining who should and should not get to provide medical services, can only 'pretend' to have the information necessary to make the kinds of decisions they claim to be making. At best, any determination of 'need' by such planners will be arbitrary and will not reflect actual market conditions. At worst, these planners can become witting or unwitting tools of entrenched interests who wish to keep competition out of the market.").

26 *See* FTC v. Phoebe Putney Health Sys., Inc., 663 F.3d 1369, 1375 (11th Cir. 2011) (noting that "on the facts alleged, the joint operation of [Phoebe Putney] and Palmyra would substantially lessen competition or tend to create, if not create, a monopoly").

27 *See* FTC v. Phoebe Putney Health Sys., Inc., 133 S. Ct. 1003, 1017 (2013).

28 *See id.* at 1010 (citing Cal. Retail Liquor Dealers Ass'n v. Midcal Aluminum, Inc., 445 U.S. 97, 105 (1980)).

29 *See id.* at 1012.

So far, so good for patients in Albany. The FTC complaint counsel resumed the administrative litigation that had been stayed pending the federal court proceedings. It did not take very long, however, before the agency recognized a potentially insurmountable hurdle to a successful resolution of this case: the Georgia certificate-of-need laws. That is, even if the Commission could have established liability—and that seemed likely, given the facts—the state CON laws would have prevented a divestiture of any hospital assets.

Now, the case took an admittedly circuitous route during its final 18 months. Unfortunately for consumers of hospital services in the Albany area, a state hearing officer ruled that the CON laws would apply to any divestiture that might take place in this matter. The fact that the Albany region is deemed "over-bedded" made it unlikely that any divestiture buyer could obtain the necessary CON approval to operate an independent hospital. Thus, last March, the Commission reluctantly finalized its consent agreement with Phoebe Putney without a divestiture.[30]

What, then, should we take away from the *Phoebe Putney* matter? First, although it is of little solace to consumers in Albany, the Supreme Court decision narrowing the state action doctrine is a significant victory for competition principles and consumer welfare going forward. That decision, along with *North Carolina Dental*, represents the culmination of a decades-long effort by the Commission to narrow state action immunity from the antitrust laws—an effort in which I was proud to participate in several roles.[31] Second, *Phoebe Putney* demonstrates the importance of obtaining preliminary relief when challenging hospital mergers in CON states. By maintaining the status quo, injunctive relief prevents the possibility of competitive harm—sometimes, as in *Phoebe Putney*, irremediable harm—from occurring during the Commission's administrative proceedings and any appeals. Similarly, the outcome in *Phoebe Putney* should give the Commission pause in challenging consummated hospital acquisitions in states with CON laws. Finally, this case is a stark reminder of the anticompetitive nature of such laws.

The Commission—both on its own and jointly with the Department of Justice, Antitrust Division ("DOJ")—has long advocated that states consider the costs that CON laws may impose on health care consumers.[32] In our most recent advocacy, we argued that CON laws "impede the efficient performance of health care markets," "create barriers to entry and expansion to the detriment of health care competition and consumers," and "weaken markets' ability to contain health care costs."[33] As a result, we expressed support for the repeal or narrowing of such laws.[34]

---

30 *See In re* Phoebe Putney Health Sys., Inc., Dkt. No. 9348, Statement of the Federal Trade Commission, at 3 (Mar. 31, 2015), *available at* https://www.ftc.gov/system/files/documents/public_statements/634181/150331phoebeputneycommstmt.pdf.

31 I was a member of the State Action Task Force, which issued a report in 2003 recommending several means for the Commission to narrow the state action doctrine (*see* Fed. Trade Comm'n, Office of Policy Planning, Report of the State Action Task Force (Sept. 2003), *available at* http://www.ftc.gov/os/2003/09/stateactionreport.pdf), testified before the Antitrust Modernization Commission on the doctrine (*see* Maureen K. Ohlhausen, Dir., Office of Policy Planning, Fed. Trade Comm'n, Prepared Statement before the Antitrust Modernization Commission on the State Action Doctrine (Sept. 29, 2005), *available at* https://www.ftc.gov/public-statements/2005/09/ftc-staff-testimony-antitrust-modernization-commission-concerning-state), and participated in several advocacy efforts at narrowing the scope of the doctrine.

32 *See, e.g.*, U.S. Dep't of Justice, Antitrust Division, & Fed. Trade Comm'n, Joint Statement before the Illinois Task Force on Health Planning Reform (Sept. 15, 2008) [hereinafter DOJ-FTC Illinois Testimony], *available at* https://www.ftc.gov/policy/policy-actions/advocacy-filings/2008/09/ftc-and-department-justice-written-testimony-illinois; Fed. Trade Comm'n, Prepared Statement before the Standing Committee on Health, Education & Social Services of the Alaska House of Representatives regarding House Bill 337 (Feb. 15, 2008), *available at* https://www.ftc.gov/policy/policy-actions/advocacy-filings/2008/02/ftc-written-testimony-alaska-house-representatives; Letter from Janet M. Grady, Reg'l Dir., Fed. Trade Comm'n, to the Honorable Mary George, Hawaii State Senate (Mar. 13, 1987), *available at* https://www.ftc.gov/policy/policy-actions/advocacy-filings/1987/03/ftc-staff-comment-governor-mary-george-concerning.

33 DOJ-FTC Illinois Testimony, *supra* note 32, at 1-2.

34 *See id.* at 2. *See also* Fed. Trade Comm'n & U.S. Dep't of Justice, Improving Health Care: A Dose of Competition ch. 8, 6 [hereinafter A Dose of Competition] (July 2004), *available at* https://www.ftc.gov/reports/improving-health-care-dose-competition-report-federal-trade-commission-department-justice ("[T]he Agencies urge states with CON programs to reconsider whether they are best serving their citizens' health care needs by allowing these programs to continue.").

These advocacies have been grounded in large part on empirical studies of the impact of CON laws conducted by Commission economists.[35] Those studies have found that, rather than keeping health care costs down, CON laws and regulations lead to higher prices and expenditures.[36] For example, one study showed that if states substantially relaxed their CON programs to subject fewer hospitals to review, annual hospital expenditures would decrease by 1.4 percent, or approximately $1.3 billion.[37] Studies conducted by several independent commissions appointed by state legislatures to evaluate the impact of CON laws have reached similar conclusions.[38] These results, of course, are rather easily predicted by economic theory. Like any barrier to entry, CON laws prevent or limit the entry of firms that could otherwise provide higher-quality or lower-priced services than those offered by incumbents. In other words, output restrictions lead to higher, not lower, costs; they also result in higher profits for incumbent firms.

Another predictable result of CON regimes is the rent-seeking behavior pursued by incumbents who are able to exploit the regulatory system to their advantage. Using the "Brother, May I?" aspects of the CON process, incumbent hospitals and other health care providers can impose substantial delays on, or thwart altogether, potential entrants coming into their markets, thus protecting their own supra-competitive revenues.[39] Returning to public choice theory, it readily predicts such incumbent exploitation of CON laws,[40] as well as incumbent efforts to keep such laws on the books.[41]

Let me also address what appears to be the primary argument that states make in support of retaining CON laws: the ability to cross-subsidize care provided to uninsured or underinsured patients.[42] The argument is that, without CON laws, new entrants will engage in cream-skimming by taking the most profitable patients, thus depriving incumbent providers of revenue that is used to provide care to otherwise under-served or unserved patients—particularly at community or safety-net hospitals. Now, the public-policy goal of ensuring access to adequate health care services for patients who cannot afford them is

---

35 The CON area is just one example of empirical work conducted by FTC economists lending support to, and thus increasing the effectiveness of, the Commission's competition advocacy efforts.

36 *See, e.g.*, DOJ-FTC Illinois Testimony, *supra* note 32, at 5 n.16 (collecting studies).

37 *See* Daniel Sherman, Bur. of Econ., Fed. Trade Comm'n, The Effect of State Certificate-of-Need Laws on Hospital Costs: An Economic Policy Analysis vi (Jan. 1988), *available at* https://www.ftc.gov/reports/effect-state-certificate-need-laws-hospital-costs-economic-policy-analysis. *See also id.* at iv ("The study thus finds no evidence that CON programs have led to the resource savings they were designed to promote, but rather indicates that reliance on CON review may raise hospital costs.").

38 *See, e.g.*, The Lewin Group, An Evaluation of Illinois' Certificate of Need Program: Prepared for State of Illinois Commission on Government Forecasting and Accountability 16 (Feb. 2007) ("A review of the evidence indicates that CONs rarely reduce health care costs, and on occasion, increase cost in some states."); William S. Custer et al., Report of Data Analyses to the Georgia Commission on the Efficacy of the CON Program 8 (Nov. 2006) ("CON regulation is associated with higher private inpatient costs. The effect is robust with respect to model specification, measures of CON rigor, and diagnoses.").

39 *See, e.g.*, DOJ-FTC Illinois Testimony, *supra* note 32, at 7; A Dose of Competition, *supra* note 34, at Exec. Summ., 22 ("Market incumbents can too easily use CON procedures to forestall competitors from entering an incumbent's market."). Incumbent providers have also entered into anticompetitive agreements that were outside of, but nonetheless facilitated by, the CON laws. *See, e.g.*, DOJ-FTC Illinois Testimony, *supra* note 32, at 7-8.

40 *See, e.g.*, Sandefur, *supra* note 14, at 176 ("Public choice theory predicts that where the government can redistribute wealth or opportunities between private groups, those groups will invest their resources in obtaining favorable legislation that will benefit them or handicap their rivals. Entry restrictions like occupational licenses or CON laws are made-to-order examples.").

41 *See, e.g.*, *id.* at 173 ("Public choice theory would also predict that as economic and technological circumstances change, CON laws would nevertheless remain on the books—vigorously defended by incumbent firms—long after the economic rationales on which they were based were rendered obsolete, even on their own terms.").

42 *See, e.g.*, Commission on the Efficacy of the Certificate of Need Program, An Analysis and Evaluation of Certificate of Need Regulations in Georgia: Final Report to the Georgia General Assembly and Governor Perdue xii-xiii (Dec. 2006) [hereinafter Georgia Commission Report] ("Hospital leaders are concerned that if they lose their ability to cross-subsidize from [the highest-margin] services, they will no longer be able to cover the fixed losses associated with inpatient Medicaid services and care of the uninsured. For this reason, hospitals, whether nonprofit or proprietary, urban or rural, have wanted to see CON rules maintained or tightened in order to maintain regulatory control over the provision of these services in non-hospital-based settings.").

certainly a laudable one. Using the blunt and anticompetitive tool of CON laws, however, is not the answer. Such a use of CON laws flies in the face of any notion of free-market competition.[43]

Clearly, there are a host of difficult issues relating to the payment and provision of health care in this country that go far beyond CON laws and that may not have easy answers. The commission established to study the efficacy of the Georgia CON program in the mid-2000s, for example, was unable to reach consensus with regard to the best policy to address the difficult issue of cross-subsidization of indigent care.[44] As the commission recognized, "When viewed in a vacuum, analysis has shown a relatively weak effect of CON, but the CON program is being used as a regulatory device in an environment involving much stronger forces."[45] Nonetheless, using CON laws as an indirect tax for funding indigent care imposes costs—in terms of price, quality, and innovation—across all consumers of health care services.[46] There are less competitively-restrictive and more politically-transparent means for pursuing the goal of indigent care. In fact, there is some evidence that CON laws do not actually advance the goal of indigent care at general community hospitals.[47] Finally, as the antitrust agencies have noted in their advocacies in this area, CON laws were not adopted as a means of cross-subsidizing health care.[48] That is an *ex post* rationale identified by CON proponents that is simply inconsistent with free-market principles. More, not less, competition is needed in the health care space.[49]

My recommendation, then, is for the Commission to re-engage with state legislatures on the issue of CON laws. With the *Noerr-Pennington*[50] doctrine rightly protecting incumbents' petitioning activity related to CON applications, there is little, if any, room for law enforcement action in this area. We have not, however, addressed this issue in our competition advocacy since 2008. Of course, the Commission typically issues advocacy comments only in response to invitations from policy makers or requests for public comments. I would urge the agency to continue that practice. Still, we ought to seek out opportunities to weigh in on the adverse impact of CON laws on consumer welfare. The Commission has been on a bit of a winning streak in challenging anticompetitive hospital mergers.[51] It would be unfortunate if any more of those victories for health care consumers were jeopardized by CON laws that preclude any meaningful remedy in those cases.

---

43 *See, e.g.*, Sandefur, *supra* note 14, at 170 ("Whatever the merits of the 'cream-skimming' and incentives rationales, they apply only to public utilities, or perhaps to markets that feature some kind of monopoly characteristics. They do not apply to private markets with healthy competition. In these markets, 'cream-skimming' is simply the ordinary competitive process on which the economy depends for innovation and growth, and encouraging investment where market demand is lacking is rightly seen as foolhardy.").

44 *See* Georgia Commission Report, *supra* note 42, at xiii.

45 *Id.*

46 *See, e.g.*, Cordato, *supra* note 25, at 18 ("If CON laws are being used to hide this tax from the electorate, then not only are they inconsistent with sound economics, they are also inconsistent with an open and democratic political process.").

47 *See, e.g.*, DOJ-FTC Illinois Testimony, *supra* note 32, at 9-10; The Lewin Group, *supra* note 38, at ii, 26-28 ("Through our research and analysis we could find no evidence that safety-net hospitals are financially stronger in CON states than other states.") (finding margins for safety-net hospitals in CON states "considerably lower" than margins for safety-net hospitals in non-CON states).

48 *See* DOJ-FTC Illinois Testimony, *supra* note 32, at 4.

49 *See* A Dose of Competition, *supra* note 34, at Exec. Summ., 4 ("Vigorous competition, both price and non-price, can have important benefits in health care as well. Price competition generally results in lower prices and, thus, broader access to health care products and services. Non-price competition can promote higher quality and encourage innovation.").

50 *See* E.R.R. Presidents Conference v. Noerr Motor Freight, Inc., 365 U.S. 127 (1961); United Mine Workers of Am. v. Pennington, 381 U.S. 657 (1965).

51 *See, e.g.*, St. Alphonsus Med. Ctr.-Nampa Inc. v. St. Luke's Health Sys., Ltd., 778 F.3d 775 (9th Cir. 2015); ProMedica Health Sys., Inc. v. FTC, 749 F.3d 559 (6th Cir. 2014); FTC v. OSF Healthcare Sys., 852 F. Supp. 2d 1069 (N.D. Ill. 2012).

IV. *McWane* and Exclusionary Conduct by Monopolists

During the remainder of my remarks, I will address a third "Brother, May I?" situation in which a would-be entrant must effectively rely on its competitor's permission before entering or expanding its business. This one involves not state regulation but private conduct by a monopolist that is exclusionary and thus maintains its monopoly and is not justified by a cognizable efficiency. The end result is that a firm looking to enter the market or expand its sales is at the whims of its monopolist-competitor to succeed in such entry or expansion. The Commission recently encountered this in its Sherman Act Section 2 action against McWane, Inc.[52]

In that case, the Commission issued a seven-count administrative complaint against McWane in January 2012[53]—prior to my arrival as a Commissioner. Ultimately, the Commission dismissed six of the seven counts, finding liability solely on the Section 2 exclusive dealing count.[54] In particular, the Commission found that McWane had used an exclusive dealing policy to prevent its sole rival, Star Pipe Products, Ltd. ("Star"), from meaningfully competing and thus maintained the monopoly that McWane enjoyed in the market for domestically-manufactured ductile iron pipe fittings.[55] (Although perhaps not the sexiest of markets the Commission has pursued of late, pipefittings are used by municipal and regional water authorities in crucial waterworks projects.)

The thrust of the case was that McWane, with over 90 percent market share, had imposed a policy on distributors that required them to purchase all of their domestic fittings from McWane; otherwise, they would lose their rebates and be cut off altogether.[56] There were two exceptions to this so-called "Full Support Program" permitting the purchase of competing domestic fittings: where McWane products were not readily available, and where the customer bought domestic fittings and accessories along with another manufacturer's ductile iron pipe.[57] The Commission found that, to the extent that Star was able to gain sales, it did so primarily under these limited exceptions, and those sales were insufficient to have a competitive impact.[58]

In finding liability on the exclusive dealing count, the Commission determined that McWane had monopoly power in the domestic fittings market,[59] that the Full Support Program constituted an exclusive dealing arrangement that substantially foreclosed its rivals' access to the most efficient sales channel,[60] and that

---

52 *See In re* McWane, Inc., Dkt. No. 9351, Opinion of the Commission (Feb. 6, 2014) [hereinafter *McWane* Commission Opinion], *available at* https://www.ftc.gov/system/files/documents/cases/140206mcwaneopinion_0.pdf.

53 *See In re* McWane, Inc., Dkt. No. 9351, Administrative Complaint (Jan. 4, 2012), *available at* https://www.ftc.gov/sites/default/files/documents/cases/2012/01/120104ccwanestaradmincmpt.pdf (alleging conspiracy, information exchange, invitation to collude, restraint of trade based on distribution agreement, conspiracy to monopolize, monopolization, and attempted monopolization).

54 *See McWane* Commission Opinion, *supra* note 52, at 2 n. 1.

55 *See id.* at 20.

56 *See id.* at 9, 16.

57 *See id.* at 9.

58 *See id.* at 28-29.

59 *See id.* at 16-18.

60 *See id.* at 20-25.

this resulted in harm to competition and consumers in the domestic fittings market.[61] As the Commission opinion concluded, "[T]he evidence that McWane's exclusive dealing policy significantly impaired the access of McWane's only rival, Star, to the main channel of distribution, thereby increasing its costs and keeping it below the critical level necessary to pose a real competitive threat, is plainly sufficient to meet the standard of harm to competition set forth in the prevailing case law."[62]

At the same time, the Commission rejected the two efficiency justifications proffered by McWane. First, McWane argued that it engaged in exclusive dealing to generate sufficient sales to operate its last domestic foundry. The Commission did not view this to be "a cognizable procompetitive justification for antitrust purposes."[63] More specifically, McWane's increased sales volume did not result from actions, such as a price reduction, that typically promote consumer welfare by increasing overall market output or lowering prices; rather, the increased sales would have come from anticompetitive reductions in Star's output.

The second justification offered by McWane was that the Full Support Program prevented customers from cherry-picking the highest-selling items from Star and forced them to purchase McWane's full line of domestic fittings. That is, if distributors were able to source from multiple suppliers, they would buy the common fittings from the limited supplier (at lower prices) and turn to the full-line supplier for less common products only, which supposedly could lead to the collapse of the full-line seller. The Commission was not convinced that this is a cognizable efficiency under the antitrust laws. To begin with, McWane never explained why it could not compete to sell the more common products by lowering its prices for them and raising its prices for the less common products, thereby reducing an implicit cross-subsidy. In any event, the Commission noted that "[e]ven if selective entry by the full-line supplier's rivals led to the collapse of the full-line seller, that itself would not constitute a harm to the market (as opposed to a single firm)."[64]

Last month, the Eleventh Circuit upheld the Commission's decision, affirming our determinations regarding market definition, McWane's monopoly power, and harm to competition.[65] The court endorsed the approach taken by the D.C. Circuit and several other courts in determining whether a monopolist's conduct has harmed competition, noting, among other things, that substantial foreclosure is just one of several factors in the analysis and that harm to one or more competitors is insufficient for purposes of Section 2.[66] The court identified the pricing evidence in the record as the "most powerful evidence of anticompetitive harm."[67] More specifically, the court observed that by keeping Star from becoming a more efficient competitor, McWane's exclusivity policy preserved its ability to charge supra-competitive prices; in fact,

---

61 *See id.* at 25-29.

62 *See id.* at 26. Commissioner Wright dissented from the Commission's opinion in *McWane*. *See In re* McWane, Inc., Dkt. No. 9351, Dissenting Statement of Commissioner Joshua D. Wright (Feb. 6, 2014), *available at* https://www.ftc.gov/system/files/documents/public_statements/202211/140206mcwanestatement.pdf. The scope of the disagreement between the majority and the dissent was largely limited to the narrow, but obviously crucial issue of whether harm to competition from McWane's exclusive dealing had been demonstrated. *See, e.g.*, *id.* at 7 n.14 (assuming monopoly power); *id.* at 27-28 n.38 (agreeing that Full Support Program amounted to exclusive dealing); *id.* at 33 n.40 (agreeing that "distributors are a key distribution channel"); *id.* at 4 (noting the "ample record evidence demonstrating that the Full Support Program harmed McWane's rival Star"). *See also* Leon B. Greenfield, *Afterword:* Lorain Journal *and the Antitrust Legacy of Robert Bork*, 79 Antitrust L.J. 1047, 1062 (2014) ("The division among the FTC commissioners in the recent *McWane* matter illustrates the narrowed scope of today's debates surrounding unilateral exclusion enforcement.").

63 *McWane* Commission Opinion, *supra* note 52, at 30.

64 *Id.* at 32.

65 *See* McWane, Inc. v. FTC, No. 14-11363, 2015 WL 1652200, at *9-12, *19-21 (11th Cir. Apr. 15, 2015).

66 *Id.* at *16 (citing United States v. Microsoft Corp., 253 F.3d 34, 58 (D.C. Cir. 2001) (en banc)). The Eleventh Circuit also endorsed the D.C. Circuit's causation standard for assessing exclusive dealing claims. *See id.* at *18 ("We agree with the Commission and our sister circuits that in these circumstances the government must show that the defendant engaged in anticompetitive conduct that reasonably appears to significantly contribute to maintaining monopoly power.").

67 *Id.* at *19.

McWane was able to raise prices and increase its gross profits, notwithstanding Star's (limited) entry.[68] Finally, much like the Commission, the Eleventh Circuit was not persuaded by McWane's efficiency arguments.[69] I understand that McWane has announced its intention to seek further review of the Eleventh Circuit's decision. I will end my discussion of the *McWane* case here.

Let me make a few general points. First, there is no question in my mind that vertical business arrangements, including exclusive dealing, are much more likely to be procompetitive than anticompetitive. Exclusive dealing can enhance competition in a number of well-documented ways, including by eliminating inter-brand free-riding, reducing the costs associated with demand and supply uncertainty, and intensifying competition for distribution.[70] Exclusive distribution arrangements can be particularly procompetitive where a manufacturer provides dealer support, discounts, or other consideration for the exclusivity, or where there is competition to be the exclusive distributor of a particular product.

In short, the economic literature clearly supports the proposition that exclusive dealing is likely to be procompetitive.[71] Exclusive dealing thus should not be a significant focus of the Commission's competition enforcement program. Nonetheless, there are some situations—particularly in monopolized markets—in which exclusive dealing can be anticompetitive and serve to maintain a firm's monopoly power.[72] Where the Commission is able to identify substantial harm to competition that is not outweighed by cognizable efficiencies, we ought to pursue such conduct.

Finally, I would like to return to the cross-subsidization point. Whether one refers to it as cream-skimming or cherry-picking, this rationale is unconvincing to me as a justification for either certificate-of-need laws or exclusive dealing by a monopolist. While cream-skimming may be a legitimate concern in very limited circumstances, such as a rate-regulated market with high fixed costs,[73] I have not seen any evidence that would justify either a CON regime or exclusive dealing by a monopolist as a procompetitive response to cream-skimming by competitors. At a more general level, it is antithetical to free-market principles to cordon off significant portions of the market from would-be competitors that may provide lower-priced, higher-quality, and more innovative products and services. Rather, we should be doing everything we can to oppose such market restrictions and to facilitate entry by new and innovative competitors.

We see this issue in the transportation area, where innovators like Uber, Lyft, Sidecar, and others are disrupting an age-old way of doing business and in the process providing consumers with expanded options, greater convenience, and often lower prices. In short, they are injecting much-needed competition into the market. For that reason, FTC staff has filed several advocacy comments to local authorities recommending that any restrictions on competition from these new transportation providers be no broader than necessary to address legitimate subjects of regulation, such as safety and consumer protection, and

---

68 *See id.*

69 *See id.* at *21-22.

70 *See, e.g.*, Benjamin Klein & Kevin M. Murphy, *Exclusive Dealing Intensifies Competition for Distribution*, 75 Antitrust L.J. 433 (2008) (explaining how exclusivity restrictions intensify competition by manufacturers for retail distribution); Jonathan M. Jacobson, *Exclusive Dealing, "Foreclosure," and Consumer Harm*, 70 Antitrust L.J. 311, 357-60 (2002) (identifying various procompetitive justifications for exclusive dealing arrangements).

71 *See, e.g.*, Alden F. Abbott & Joshua D. Wright, *Antitrust Analysis of Tying Arrangements and Exclusive Dealing*, *in* Antitrust Law and Economics 183, 200-01 (Keith N. Hylton ed., 2d ed. 2010) ("[T]he potential efficiencies associated with both tying and exclusive dealing ... lead most commentators to believe that they are generally procompetitive and should be analyzed under some form of rule of reason analysis."); James C. Cooper et al., *Vertical Antitrust Policy as a Problem of Inference*, 23 Int'l J. Indus. Org. 639, 658 (2005) ("Most studies find evidence that vertical restraints/vertical integration are precompetitive. . .").

72 *See* Eastman Kodak Co. v. Image Tech. Servs., Inc., 504 U.S. 451, 488 (1992) (Scalia, J., dissenting) ("Where a defendant maintains substantial market power, his activities are examined through a special lens: Behavior that might otherwise not be of concern to the antitrust laws—or that might even be viewed as procompetitive—can take on exclusionary connotations when practiced by a monopolist.").

73 *See, e.g.*, *supra* text accompanying note 43.

narrowly crafted to minimize any potential anticompetitive impact.[74] Implicit in our advocacies is a rejection of the cream-skimming argument made by some taxi competitors[75] and regulators[76] in justifying opposition to Uber and others seeking to enter transportation markets throughout the country. These new firms ought to be treated the same as incumbents, in terms of applying existing regulations; however, they should not be locked out of the market because they are skimming cream or picking cherries. What they are really doing is competing.

V. Conclusion

Thank you for your attention this morning. I hope my remarks have shed some light on the problems that these "Brother, May I?" approaches create for free-market competition and how targeted antitrust enforcement and advocacy, supported by sound economic analysis, can help limit the damage. I also hope that my call to reduce these barriers, which particularly harm those on the bottom rung of the economic ladder, will encourage others to take up the challenge.

---

74 *See, e.g.*, Staff Letter from Fed. Trade Comm.n to Brendan Reilly, Alderman, Chi. City Council, regarding Proposed Ordinance O2014-1367 (Apr. 15, 2014), *available at* https://www.ftc.gov/policy/policy-actions/advocacy-filings/2014/04/ftc-staff-comment-honorable-brendan-reilly-concerning; Staff Letter from Fed. Trade Comm'n to Jacques P. Lerner, Gen. Counsel, D.C. Taxicab Comm'n regarding Second Proposed Rulemakings regarding Chapters 12, 14, and 16 of Title 31 (June 7, 2013), *available at* https://www.ftc.gov/policy/policy-actions/advocacy-filings/2013/06/ftc-staff-comments-district-columbia-taxicab; Staff Letter from Fed. Trade Comm'n to Colo. Pub. Utilities Comm'n regarding Docket No. 13R-0009TR (Mar. 6, 2013), *available at* https://www.ftc.gov/policy/policy-actions/advocacy-filings/2013/03/ftc-staff-comment-colorado-public-utilities.

75 *See, e.g.*, Andrew Zaleski, *Welcome to the Uber Wars*, Politico Magazine (Sept. 2, 2014), http://www.politico.com/magazine/story/2014/09/welcome-to-the-uber-wars-110498.html#.VWcQHrHD83E ("'Skimming the cream' is the way [a taxi company executive] describes what Uber does to taxi competitors.").

76 *See, e.g.*, *Community-wide Taxi Service Endangered by "Ridesharing,"* Who's Driving You? (June 30, 2014), *available at* http://www.whosdrivingyou.org/wp-content/uploads/2015/06/community-wide-access-fact-sheet.pdf ("'Uber, Lyft and Sidecar simply do not serve all areas of a community at all hours of the day. By stealing more lucrative fares, they will ultimately leave transportation deserts in under-privileged neighborhoods where people rely on taxicabs for daily errands.' — Robert Werth, President of the Taxicab, Limousine & Paratransit Association.").

Signaling and Agreement under Section 1 of the Sherman Act

William H. Page
page@law.ufl.edu
Professor, Levin College of Law, University of Florida

Abstract

Oligopolists look for signals from one another in planning strategies. Some signals solicit cooperation to achieve noncompetitive equilibria. In this essay, I try to identify what sorts of signaling in this latter category bring about agreement under Section 1 of the Sherman Act. *Conventional* signals are actions, like nods of the head, that a culture has recognized as having a specific meaning; *prearranged* signals are actions or events that parties have agreed to treat as having special significance. Both conventional and prearranged signals may form or implement an express agreement in the same way as words, although rivals sometimes prefer to use the signals in order to conceal a surreptitious conspiracy. *Implicit* signals are actions with meanings for multiple audiences, but that rivals understand as conveying a special meaning for them. Where the action's meanings for multiple audiences (especially consumers) have important efficiency consequences—like a bare public announcement about present or even future prices—courts do not treat the specialized meaning for rivals as triggering a Sherman Act agreement, even if the conduct facilitates noncompetitive pricing. On the other hand, even a formally public announcement may bring about an agreement, if its implicit meaning targets rivals without providing useful information to other audiences.

I. Introduction

Judge Richard Posner observed in his recent opinion in *Text Messaging* that oligopolists "watch each other like hawks."[1] They do so because they are looking for *signals*: actions that convey messages about their rivals' intentions and other information they can use to plan their own competitive behavior. In some instances, oligopolists signal and interpret signals in ways that coordinate their competitive choices; in a subset of those instances, the coordination restrains trade. Even within this last subset, however, Section 1 of the Sherman Act[2] applies to signaling only if it results in something courts are willing to call an agreement. In this essay, I try to identify what sorts of coordination fall within this last and narrowest category: signaling that equals agreement. In a related paper, I examine what sorts of communication and responsive conduct are necessary to bring about an agreement. After summarizing the lessons of that study, I will offer a typology of signaling and examine how courts have treated instances of the various types.

II. Agreement and Signals

After 125 years, the meaning of agreement remains among the most contested and litigated issues under the Sherman Act. One longstanding problem for both the courts and antitrust scholars has been how to treat oligopolistic interdependence or tacit collusion. Despite sophisticated arguments by Richard Posner (until last year)[3] and Louis Kaplow in his excellent 2013 book,[4] the Supreme Court has made clear that this sort of coordination, or "mere interdependence" is not agreement. In *Twombly*,[5] the Court characterized evidence of interdependent conduct as simply "business strategy unilaterally prompted by common perceptions of the market."[6] So, if gas stations at a remote intersection manage to coordinate a noncompetitive price increase by announcing a series of price increases, their conduct is only tacit collusion and not a Section 1 agreement, even if it involves a kind of meeting of the minds on the new price; it is not only not *per se* unlawful as a price-fixing agreement—but *per se* lawful. Similarly, if, as in *Twombly*, incumbent telephone monopolies choose not to enter one another's territories and thus retain a degree of monopoly power, they are merely "sitting tight expecting their neighbors to do the same thing;"[7] even if those decisions are interdependent, they are not an agreement in a legal sense. Not only that, the Court has "hedged against false inferences from identical behavior at a number of points in the trial sequence,"[8] by requiring plaintiffs to plead facts and to produce evidence that distinguish their cases from mere interdependence in order to avoid dismissal on the pleadings or summary judgment, as the case may be. So, if all the plaintiff pleads is conduct that the court can explain as mere interdependence, the court will dismiss the case.

---

1 *In Re* Text Messaging Antitrust Litigation, 782 F.3d 867, 875 (7th Cir. 2015).

2 15 U.S. Code § 1.

3 Richard A. Posner, *Review of* Kaplow, Competition Policy and Price Fixing, 79 Antitrust L.J. 761 (2014).

4 Louis Kaplow, Competition Policy and Price Fixing (2013).

5 Bell Atlantic Corp. v. Twombly, 550 U.S. 544 (2007).

6 *Id.* at 554.

7 *Id.* at 568.

8 *Id.* at 554.

If tacit collusion is not an agreement, what is? Quoting *Theatre Enterprises*, the Court in *Twombly* wrote that the "'crucial question' is whether the challenged anticompetitive conduct 'stem[s] from independent decision [including a merely interdependent decision] or from an agreement, *tacit* or express."[9] This passage excludes independent and interdependent conduct from the agreement category and includes express or verbal agreement—so a plaintiff can survive a motion to dismiss by alleging (or reach a jury by offering) direct or circumstantial evidence from which a jury can reasonably find that an express agreement occurred.

But the Court also included tacit agreement within Section 1. In the passage quoted from *Theatre Enterprises*, the term tacit agreement means some form of coordination that is more formal than mere interdependence, but less formal than an express exchange of promises.[10] "Tacit agreement" is perhaps not the best choice of terms; many commentators have expressed their dissatisfaction with the term. Nevertheless, the Court has persisted in using it so it seems best to try to make sense of it. Lower courts typically do not explain what a tacit agreement is with any clarity. They use a variety of formulations in stating the agreement requirement, some that seem to require express agreement and some that seem to include interdependence. In other instances, they just use "agreement" as if its meaning is self-evident. Nevertheless, there are several forms of conduct that the courts have characterized as Section 1 agreements, even though they do not involve an express agreement.

An important historical example was the Gary Dinners episode, in which Judge Elbert Gary, the Chairman of US Steel, conceived of series of organized dinners and related meetings in which rivals in various lines of fabricated steel coordinated their prices.[11] At the meetings, the rivals stated their pricing intentions, without making any promises or expecting any in return. After the meetings, the rivals would, if all went well, set their prices as they had stated. Although Gary thought his system avoided the formation of any agreements, the district court and later the Supreme Court held that this form of coordination satisfied the agreement requirement of Section 1.[12] It was just as effective as the explicit cartels in which the steel fabricators had participated before the epic merger that created US Steel.

In *Esco*,[13] the court described essentially the same scenario[14] and held that it could amount to sufficient evidence of an agreement in a criminal case. It added that an "express agreement" and written or oral assurances are not required "if a course of conduct, or a price schedule, once suggested or outlined by a competitor in the presence of other competitors, is followed by all—generally and customarily—and continuously for all practical purposes, even though there be slight variations."[15] Since it is not express, the resulting agreement is tacit: although the agreement involves communication, the assent is conveyed not by words but by compliance with the suggested course of conduct. Or, as the First Circuit recently put it, a "tacit agreement—one in which only the conspirators' actions, and not any express communications, indicate the existence of an agreement—is distinguished from mere conscious parallelism by 'uniform

9 *Id.* at 553 (emphasis added) (quoting Theatre Enterprises, Inc. v. Paramount Film Distributing Corp., 346 U.S. 537, 540 (1954)).

10 William E. Kovacic et al., *Plus Factors and Agreement in Antitrust Law*, 110 Mich. L. Rev. 393, 405 (2011) ("The line that distinguishes tacit agreements (which are subject to section 1 scrutiny) from mere tacit coordination stemming from oligopolistic interdependence (which eludes section 1's reach) is indistinct."); William E. Kovacic, *Antitrust Policy and Horizontal Collusion in the 21st Century*, 9 Loy. Consumer L. Rev. 97, 100 (1997) (agreement may be formed by "means other than a direct exchange of assurances"). Kovacic refers to the "safe harbor that *Theatre Enterprises* recognized." *Id.* at 102.

11 *See* William H. Page, *The Gary Dinners and the Meaning of Concerted Action*, 62 S.M.U. L. Rev. 597, 616-18 (2009).

12 United States v. U.S. Steel Corp., 223 F. 55, 159 (D.N.J. 1915), *aff'd*, 251 U.S. 417 (1920).

13 Esco Corp. v. United States, 340 F.2d 1000 (9th Cir. 1965).

14 *Id.* at 1007.

15 *Id.* at 1008.

behavior among competitors, preceded by conversations implying that later uniformity might prove desirable or accompanied by other conduct that in context suggests that each competitor failed to make an independent decision.'"[16]

This brings us to signaling. Signaling is a form of communication, so it is certainly broadly relevant to whether rivals have engaged in communications and related conduct that formed an express or tacit agreement. Yet the term is at least as vague as agreement and says little, by itself, about whether rivals' signaling behavior amounts to a Sherman Act agreement. Courts use the term signal to mean different things and often do not use the term when the conduct at issue appears to involve signaling in a meaningful sense. In the remainder of this paper, I offer a typology of forms of signals, then try to identify which are most relevant to the analysis of Section 1 agreements. I distinguish between *conventional* signals, *prearranged* signals, and *implicit* signals.

III. Conventional Signals

A signal can be conventional action that individuals within a culture use exclusively as a form of nonverbal communication, like turn signals, hand waves, or obscene gestures.[17] The courts have likewise recognized that rivals may form agreements by using conventional signals. *Esco* famously recognized that "[a] knowing wink can mean more than words."[18] Judge Posner suggested that a grunt may also convey sufficient meaning in the vertical context.[19] Similarly, "[t]he law forbids nonverbal agreements in restraint of trade, as well as express ones; otherwise, the law would be emasculated as competitors accomplished the forbidden goal with a wink and a nod."[20] There are drug cases, for example, that hold that these sorts of signals in clandestine meetings can indicate that a defendant joined a criminal conspiracy.[21]

But in the antitrust context, there are no cases that I can find in which a wink or nod alone formed an express conspiracy. Unlike the actions of some nonhuman species, which can signal a great deal of information by body movements and even sonar, human conventional signals—those shared by an entire society—convey only as much information as a few words, so they cannot by themselves negotiate an agreement;[22] they can at best indicate assent to a fairly complete proposal or arrangement. Equally important, by their very nature they are as public and as well understood by bystanders as words, so they cannot conceal the actor's participation in a conspiracy from witnesses any more than words.

---

16 White v. R.M. Packer Co., 635 F.3d 571, 576 (1st Cir. 2011) (quoting Brown v. Pro Football, Inc., 518 U.S. 231, 241 (1996)).

17 As an illustration of the power of such a signal, *see* Arek Sarkissian, "Alachua County's Armored Vehicle Makes Traffic Stop After Driver Flips the Bird," Ocala Star Banner, Apr. 13, 2015, *available at* http://www.ocala.com/article/20150413/ARTICLES/150419881.

18 Esco Corp. v. United States, 340 F.2d 1000, 1007 (9th Cir. 1965).

19 Isaksen v. Vermont Castings, Inc., 825 F.2d 1158, 1164 (7th Cir. 1987).

20 Blomkest Fertilizer, Inc. v. Potash Corp. of Sask., 176 F.3d 1055 (8th Cir. 1992)), superseded en banc on other grounds, 203 F.3d 1028, 1037 (8th Cir. 2000).

21 *See, e.g.*, United States v. Grajeda-Encinas, 474 Fed. App'x 506, 508-09 (9th Cir. 2012); United States v. Torres, 114 F. 3d 520, 525 (5th Cir. 1997); Hamilton v. Arnold, 29 Fed. App'x 614, 618 (1st Cir. 2002) (evidence that the defendant was present at a meeting and "nodded his head during the discussion of transporting drugs" was "barely" sufficient to support a conviction).

22 *Cf.* Brunette v. Humane Soc'y, 294 F.3d 1205, 1212 (9th Cir. 2002) ("The generalized allegation of a wink and a nod understanding . . . does not amount to an agreement or conspiracy to violate [plaintiff's] rights in particular.").

IV. Prearranged Signals

Far more significant are signals that parties have *prearranged* to function as private communication. Familiar examples would include, as described in the Bible, Jonathan's use of arrows and shouts to tell David that Saul means to kill him;[23] or, as described by Shakespeare, Lady Macbeth's use of a bell to tell Macbeth the chamberlains are drunk so he can kill Duncan.[24] These sorts of signals are actions that, to outward appearances, serve benign functions, but function as signals because of a prior agreement to use them at a critical moment to convey information necessary for a decision. In some instances, like a third-base coach's signs to a batter, everyone can see that signals are being given, but only the parties to a prior arrangement know what they mean. These sorts of signals are less useful for clandestine arrangements because they publicly announce the existence of the prearrangement between the parties; far more useful are actions that appear to mean something else, but, by prearrangement, the parties know the actual intended meaning.

Prearranged signals in this last category are more useful for antitrust conspiracies than conventional signals because they can convey a triggering mechanism that implements a much more detailed prior agreement to use the mechanism to limit competition. If the signals are outwardly benign, they convey the information without others' awareness. A famous example was the arrangement among participants in the electrical equipment conspiracy in the 1950s to rotate the winning bidder at two-week intervals, or by the phases of the moon.[25] Under the plan, each manufacturer was assigned a code number and bidding order. As each rival moved into the winning position, the others would, following another coded list, bid above its collusively established list price by assigned amounts. According to the indictment, the "formula was so calculated that submitting prices to these customers, the price spread between defendant manufacturers' quotations would be sufficiently narrow so as to eliminated actual price competition among them, but sufficiently wide so as to give an appearance of competition."[26] The phase-of-the-moon aspect of the conspiracy was designed specifically to avoid detection. A later court held that it was part of a pattern of fraudulent concealment sufficient to toll the statute of limitations in private litigation.[27] A knowing wink, by contrast, is unlikely to convey enough information to form an agreement, unless what is known is a prearranged system in which the wink means more than what convention typically assigns it. Worse, a nod or a wink, without more, tells everyone not only that the parties are signaling but also the content of what is signaled.

Perhaps more important, as a matter of law, the element of prearrangement can serve as the relevant Section 1 agreement. The electrical equipment conspiracy is an example. Another classic example is *Eastern States Retail Lumber Dealers*,[28] where an association circulated a list of wholesalers that were selling directly to consumers. These so-called blacklists predictably led retailers to refuse to buy from listed suppliers. The government conceded that "there is no agreement among the retailers to refrain from dealing with listed wholesalers," but argued that "he is blind indeed who does not see the purpose in the

---

23 1 *Samuel* 20:17-23.

24 William Shakespeare, Macbeth act II, sc. 1 ("I go, and it is done. The bell invites me. Hear it not, Duncan, for it is a knell. That summons thee to heaven or to hell."). Earlier, Macbeth had told a servant "Go bid thy mistress, when my drink is ready, She strike upon the bell." *Id.*

25 Richard Austin Smith, *The Incredible Electrical Conspiracy, Part II*, Fortune, May 1961, 161, at 164, 210.

26 *Quoted in* John G. Fuller, The Gentlemen Conspirators: The Story of the Price-Fixers in the Electrical Industry 65 (1962).

27 Kan. City v. Fed. Pac. Elec. Co., 310 F.2d 271, 284 n.2 (8th Cir. 1962).

28 Eastern States Retail Lumber Dealers' Ass'n v. United States, 234 U.S. 600 (1914).

predetermined and periodical circulation of this report to put the ban upon wholesale dealers whose names appear in the list."[29] The Supreme Court concluded that "when, in this case, by concerted action the names of wholesalers who were reported as having made sales to consumers were periodically reported to the other members of the associations, the conspiracy to accomplish that which was the natural consequence of such action may be readily inferred."[30] In other words, the association prearranged the use of a blacklist to signal which suppliers to boycott.[31]

More recently, the Justice Department alleged that bidders in Federal Communications Commission auctions of regional licenses signaled to rivals by making, and then withdrawing, high bids in other auctions in which the rival had been the higher bidder. The transitory high bids were in amounts that ended in three digit numbers corresponding to the number of the region that was the subject of the target auction. The bids signaled offers to refrain from bidding in the other auctions in return for the rivals' forbearance in the primary auction.[32] As Gregory Werden has observed, by using the signals, the rivals were able to use outwardly minimal communication in order to negotiate an express agreement to fix prices.[33] The formulation of the system may require detailed verbal communication, but it economizes on the need for communication at the critical moment; it allows seemingly public communication to serve as communication of a private meaning.

In the accounts of the arrangements between Jonathan and David and between Macbeth and Lady MacBeth, we see the parties agree on their systems of signals. In the electrical equipment cases, the government was able to uncover documentary evidence of the system in the codes that prescribed the conspirators' timing and calculations of their bids. In other cases, we may see only the signals of the rivals and their apparent consequences, but it may still be possible to infer the earlier communications. An awareness of the function of prearranged signaling can affect the sufficiency of the evidence necessary to infer an agreement. One case,[34] for example, analyzed "an e-mail from a Hitachi employee to a Samsung employee asking, 'Are you willing to exchange product roadmaps again?'" The defendants minimized the email, arguing that it actually suggested that the defendants had no agreement to share confidential information. The court, however, found it plausible to infer "that the companies had an agreement to exchange the information from time to time and Hitachi was inquiring whether it was time for the next exchange."[35] The court continued:

> Plaintiffs need not allege that Defendants actually discussed the prices they exchanged. These emails support Plaintiffs' allegation that Defendants had an ongoing agreement to exchange price and demand information for SRAM and that Defendants were aware that the purpose of sharing this information was to 'stabilize or raise the price of SRAM sold in the United States and elsewhere.'"[36]

---

29 *Id.* at 608-09.

30 *Id.* at 612.

31 *See* Comment, *Sherman Anti-Trust Act—What Constitutes Restraint of Trade*, 1 Tex. L. Rev. 355, 356 (1923) (the *Eastern States* arrangement "savored of a tacit agreement on the part of retail dealers to boycott any wholesaler who dared to deal directly with the consumer").

32 Gregory J. Werden, *Economic Evidence on the Existence of Collusion: Reconciling Antitrust Law With Oligopoly Theory*, 71 Antitrust L.J. 719, 766 (2004).

33 *Id.* at 766-67.

34 *In re* Static Random Access Memory (SRAM) Antitrust Litig., 580 F. Supp. 2d 896 (N.D. Cal. 2008).

35 *Id.* at 901 (citing United States v. Container Corp., 393 U.S. 333 (1969)).

36 *Id.* at 902 (citing United States v. Container Corp., 393 U.S. 333 (1969)). "[Furthermore,] Plaintiffs have plead sufficient facts plausibly to suggest a § 1 price fixing conspiracy . . . [because] . . . [t]hey have plead that Defendants had an ongoing agreement to exchange price information and intended that this exchange would lead to price stabilization or increases . . . [and] . . . the SRAM market was one in which such information exchanges would lead to price stabilization or increases." *Id.* at 903.

In this reasoning, the email, despite its relatively innocuous surface meaning, served as a prearranged signal to resume more explicit exchanges.

V. Implicit Signals

Finally, a signal can be an action that has a more general purpose, but that functions *implicitly* to convey more specific information to a perceptive observer. In daily life, especially in personal relationships, body movements, facial expressions, tones of voice, clothing, physical proximity, and touching, among many other actions, may convey important information.[37] Implicit signals may be unintentional if "unintentional actions . . . are decoded accurately, often because they have shared social meanings."[38] An example is a "tell" in poker, a player's facial expression or other action that unintentionally reveals something about the player's hand. Another might be behavior by a child that indicates a need that the child is not expressing verbally. The law has recognized the possibility of these sorts of unintentional signals. The demeanor of a driver or pedestrian can supposedly provide signals of intent that justify a police stop.[39] The demeanor of a witness can supposedly signal his or her truthfulness or deceit.[40]

Similar implicit signals may occur in market activities.[41] The classic example studied in the economics literature is a graduate degree, which a prospective employee may acquire at great cost in part as a signal of unusual productivity to potential employers.[42] A similar phenomenon may occur in initial public offerings, in which entrepreneurs may keep control of a larger share of their company, again at some cost, in order to signal that the company has good profit potential.[43] Law schools, believe it or not, may undertake costly, sometimes questionable practices in order to boost their *US News* rankings, as a signal (also questionable) of more general quality to both prospective students and employers.[44] Firms may undertake a "price reduction, a new marketing campaign, or the building of a new plant . . . [in order to signal] . . . the intent of the firm to pursue an aggressive strategy of market penetration or to enter into another market segment . . . [or to provide] . . . information regarding product quality."[45]

---

37 Judee K. Burgoon et al., *Nonverbal Signals*, *in* The Sage Handbook of Interpersonal Communication 239, 241 (Mark L. Knapp & John A. Daly eds., 4th ed. 2011).

38 *Id.* at 240.

39 Brown v. Texas, 443 U.S. 47, 52 (1979) ("We have recognized that in some circumstances an officer may detain a suspect briefly for questioning although he does not have 'probable cause' to believe that the suspect is involved in criminal activity, as is required for a traditional arrest [if the officer has] a reasonable suspicion, based on objective facts, that the individual is involved in criminal activity.").

40 *See* Fed. R. Civ. P. 43, advisory committee note to 1996 amendment. ("The importance of presenting live testimony in court cannot be forgotten. The very ceremony of trial and the presence of the factfinder may exert a powerful force for truth telling. The opportunity to judge the demeanor of a witness face-to-face is accorded great value in our tradition."). *But see* Jeremy A. Blumenthal, *A Wipe of the Hands, a Lick of the Lips: The Validity of Demeanor Evidence in Assessing Witness Credibility*, 72 Neb. L. Rev. 1157, 1159 (1993) ("The [scientific] studies establish that typical subjects are unable to use the 'manner and conduct' of a speaker to successfully detect deceptive information on any reliable basis.").

41 Paul Herbig & John C. Milewicz, *Market Signalling and Its Role in Business-to-Business Communications*, 12(4) Marketing Intel. & Plan. 27, 27 (1994) ("A marketing signal is a marketing activity that provides information beyond its mere form and reveals insights into the unobservable.").

42 *See, e.g.*, Michael Spence, *Job Market Signaling*. 87 Q.J. Econ. 355 (1973). *See also* Michael Spence, *Signaling in Retrospect and the Informational Structure of Markets*, 92 Am. Econ. Rev. 434 (2002).

43 Hayne E. Leland & David H. Pyle, *Informational Asymmetries, Financial Structure, and Financial Intermediation*, 32 J. Fin. 371 (1977).

44 *See, e.g.*, Darren Bush & Jessica Patterson, *Jukin' the Stats: The Gaming of Law School Rankings and How to Stop It*, 45 Conn. L. Rev. 1235 (2013).

45 Paul Herbig & John Milewics, *Market Signaling: A Review*, 34 Mgmt. Decision 35, 35 (1996).

Market signals may be unintentional—rivals watch each other like hawks, as Judge Posner notes, in part for actions that unintentionally reveal their plans. If a firm cancels an important equipment order or announces a hiring freeze, for example, its rivals may infer that it is changing business strategy in other, more fundamental ways. Signals may also be false. A firm may take actions in hopes that rivals interpret them as messages, but with the intent to mislead rivals about the firm's true intent. The firm may, for example, announce a product introduction as a bluff in order to mislead rivals. Microsoft, most famously, allegedly used a policy of vaporware, i.e., it would use "the public announcement of a computer product before it is ready for market for the sole purpose of causing consumers not to purchase a competitor's product that has been developed and is either currently available for sale or momentarily about to enter the market."[46]

For our purposes, however, we can limit consideration to cases in which, at least eventually, the announcements are intentional and truthful and the rival believes them and acts collusively. Unintentional signals, by their very nature, do not convey a specific intent, proposal, or assurance that can be the basis for a Sherman Act agreement, whether tacit or express. False signals also do not result in an agreement, at least in the near-term. Vaporware, if it is ever an appropriate theory of monopolization, has no relevance to claims of collusion. Bluffing aimed at misleading buyers may be illegal as fraud, but the harms it inflicts on rivals are not the result of collusion. Bluffing, by its nature, is aimed at gaining a competitive advantage by deterring rivals from taking actions that undermine a firm's competitive position; calling a bluff thwarts that strategy to the rival's benefit. In either instance, the outcome cannot be concerted. It only becomes concerted if the process of bluffing and calling leads rivals to learn one another's intentions and their outcomes, and leads them eventually to reach an agreement on a mutually preferred noncompetitive outcome.

A price increase announcement may signal a multitude of things to various constituencies, but, in oligopolies, it can have a specific meaning to rivals depending upon its context, its content, and the experience of firms in the market over time. In some instances, like the gas station hypothetical I described in Part II, the announcement can signal a proposal to coordinate the rivals' competitive choices. In a one-shot game, the rivals' intention by a price increase is so opaque that it is unlikely that its counterpart can interpret it as a proposal to collude. In repeated games, however, it is more likely that rivals can indicate their intention by patterns of price movements. In some instances, they will be able to achieve tacit collusion. Economists, for example, commonly use the term signaling to refer to simple posting of prices in the process of tacit collusion. Joseph Harrington, for example, wrote recently that a "common form of tacit collusion is indirect communication through price signaling."[47] In *Brooke Group*, the Supreme Court used the term in a similar way:

> Firms that seek to recoup predatory losses through the conscious parallelism of oligopoly must rely on uncertain and ambiguous signals to achieve concerted action. The signals are subject to misinterpretation and are a blunt and imprecise means of ensuring smooth cooperation, especially in the context of changing or unprecedented market circumstances. This anticompetitive minuet is most difficult to compose and to perform, even for a disciplined oligopoly.[48]

---

46 United States v. Microsoft Corp., 159 F.R.D. 318, 334 (D.D.C. 1995) (Sporkin, J.), *rev'd*, 56 F.3d 1448 (D.C. Cir. 1995). For discussion, *see* William H. Page & John E. Lopatka, *Microsoft, Monopolization, and Network Externalities: Some Uses and Abuses of Economic Theory in Antitrust Decision Making*, 40 Antitrust Bull. 317, 356-61 1995. For more general discussion, *see* Maurice E. Stucke, *When a Monopolist Deceives*, 76 Antitrust L.J. 823, 824 (2010). *Cf.* Heonsoo Jung, *Signaling Quality with New Product Preannouncements: Vaporware and the Role of Reference Quality*, 64 J. Bus. Res. 1251 (2011) (studying the benefits and costs to firms of exaggerating product quality).

47 Joseph E. Harrington & Wei Zhao, *Signaling and Tacit Collusion in an Infinitely Repeated Prisoner's Dilemma*, 64 Mathematical Soc. Sci. 277, 277 (2012).

48 Brooke Group Ltd. v. Brown & Williamson Tobacco Corp., 509 U.S. 209, 227-28 (1993). Justice Stevens objected that "professional performers who had danced the minuet for 40 to 50 years would be better able to predict whether their favorite partners would follow them in the future than would an outsider, who might not know the difference between Haydn and Mozart." *Id.* at 257.

Given these limitations, in what circumstance does this kind of implicit signal result in a Sherman Act agreement? The cases suggest that the answer depends on whether the signals are sufficiently clear to convey the necessary intent, without providing compensating social benefit. There are a variety of factors, but the Gary Dinners example provides a starting point. The statements of intention in the various meetings of fabricators were private and thus provided no benefit to consumers. Moreover, they were about future competitive behavior and thus were more likely to limit uncertainty about strategic choices. Consequently, the court was willing interpret the statements as signals inviting a tacit agreement. The gas station hypothetical, mentioned earlier, provides a clear contrast: the posting of price changes can be viewed as a signal, which the rivals use to restrict competition. But courts do not infer a tacit agreement in these circumstances. As one court put it, a "public announcement of a pricing decision cannot be twisted into an invitation or signal to conspire; it is instead an economic reality to which all other competitors must react."[49] The posting of prices is indistinguishable from ordinary oligopoly pricing. Price announcements are essential in virtually every market because they provide the information sellers and buyers need to make choices.[50] Oligopolists watch one another's price movements and decide their most profitable response. Even though this process may result in noncompetitive pricing, the courts have placed it within the safe harbor for mere interdependence.[51] Courts only find agreement in more limited circumstances where the meaning of the signal is clearer.[52]

Joseph Harrington usefully identifies the benefits of a certain kind of price announcement in reducing buyers' search costs and both buyer and sellers' transaction costs.[53] He also notes, however, that these are likely to be most significant in consumer markets with standardized products—typified by the gas station hypothetical. In markets for differentiated products with few sellers and knowledgeable commercial buyers, the cost savings are likely to be far lower. In those markets, he argues that competitive firms will choose a quoted price format and that firms' adoption of a set list price, contrary to their individual interest, can be the basis for inferring an agreement if it results in a price increase.[54]

Similar reasoning applies to advance price announcements, which usually provide useful information to both rivals and consumers. On a number of occasions, enforcement authorities have sought to characterize oligopolists' announcement of future price increases as signals inviting price coordination by rivals. In most cases, however, the courts have rejected the characterization because the announcements serve benign purposes and may benefit consumers.[55] In *Ethyl*, for example, the Federal Trade Commission ("FTC") alleged that rivals' practice of publicly announcing price changes 30 days in advance allowed them to coordinate their pricing decisions.[56] The court concluded, however, that the practice was not an

---

49 United States v. General Motors Corp., No. 38219, 1974 WL 926, *21 (E.D. Mich. Sept. 26, 1974). *See also* Williamson Oil Co., Inc. v. Philip Morris USA, 346 F.3d 1287, 1310 (11th Cir. 2003) ("None of the [price changes] by PM, RJR or B&W that appellants label 'signals' tend to exclude the possibility that the primary players in the tobacco industry were engaged in rational, lawful, parallel pricing behavior that is typical of an oligopoly. Nor, conversely, do they tend to establish that a price fixing conspiracy was afoot.").

50 Joseph Kattan, *Beyond Facilitating Practices Price Signaling and Price Protection Clauses in the New Antitrust Environment*, 63 Antitrust L.J. 133, 138-39 (1994) (a price increase cannot "be viewed predominantly as a signal to competitors rather than as a notice to customers).

51 *Id.* at 139 (observing that "[f]irms must be able to react to market conditions, including the prices charged by rivals;" they cannot "put blinders on and pretend that it does not know what its rivals are charging;" consequently, "the interdependent outcome may be unavoidable").

52 Jacobs v. Tempur-Pedic Int'l, 626 F.3d 1327, 1343 (11th Cir. 2010) ("[I]n addition to tacitly colluding, [rivals must have] signaled each other on how and when to maintain or adjust prices.").

53 Joseph E. Harrington, *Posted Pricing as a Plus Factor*, 7 J. Competition L. & Econ. 1 (2011).

54 *Id.* at 16.

55 E.I. du Pont de Nemours & Co. v. FTC (Ethyl), 729 F.2d 128, 133-04, 140-42 (2d Cir. 1984) (finding no violation when defendants' use of advance price announcements, price protection clauses, and delivered pricing had independent justifications and benefited consumers). *See also* Blomkest Fertilizer, Inc. v. Potash Corp. of Sask., 203 F.3d 1028, 1037 (8th Cir. 2000) (characterizing these actions as simply dissemination of price information and "far too ambiguous to defeat summary judgment").

56 E.I. du Pont de Nemours & Co. v. FTC (Ethyl), 729 F.2d 128 (2d Cir. 1984).

unfair method of competition because it had independent competitive justifications.[57] The court observed that the announcements could not primarily have been to coordinate prices, because one of the rivals began issuing "advance notice of price increases both to buyers and to the press" decades before, when it was the only producer in the industry, "as a means of aiding buyers in their financial and purchase planning."[58] Moreover, the court noted, the practice did little to facilitate price coordination because rivals have other ways of quickly finding out about rivals' prices and the announcements did not prevent firms from rescinding the announced changes based on new information.[59]

In some instances, however, the form and content of the announcement can clarify the intention sufficiently to justify a plausible inference of tacit agreement.[60] Even in these circumstances, however, it is hard to set meaningful boundaries on the principle. In *Petroleum Products*,[61] for example, the court found that where wholesale buyers were under contract to individual refiners, the refiners' practice of posting wholesale tank-wagon prices, in some instances before they became effective, served only to coordinate higher prices. The refiners' officers testified that the only reason to post the prices was "for the purpose of quickly informing competitors of the price change, in the express hope that these competitors would follow the move and restore their prices."[62] Leading price increases without public announcements was costly because it took time for rivals to learn of it and to detect its significance; publicly announcing the future prices greatly reduced those costs. Moreover, "the public dissemination of information concerning dealer tank-wagons and discounts could hardly be described as fostering the efficient or rational operation of the market inasmuch as there simply was no wholesale market to rationalize; the branded dealers were not free to shop around for their oil."[63] The Ninth Circuit, however, later expressed its discomfort with this decision by characterizing it as dicta.[64]

In *Airline Tariff Publishing*, the Justice Department alleged that airlines used a jointly operated computerized listing of fare information to coordinate noncompetitive pricing. The posted fares were not only present ones, but proposals of future fares, with footnotes indicating the dates on which they would be available and "linkages" of the fares among routes. According to the Justice Department, the airlines used the announcements of future fares to negotiate fare increases and to indicate retaliation for fare changes on linked routes.[65] According to its description in the Competitive Impact Statement that accompanied the eventual consent decree, in one scenario:

> [O]ne airline began the process by filing its proposed higher fares in particular markets with a first ticket date in the future. . . . Other airlines responded to such a proposal in different ways. If an airline wanted that increase, it conveyed its agreement by filing the same proposed increase

---

57 *Id.* at 140.

58 *Id.* at 134.

59 *Id.*

60 Advance announcements of commission increases at trade association meetings, in circumstances in which other communications were occurring, may be interpreted less as taking "the lead in raising its commissions, with the blind hope that other members would follow" than as seeking "some guarantee that the other defendants would acquiesce, to ensure that its clients would not segregate against them." Fears v. Wilhelmina Model Agency, Inc., No. 02 Civ. 4911(HB), 2004 WL 594396, *8 (S.D.N.Y. Mar. 23, 2004). It is unclear whether the court saw these announcements as implicit or prearranged signals. There was evidence in earlier minutes of agreements on variables other than fees that raised an inference of "an industry inundated with collusion." *Id.* at *13.

61 *In re* Coordinated Pretrial Proceedings in Petroleum Prods. Antitrust Litig., 906 F.2d 432, 444 (9th Cir. 1990).

62 *Id.* at 446.

63 *Id.* at 448.

64 *In re* Citric Acid Litig., 191 F.3d 1090, 1096 (9th Cir. 1999) (observing that the result was also supported by direct evidence of conspiracy).

65 Werden, *supra* note 33, at 765-66.

> in the same city pairs with the same first ticket date. If an airline wanted a different increase, it made a counterproposal, filing fares with first ticket dates in the future to communicate which fares it wanted to increase, by how much and in what city pairs. To facilitate negotiations, an airline typically used a common footnote designator on the fares included in its proposal, such as all leisure fares or all fares in certain city pairs. This highlighted for the other airlines which fares it wanted bundled together to receive common treatment.
>
> Often, the airlines exchanged proposals over several weeks, with the first ticket dates repeatedly postponed ("rolled") in order to allow more time for negotiation. At times they took steps to secure the agreement of recalcitrant airlines. . . . The negotiation process continued until all significant airlines were lined up with the same proposed fare increase and the same first ticket date, thus providing each other with commitments and assurances as to the amount, scope, and timing of the proposed fare increase. On that first ticket date, the fares for all the airlines increased.[66]

The consent decree prohibited airlines from posing fares with first ticket dates, and only permitted listing last ticket dates if they were generally advertised to consumers; it also prohibited use of footnotes to link fares.[67] Interestingly, travel agents and consumer groups objected that these provisions would limit their access to useful information, but the Justice Department persuaded the court that the postings to which it applied were of little use to consumers because they were mainly signals among airlines, and not reliable for reservations.[68]

Later, in response to a letter inquiry from American Airlines, however, the Justice Department stated that the decree did not prohibit posting "bona fide fares" then withdrawing them if other airlines did not match them, but maintaining them if they did.[69] The Department explained that:

> [A]lthough there may be an element of communication inherent in fares that are actually available and intended to be sold, . . . the Decree specifically provides that it does not prohibit a defendant, "in unilaterally determining its own fares, from considering all publicly available information relating to the fares of other airlines." Section V(G). Publicly available information encompasses information concerning other airlines' current and prior bona fide fares and fare changes, as well as any "pattern" that emerges from changes in such fares.[70]

Based on this sequence of allegations and qualifications, Joseph Kattan observed at the time that "[a] dvance price announcements may not be safe from antitrust attack . . . simply because they have some business justification. To the extent that the business justification appears weak in comparison to the anticompetitive potential of a practice, the practice may be vulnerable to attack."[71]

---

66 United States v. Airline Tariff Publishing Co., Proposed Final Judgment and Competitive Impact Statement, 59 Fed. Reg. 15,225, 15,230-31 (Mar. 31, 1994).

67 United States v. Airline Tariff Pub. Co., 836 F. Supp. 9, 12 (D.C. Cir. 1993).

68 *Id.* at 13.

69 United States v. Airline Tariff Publishing Co., Proposed Consent Decree and Competitive Impact Statement, 59 Fed. Reg. at 15,235.

70 *Id.* at 15,236.

71 Kattan, *supra* note 50, at 145.

More specific signals may also occur during earnings calls with stock analysts.[72] Although public, they are far more detailed than a bare announcement of a future price increase. They allow a rival to discuss their reasoning about future price and output decisions in a setting typically monitored by competitors and generally not by consumers. Nevertheless, the same considerations recur in the courts' analysis of allegations of signaling during the calls. If the statements provide legitimate information to a range of market constituencies, courts refuse to interpret them as forming tacit agreements simply because rivals monitor the calls and adapt their strategic behavior.[73]

The most detailed expression of the benign view of implicit signaling during analyst calls is in the district court opinion in *Holiday Wholesale*.[74] In a lengthy section on signaling, the court considered the wholesalers' allegations that the cigarette manufacturers, through an intermediary, monitored one another's signals made during their presentations to analysts to coordinate specific price increases.[75] The court was at pains to distinguish the connotation of the word signaling from the specific alleged conduct. The term insinuates, according to the court, "either that a competitor is inviting all to make a traditional price-fixing agreement," apparently using something like an implicit signal, or "that there already exists such an agreement and it is being carried out through indirect communications,"[76]—what I am calling a prearranged signal.

But despite plaintiffs' use of terms like nods and olive branches, they showed only that "in an oligopoly, each company is aware of the others' actions" and takes them into account in their competitive decisions.[77] The court reasoned that "[b]ecause in competitive markets, particularly oligopolies, companies will monitor each other's communications with the market in order to make their own strategic decisions, antitrust law permits such discussions even when they relate to pricing."[78] For there to be an "inference of traditional agreement from indirect communications," there must be "communications with no public purpose,"[79] like "internal competitive memos" and "supply and demand forecasts."[80] "Signals," as plaintiff used the term, conveyed too little information in too noisy and complex a setting to form and police a conspiracy.[81]

The court of appeals agreed with the district court's interpretation of the evidence. By the plaintiffs' account, when Phillip Morris drastically cut its prices on "Marlboro Friday," it signaled rivals that it would

---

72 *Cf.* Howard Rosenblatt & Tomas Nilsson, *Analyst Calls and Price Signaling under EU Law*, Antitrust Source at 1-3 (June 2012) (discussing enforcement actions against firms for anticompetitive announcements during telephone calls with analysts, but monitored by rivals), *available at* http://www.americanbar.org/content/dam/aba/publishing/antitrust_source/jun12_full_source.authcheckdam.pdf.

73 Similar considerations apply to other ostensibly public, detailed communications that primarily address rivals. For example, "pricing letters," ostensibly to customers, may offer rivals detailed plans for anticipated increases in prices. *In re* McWane, Inc. and Star Pipe Prods., Ltd., Docket No. 9351, 2012 WL 4101793 (F.T.C. Sept. 14, 2012), the FTC denied a summary decision on the ground that there was sufficient evidence to support allegations that producers of pipe fittings fixed prices by following a plan set out in one rivals' pricing letters:

> While McWane denies that it ever intended to convey any plan to its competitors, there is evidence suggesting otherwise. [The letters] contained language that Complaint Counsel contends was aimed at competitors and would have been meaningless to customers. Thus, a reasonable inference could be that McWane intended to use its pricing letters to communicate a plan to its competitors. *Id.* at *12.

The alleged conspiracy included the creation of an information exchange to monitor rivals' pricing. *Id.* at *16-17. *See also In re* Ductile Iron Pipe Fittings (DIPF) Direct Purchaser Antitrust Litigation, No. 12-711, 2014 WL 3971620 (D.N.J. Aug. 13, 2014) (denying a motion to dismiss in follow-on private litigation).

74 Holiday Wholesale Grocery Co. v. Philip Morris, Inc., 231 F. Supp. 2d 1253, 1276 (2002), *aff'd sub nom.* Williamson Oil Co. v. Philip Morris USA, 346 F.3d 1287 (11th Cir. 2003).

75 *Id.* at 1275.

76 *Id.*

77 *Id.*

78 *Id.* at 1276.

79 *Id.* at 1277.

80 *Id.*

81 *Id.*

not tolerate erosion of its leading market share, and invited them instead to collude to return to profitability.[82] Phillip Morris also announced that it would permanently reduce the prices of its premium brands, narrow the price gap between premium and discount cigarettes, and consolidate the wholesale prices of its various products so that there were fewer price points in the market.[83] In response to these "signals," rivals made announcements during analyst calls suggesting that they did not want to continue the price war and expected to raise prices in the future.[84] Over a five year period, the rivals followed one another's price increases 11 times.[85]

The court rejected the plaintiffs' characterization of each of these actions and statements as *collusive* signals, finding that in context they all were explicable as part of rational oligopoly pricing. For example, the wholesalers contended that the manufacturers' "signaling reached a peak . . . when RJR increased wholesale prices in equal amounts for both the premium and discount price tiers" when it would have been in its "economic interest to attempt to widen the price gap."[86] On the contrary, the court reasoned, RJR "knew as a result of Marlboro Friday that PM would not readily accept such a strategy, and that any effort to re-widen the price gap ultimately would have further depressed industry revenues without increasing their market shares, [so] economic self-interest dictated that they raise premium and discount prices as much as they could."[87]

Interestingly, the court here agreed that firms' price moves convey implicit meanings that may influence their rivals' pricing behavior and lead to price increases. It reasoned that Phillip Morris's "premium price cuts strongly suggested to its competitors that any attempt to gain market share for discount brands through further price cuts would not be accepted."[88] Phillip Morris would meet the price cuts, so they would only reduce industry revenues. Consequently, the rivals could only increase their own revenues by raising their "prices in a manner that would not provoke a competitive response from PM, which is precisely the action that the class labels a signal of conspiracy." The very actions that the plaintiffs characterized as a pattern of collusive signaling were simply "lawful, rational pricing behavior."[89]

In some instances, the signals in earnings calls are far clearer and may support a finding of agreement.[90] In one recent case, for example, competing firms allegedly proposed during earnings calls and industry meetings to reduce output and raise fees, and then acted consistently with the proposals.[91] One announced that "we strongly believe that more industry capacity needs to be removed,"[92] and its rival the next day stated it wanted to remove capacity, but had "to do it in conjunction with the other carriers" and that "if

82 Williamson Oil Co. v. Philip Morris USA, 346 F.3d 1287, 1306 (11th Cir. 2003).

83 *Id.* at 1307.

84 *Id.* at 1307-09.

85 *Id.* at 1294.

86 *Id.* at 1309.

87 *Id.*

88 *Id.* at 1307.

89 *Id.*

90 The signals may, according to the FTC, constitute an invitation to collude in violation of Section 5. *See, e.g.*, *In re* Valassis Commc'ns, Inc., FTC File No. 051–0008, 2006 WL 1367833 (Apr. 19, 2006) (where the FTC found that statements by a producer of discount coupon books detailing its goals of reducing its market share targets and increasing prices invited a rival to collude. The producer also promised to monitor its rival's response to the proposal and threatened reprisals if the response was not favorable: "We expect that concrete evidence of News America's intentions will be available in the marketplace in short order. If News continues to pursue our customers and market share then we will go back to our previous strategy." *Id.* at *3. Had the rival responded favorably by its own announcements and conduct, a court would likely have found a Section 1 agreement.)

91 *In re* Delta/AirTran Baggage Fee Antitrust Litig., 733 F. Supp. 2d 1348, 1352 (N.D. Ga. 2010).

92 *Id.* at 1352.

the industry could achieve a 10% reduction in capacity year-over-year by the fall that we'd be in pretty good shape given today's fuel environment."[93] They made similar statements concerning prices and fees in subsequent earnings calls and industry meetings, then simultaneously increased fees and reduced capacity during a recession in which oil prices were falling.[94] The court concluded that the complaint sufficiently alleged a Section 1 agreement. It distinguished the case from "mere price announcements" on the ground that the complaint alleged "that each Defendant signaled its willingness to cut capacity and increase prices if the other Defendant acted in concert."[95]

Another case illustrates some of the challenges of this approach and the importance of correctly classifying the alleged signaling.[96] Private equity firms allegedly conspired to allocate leveraged buyout deals by withdrawing or "standing down" from bidding for the contract once another firm's deal was announced, even though the deals permitted the seller to shop the agreement. In one of the episodes, one consortium announced that it had reached a proprietary agreement to purchase a hospital chain; another consortium reached a deal to purchase a semiconductor firm. Once the deals were announced, after a "flurry of activity,"[97] each of the winning firms stood down in their efforts to take the other's deal. One of the grounds the court offered for finding a conspiracy was that, regardless of whether there was evidence of a *quid pro quo* in the two deals, it was sufficient that there was evidence that one of the firms had issued a "request to the industry" to stand down in their bids for the hospital chain, and the others had done so—an instance of tacit agreement, or "uniform behavior among competitors, preceded by conversations implying that later uniformity might prove desirable."[98] The defendants requested interlocutory review, arguing that the court seemed to be adopting a novel definition of agreement as "a request followed by uniform action," but the court denied the motion, first on the ground that the tacit agreement rationale was not an exclusive holding, and, second, because *White* had characterized its' account of the concept of tacit agreement as "settled."[99]

---

93 *Id.* at 1353.

94 *Id.* at 1356.

95 *Id.* at 1362. *See also* Federal Trade Commission, U–Haul Int'l, Inc. and AMERCO, 75 Fed. Reg. 35,033, 35,034 n.3 (June 21, 2010) (where U-Haul allegedly announced that it had raised rates and suggested that Budget's failure to match the price increases, within 3-5 percent, was unfortunate and would require U-Haul to cut its rates in order to maintain market share.). *Cf.* Liu v. Amerco, 677 F.3d 489, 494 (1st Cir. 2012) (holding the same conduct could support a private right of action under a Massachusetts statute that "parallels" the FTC Act).

96 Dahl v. Bain Capital Partners, LLC, 937 F. Supp. 2d 119 (D. Mass. 2013).

97 *Id.* at 131.

98 *Id.* at 142 (quoting White v. R.M. Packer Co., Inc., 635 F.3d 571, 576 (1st Cir.2011)).

99 Dahl v. Bain Capital Partners, LLC, 983 F. Supp. 2d 185, 187-88 (D. Mass. 2013).

VI. Conclusion

Collusion requires communication. Oligopolists converse and sometimes reach noncompetitive understandings by public communications with the market. While those sorts of communications may contain signals in an economic sense, they are also necessary for markets to function at all, so courts have resisted characterizing the resulting anticompetitive understandings as agreements in a legal sense. To form a Sherman Act agreement, signals to rivals must be more specific in content, without providing useful information to consumers. In this article, I have examined how various forms of signals—conventional, prearranged, and implicit—might accomplish anticompetitive coordination. The most important, in practical terms, are implicit signals—those conveyed in actions that have an outwardly neutral meaning, but also a meaning that rivals understand as directed to them. I have argued that, even if a signal causes in a noncompetitive market outcome, it only forms a Sherman Act agreement only if the signal conveys specific information, useful only rivals, about the sender's intent and its expectations about the rivals' competitive choices.

Improving Antitrust Sanctions

Daniel L. Rubinfeld*
drubinfeld@law.berkeley.edu
Robert L. Bridges Professor of Law and Professor of Economics Emeritus
University of California, Berkeley
Professor of Law, New York University School of Law

Abstract

Our current systems of private and public enforcement can be improved if more attention is given towards increasing individual incentives. Public enforcement can benefit from appropriate targeted prison sentences, while private enforcement would benefit from a more expansive set of whistle blower opportunities and rewards.

* Sarah Tang provided valuable research assistance.

I. Introduction

In a recent paper, Doug Ginsburg and Josh Wright have made a number of provocative comments and suggestions concerning corporate liability.[1] The suggestions move us in the right direction by focusing on the distinction between individual and corporate liability and by emphasizing the importance of individual incentives.

Based on the current empirical evidence relating to public enforcement, Ginsburg and Wright proceed from a starting point that presumes under-enforcement. This is appropriate. It is well known that in recent years US enforcement agencies have increased corporate fines to deter anticompetitive activity. The average fine levied on corporations participating in anticompetitive conduct has grown from $28 million in the early 1990s, to well over $500 million in recent years.[2] Yet, despite this dramatic increase in corporate fines, studies have shown that cartel activity has remained constant over the past four decades.[3] This suggests that financial penalties alone generate only partial deterrence.[4]

I offer no evidence to the contrary. Rather, I explain why the question of optimal enforcement becomes especially complex once one takes into account the overlap between public and private enforcement. I also offer some thoughts as to how the current system of public enforcement might be improved.

II. Improving Deterrence

Persistent recidivism reveals shortcomings in the current public enforcement system. From 1999 to 2009, the top 10 recidivist firms in the US were cited for multiple counts of anticompetitive conduct.[5] To illustrate, Ajinomoto, Bayer, and Coca Cola all faced multiple citations each within a two year period.[6] In the current landscape, the probability of detection may not be very high and for some the expected gain of collusion may outweigh the expected fine.[7] It is plausible to expect that relatively high rates of recidivism result, at least in part, from the fact that current measures do not impose sufficient costs on companies or corporate executives.[8]

---

1 Douglas H. Ginsburg & Joshua D. Wright, *Antitrust Sanctions*, 6 Competition Pol'y Int'l 3, 3 (2010).

2 *Id.* at 10.

3 Alla Golub, Joshua Detre & John M. Connor, *The Profitability of Price Fixing: Have Stronger Antitrust Sanctions Deterred?*, Presented at the International Industrial Organization Conference 3, at 11 (Apr. 8-9, 2005), *available at* http://papers.ssrn.com/sol3/papers.cfm?abstract_id=1188515&download=yes.

4 Letter from Douglas H. Ginsburg, Senior Cir. J., U.S. Ct App. D.C. Cir., & Joshua D. Wright, Comm'r, Fed. Trade Comm'n, to the U.S. Sentencing Comm'n (July 28, 2014), *available at* http://www.ussc.gov/sites/default/files/pdf/amendment-process/public-comment/20140729/Ginsburg_Wright.pdf; Letter from Albert Foer, President, American Antitrust Inst., & Robert H. Lande, Dir., American Antitrust Inst., to the US Sentencing Comm'n 2 (July 18, 2014), *available at* http://papers.ssrn.com/sol3/papers.cfm?abstract_id=2610780.

5 Ginsburg & Wright, *supra* note 1 at 15.

6 *See* United States v. Bayer AG, No. CR 04-0331 (N.D. Cal. Oct. 13, 2004), *available at* http://www.justice.gov/atr/cases/f205900/205904.pd; United States v. Bayer Corp., No. CR 04-0318, *available at* http://www.justice.gov/atr/cases/f206100/206198.pdf; United States v. Bayer AG, No. CR 04-0235, *available at* http://www.justice.gov/atr/cases/f204800/204899.pdf. *See also* United States v. Ajinomoto Co., Inc., No. 301-CR-279, *available at* http://www.justice.gov/atr/cases/f9300/9301.pdf; United States v. Ajinomoto Co., Inc., No. 96-CR-520, *available at* http://www.justice.gov/atr/ cases/f0900/0918.pdf.

7 An early study found that only 13-17% of cartels are detected and prosecuted. *See* Peter G. Bryant & Edwin Eckard, *Price Fixing: The Probability of Getting Caught*, 73 Rev. Econ. & Stat. 531 (1991).

8 One mechanism that could increase deterrence is to increase penalties for repeat offenders. For an analysis, *see* Mitchell A. Polinsky & Daniel L. Rubinfeld, *A Model of Optimal Fines for Repeat Offenders*, 46 J. Pub. Econ. 291 (1991).

There is reason to believe that fines are less effective than prison sentences, at least with respect to key individual offenders. One response is to augment corporate fines with fines on individual perpetrators.[9] This is an apt approach because corporate fines are typically borne by shareholders who do not directly participate in decision making processes. I expect that imposing consequences on parties with direct decision making powers (such as directors and officers) will produce greater deterrence than corporate fines alone.

Of course, individual fines do not present the perfect solution, especially if corporations indemnify individual perpetrators. I am sympathetic with Ginsburg and Wright's suggestion that we increase the length of prison sentences associated with white collar crimes. Executives are more likely to be responsive to the threat of incarceration, given that it introduces real, lifestyle-altering consequences.[10] Apart from the stigma associated with a criminal conviction, offenders are deprived of their privacy, rights, and future earnings.[11] For members of the bar, disbarment may also present a viable alternative to a prison sentence. Disbarment produces similar deterrent effects by publicizing the offense and imposing reputational and financial punishment on offenders without the social costs of criminal trials.[12] Both of these punishments force the individual responsible to internalize the costs of his or her actions and, therefore, are reasonable deterrence mechanisms.[13]

We can also further improve on the current system by implementing whistleblower rewards.[14] Empirical evidence reveals a strong link between financial rewards and increased cartel reporting.[15] Unfortunately, the Antitrust Criminal Penalty Enhancement and Reform Act ("ACPERA") currently does not include a whistleblower rewards provision.[16] While the topic remains controversial, many experts agree that some form of reward is vital to compensate whistleblowers for the various risks they face in assisting authorities in cartel investigations.[17] Therefore, a logical next step would be to improve the incentives that encourage employees to report anticompetitive behavior. This could improve deterrence by increasing the pool of potential informants.[18]

---

9 Ginsburg & Wright, *supra* note 1 at 5.

10 Stephen A. Yoder, *Criminal Sanctions for Corporate Illegality*, 69 J. Crim. L. & Criminology 40, 46 (1978).

11 Gregory J. Werden, Scott D. Hammond & Belinda A. Barnett, *Deterrence and Detection of Cartels: Using All the Tools and Sanctions*, Presented at the 26th Annual National Institute of White Collar Crime at 15 Mar. 1, 2012), *available at* http://www.justice.gov/atr/file/518936/download; Daniel R. Fischel & Alan O. Sykes, *Corporate Crime*, 25 J. Legal Stud. 319, 319 (1999).

12 Ginsburg & Wright, *supra* note 1 at 15, 19.

13 *Id.* at 13.

14 Gordon Schnell, *Bring In the Whistleblowers and Pay Them – The Next Logical Step in Advancing Antitrust Enforcement*, 2 Competition Pol'y Int'l Antitrust Chron. 5 (2013).

15 Bill Libit, Todd Freier & Walt Draney, *Elements of an Effective Whistleblower Hotline*, Harvard Law School Forum on Corporate Governance and Financial Regulation (Oct. 25, 2014), *available at* http://corpgov.law.harvard.edu/2014/10/25/elements-of-an-effective-whistleblower-hotline/.

16 U.S. Gov't Accountability Office, Criminal Cartel Enforcement: Stakeholder Views on Impact of 2004 Antitrust Reform (2011), *available at* http://www.gao.gov/assets/330/321794.pdf. For a breakdown of arguments for and against whistleblower incentives, *see* Kevin R. Sullivan, Kate Ball & Sarah Klebolt, *The Potential Impact of Adding a Whistleblower Rewards Provision to ACPERA*, Antitrust Source, Oct. 2011, *available at* http://www.americanbar.org/content/dam/aba/publishing/antitrust_source/oct11_sullivan_10_24f.authcheckdam.pdf.

17 Eleanor Bloxham, *How to Encourage the Right Kind of Whistleblowers*, Fortune (June 15, 2011, 4:15 PM), http://fortune.com/2011/06/15/how-to-encourage-the-right-kind-of-whistleblowers/; Cecile Aubert, Patrick Rey & William E. Kovacic, *The Impact of Leniency and Whistle-Blowing Programs on Cartels*, 24 Int'l J. Indus. Org. 1241 (2006), *available at* https://www.ftc.gov/system/files/documents/public_statements/418011/2006leniency.pdf.

18 *See* Libit, Freier & Draney, *supra* note 15.

III. Private Enforcement

Despite its many flaws, private enforcement continues to serve an important function. Private and public enforcement play complementary roles in deterring anticompetitive conduct, with private enforcement emphasizing compensation and public enforcement focused on penalizing and deterring anticompetitive behavior. Private enforcement also adds to the deterrence effect, especially when private parties face lower information costs than their public counterparts and have the potential to uncover otherwise undetected cartel activity.[19]

In terms of consumer compensation, the US Department of Justice ("DOJ") has relied primarily on private litigation for damage recovery since 1960.[20] A comparison of public and private recoveries from 1990 through 2011 reveals that private litigators recovered $35.8 billion in damages for consumers, three times the amount the DOJ collected in the same period.[21] Private litigation, particularly through class action lawsuits, can impose steep damage awards on offending corporations, imposing fiscal consequences beyond the limits of public enforcement.

Private litigation has also been successful in prosecuting cases which have not been pursued by federal or state agencies. In a study of 40 antitrust cases with $23 billion in cumulative recoveries, 46% of recoveries were a result of non-follow on cases.[22]

Of course, private enforcement is not a panacea. While empirical evidence has proven that private action can expand and complement the scope of public litigation, the current system has many flaws that can and should be corrected. A key complaint regarding private litigation is that its high payouts invite excessive and unnecessary litigation.[23] There are clearly avenues for potential improvement and, in recent years, the US judicial system has taken steps to eliminate meritless lawsuits.

Of the other areas of potential improvement, two strike me as worthy of consideration: (1) reforming the complexities that flow from *Illinois Brick*; and (2) employing a variant of the loser pays system.[24]

In June 1977, the US Supreme Court in *Illinois Brick* ruled that indirect purchasers could not file a suit or claim trebled damages from firms that had engaged in anticompetitive behavior.[25] The indirect purchaser rule was aimed at protecting defendants from paying double recoveries. The ruling assumed that indirect purchasers would pass on overcharges to direct buyers, making it unnecessary to compensate both parties. While *Illinois Brick* was certainly a step in the right direction in minimizing unnecessary class action lawsuits, the ruling's lack of clarity and the complications created by the various state laws that repealed the ruling in *Illinois Brick* must be addressed if it is to be a cornerstone of the law.[26] Recent cases such

---

19 For a thoughtful discussion of this and related issues, *see* Ilya R. Segal & Michael D. Whinston, *Public vs. Private Enforcement of Antitrust Law: A Survey*, 28 Eur. Competition L. Rev. 306, 323-32 (2006).

20 Robert H. Lande & Joshua P. Davis, *Benefits from Private Antitrust Enforcement: Forty Individual Case Studies*, 80 U.S.F. L.Rev. 879 (2008).

21 Joshua P. Davis, & Robert H. Lande, *Defying Conventional Wisdom: The Case for Private Antitrust Enforcement*, 48 Ga. L. Rev. 1, 17 (2013).

22 Lande & Davis, *supra* note 21 at 897.

23 Jessica Beess und Chrostin, The Future of Collective Redress in Europe: Where We Are and How to Move Forward 9 (Apr. 2011) (unpublished student paper, Harvard Law School), *available at* http://blogs.law.harvard.edu/hnmcp/files/2012/02/Fisher-Sander-Prize-2011-Winner-Jessica-Beess-und-Chrostin-May-2011.pdf.

24 For one analysis of the efficacy of a loser pays system, *see* Mitchell A. Polinsky & Daniel L. Rubinfeld, *Does the English Rule Discourage Low-Probability-of-Prevailing Plaintiffs?*, 27 J. Legal Stud. 519 (1998).

25 Illinois Brick Co. v. Illinois, 431 U.S. 720, 726–727 (1977).

26 Jeffery L. Harrison, *Reexamining the Role of* Illinois Brick *in Modern Antitrust Standing Analysis*, 68 Geo. Wash. L. Rev. 1, 42-43 (1999).

as *Bell Atlantic v. Twombly* and *AT&T Mobility LLC v. Concepcion* have added clarity while generating continued controversy by: (i) taking a more aggressive stance toward dismissing meritless cases; and (ii) disallowing class actions in cases in which contracts have arbitration clauses.[27]

With respect to other possible reforms, I support procedures that would move the current opt-out system to an opt-in system. In the United States, individuals who do not wish to be involved in class proceedings must affirmatively opt-out.[28] While opt-out systems inarguably favor victim compensation, they also often result in large costly-to-litigate classes. Indeed, risk-averse defendants have a strong incentive to settle post-certification to avoid lengthy and potentially expensive litigation.[29] Opt-in systems prevent abusive litigation by producing a smaller class, and thus smaller contingency fees, which discourage law firms from bringing frivolous suits to court. They do, however, leave open the risk that some (uninformed) consumers will not be compensated and there will be inadequate deterrence.

IV. Concluding Remarks

While double paying may not be ideal, I do not see it as a major concern given that public sanctions primarily serve a deterrence function, while private enforcement is more directed towards compensation. There is reason to believe that private litigation has uncovered and prosecuted antitrust violations that were beyond the resources of public enforcers, thereby increasing overall detection and deterrence. Despite its merits, however, private litigation has serious shortcomings. Some of these can be addressed through substantive changes such as those I have suggested.

27 AT&T Mobility LLC v. Concepcion, 563 U.S. 321 (2011); Bell Atlantic Corp. v. Twombly, 550 U.S. 544 (2007). *See also* Ashcroft v. Iqbal, 56 U.S. 662 (2009).

28 Chrostin, *supra* note 23 at 11.

29 Guido Calabresi & Kevin S. Schwartz, *The Costs of Class Actions: Allocation and Collective Redress in the U.S. Experience* 10 (IEL Working Paper No. 1, 2011), *available at* http://econpapers.repec.org/scripts/redir.pf?u=http%3A%2F%2Fpolis.unipmn.it%2Fpubbl%2FRePEc%2Fuca%2Fucaiel%2Fiel001.pdf;h=repec:uca:ucaiel:1.

The Prominence of Market Definition in Antitrust Evaluation and Litigation*

LOREN SMITH
lsmith@compasslexecon.com
Senior Vice President, Compass Lexecon

MARIA STOYADINOVA
mstoyadinova@compasslexecon.com
Vice President, Compass Lexecon

Abstract

In recent years antitrust agencies have placed more emphasis on direct analyses of the likely competitive effects of horizontal mergers, relying less on structural indicators of likely merger harm such as market shares, particularly when the most likely theory of anticompetitive harm is unilateral competitive effects. This shift in emphasis is reflected in the 2010 Horizontal Merger Guidelines as well as in speeches and writings by agency officials. Courts, however, have maintained a strong reliance on market definition and market shares, as indicated by review of the court decisions in litigated merger transactions between 2005 and 2014. This is true even when direct analyses of competitive effects likely were the focus of the antitrust review prior to litigation. The adherence of courts to structural indicators of merger harm can cause the agencies and merging parties to shift focus and effort to rigorous analyses of market definition and market shares even when such analyses are redundant to direct analyses of competitive effects.

---

* The views and opinions expressed in this paper are solely those of the authors and do not necessarily reflect the views and opinions of Compass Lexecon or any of the organizations with which the authors are or have previously been associated.

I. Introduction

Modern antitrust investigations utilize a wide array of theoretical and empirical tools to analyze the likely competitive effects of horizontal mergers. As theoretical and econometric tools have been developed to directly analyze the likely competitive effects of mergers, antitrust practitioners' reliance on formal market definition and related indirect measures of likely competitive effects (e.g., market shares) has lessened. This shift in focus is reflected in the 2010 Horizontal Merger Guidelines (the "Merger Guidelines")[1] and in subsequent writings and speeches by US antitrust agency officials.[2]

By contrast, decisions from litigated mergers indicate that the courts still rely heavily on market definition and market shares. As we show below, the decisions of all mergers that were litigated in federal court in the 10-year period from 2005 to 2014 indicate a strong reliance on market definition and market shares.

The divergence between the analyses of mergers at the investigation and litigation stages can cause unnecessary redundancy, confusion, and wasteful effort and focus. Most merger investigations begin with an informal review of market definition/concentration, which helpfully separates for decision-makers and courts markets that potentially matter from those that clearly do not.[3] However, typically transactions that require a more in-depth investigation quickly move past this initial screening phase to focus on direct analyses of competitive effects. In many of these cases, formal market definition and related analyses are not given serious consideration until the issue of potential litigation is raised.

When litigation becomes likely, the US Department of Justice ("DOJ") and the Federal Trade Commission ("FTC") (collectively the "Agencies") and outside practitioners are compelled to formally define markets and compute market shares because there is a general feeling that the courts will weigh heavily evidence on market definition and market shares. In our experience, the shift in focus to market definition is driven by at least three factors: (i) legal precedent; (ii) the implications of high market shares are familiar and easy to understand; and (iii) market definition/market shares give advocates on both sides of a merger litigation an additional way to present their case. However, in those cases where unilateral competitive effects are the primary theory of harm, courts focusing more attention on direct analyses of competitive effects likely would be more efficient and potentially lead to a more informed outcome.[4]

---

1 U.S. Dep't of Justice & Fed. Trade Comm'n, Horizontal Merger Guidelines (2010), *available at* https://www.ftc.gov/sites/default/files/attachments/merger-review/100819hmg.pdf.

2 *See, e.g.*, Carl Shapiro, *The 2010 Horizontal Merger Guidelines: From Hedgehog to Fox in Forty Years*, 77 Antitrust L.J. 701 (2010). Jon Leibowitz, Chairman, Fed. Trade Comm'n, *Making the Grade? A Year at the FTC*, Remarks at the Fourth Annual Global Antitrust Enforcement Symposium 4 (Sept. 21, 2010), *available at* https://www.ftc.gov/sites/default/files/documents/public_statements/making-grade-year-ftc/100921makingthegradespeech.pdf ("[the 2010 Horizontal Merger Guidelines] reflect the reality that market definition is an important part of the analysis, but not necessarily the starting point and certainly not the end. . . . [T]he revised Guidelines explain in more detail the economic basis of unilateral effects.").

3 These benefits of market definition are highlighted in, *e.g.*, Gregory J. Werden, *Why (Ever) Define Markets? An Answer to Professor Kaplow* (2012), *available at* http://ssrn.com/abstract=2004655; Dennis W. Carlton & Mark Israel, *Response to Gopal Das Varma's* Market Definition, Upward Pricing Pressure, and the Role of Courts: A Response to Carlton and Israel, Antitrust Source (December 2010), *available at* http://www.americanbar.org/content/dam/aba/publishing/antitrust_source/Dec10_Carlton12_21f.pdf.

4 Of course it is not always the case that formal market definition and associated market shares are counterproductive. Some matters lack sufficient information to analyze competitive effects directly, in which case market shares may be the best indicator of likely merger harm.

II. Migration toward Direct Competitive Effects Analyses

1. US Antitrust Agency Staff and Outside Practitioners

Long before a horizontal merger in the United States is litigated in a federal or administrative court, lawyers and economists at the Agencies engage with outside lawyers and economists in an attempt to find a common ground that will resolve any competitive concerns while allowing the proposed merger to proceed. These talks often move quickly from informal market definition and market shares to discussions and analyses of the likely competitive effects of the merger. It is rare for merger investigations prior to litigation to involve formal market definition.

The Agencies and outside practitioners tend to focus on analyses of competitive effects for at least two reasons. First, the Merger Guidelines make it clear that market definition and market shares are only a preliminary step in merger analysis, and that, even if one were able to confidently define relevant markets, further analysis of likely competitive effects is required. Second, formal market definition is not a trivial task; it often raises difficult and valid questions about what should be the correct approach. Modern economic and econometric tools often allow for the assessment of likely competitive effects without resolving these tough questions about market definition.

The Agencies and practitioners understand that to come to a resolution on a merger that makes it past the initial market share screen, the principal task will be to find a middle ground on the merger's likely competitive effects. Hence, the more quickly both sides can focus on a discussion of likely competitive effects, the more quickly merger concerns can be resolved. Both sides benefit from minimizing the time they spend on defining relevant markets and computing market shares, so that they may spend more time and effort on analyzing the likely competitive effects of the proposed merger.

A benefit of market definition is that it allows the relevant competitors to be identified. However, the issue with market definition is often that the facts surrounding competition are inconsistent with the sharp delineations of markets prescribed by market definition. Market definition is a heuristic drawing of a line that separates the players that are relevant competitors to the merging parties from those that are not. Often there are valid debates to be had about where this line should be drawn. Relevant competitors still need to be identified even when market definition is not performed. However, modern techniques for analyzing likely competitive effects directly can often obviate this function of market definition and can allow likely competitive effects to be analyzed assuming several possible groupings of putative relevant competitors (i.e., several possible relevant markets). In other words, econometric techniques can allow practitioners to analyze whether hypothesized relevant competitors matter to the likely competitive outcomes, and thus should be considered in direct analyses of competitive effects. For instance, if the Agencies hypothesized that the relevant geographic markets are circles with two mile radii, while outside parties claim that the relevant geographic markets have larger radii, econometric analyses of direct competitive effects may allow both sides to see how changing from one assumption to the other affects predicted outcomes.

2. The 2010 Merger Guidelines

The 2010 Merger Guidelines deemphasize market definition and place more focus on direct analysis of competitive effects. For example, the Market Definition section of the Guidelines (Section 4) begins by describing situations where direct forms of evidence regarding competitive effects should receive more attention than market definition, stating:

> The Agencies' analysis need not start with market definition. Some of the analytical tools used by the Agencies to assess competitive effects do not rely on market definition, although evaluation of competitive alternatives available to customers is always necessary at some point in the analysis.
>
> ... [Direct evidence of competitive effects] also may more directly predict the competitive effects of a merger, reducing the role of inferences from market definition and market shares.
>
> Where analysis suggests alternative and reasonably plausible candidate markets, and where the resulting market shares lead to very different inferences regarding competitive effects, it is particularly valuable to examine more direct forms of evidence concerning those effects.[5]

These notions are then echoed in the Unilateral Competitive Effects section of the Guidelines (Section 6), which state, for example, that:

> Diagnosing unilateral price effects based on the value of diverted sales need not rely on market definition or the calculation of market shares and concentration. The Agencies rely much more on the value of diverted sales than on the level of the HHI for diagnosing unilateral price effects in markets with differentiated products.[6]

These passages clearly indicate that the Agencies have a preference for direct analysis of competitive effects when possible. Yet, in our experience, even when direct analysis of competitive effects is possible, when a matter reaches federal or administrative court, the Agencies and outside parties still rely heavily on market definition and associated market shares.

III. Analysis in the Courts

A review of litigated merger transactions for the 10-year period from 2005 to 2014 reveals that courts do consider direct competitive effects analysis. Ten out of the twelve litigated merger transactions during this period contain some discussion of direct analysis of unilateral competitive effects.[7] However, courts still depend on market definition and related market concentration analyses, even as the Agencies shift toward direct analysis of unilateral effects. In six of the 12 litigated mergers, market definition and market concentration were central to the court's final decision, even when direct effects were also considered.

---

5 Merger Guidelines, *supra* note 1, at 7.

6 *See id.* at 21.

7 These are the transactions discussed in the Hart-Scott-Rodino Annual Reports for fiscal years 2005 to 2014 filed by the Agencies. We exclude litigated merger transactions that ended in a consent order or abandonment or restructuring of the transaction prior to a court decision. Two of the 12 transactions have no official court opinions that discuss the economic factors affecting the court's decision; in these two instances, we analyze the economic arguments put forth by the plaintiffs' competitive impact statements instead.

In the remaining six litigated mergers, unilateral competitive effects played a larger role, though market definition was still a key factor.[8] Table 1 below summarizes these findings.

Table 1

2005-2014 Merger Transactions Litigated in Federal Court by the US Antitrust Agencies				
No. of Litigated Transactions	**Transaction in Effect before Litigation**	**Theory of Harm in Court's Opinion**	**Direct Effects Discussed in Court's Opinion**	**Direct Effects Important to Agency's Case**
4	No	Market Definition/ Concentration & Direct Effects	Yes (with empirical results)	Yes
2	Yes	Market Definition/ Concentration & Direct Effects	Yes (observed effects)	Yes
2	No	Market Definition/ Concentration Only	Yes (with empirical results)	Yes
1	No	Market Definition/ Concentration Only	No	Yes
2	No	Market Definition/ Concentration Only	Yes (theoretical discussion only)`	No
1	No	Market Definition/ Concentration Only	No	No

1. Direct Analysis of Competitive Effects in Litigation

In half of the litigated cases in the 10-year period from 2005 to 2014, the courts considered empirical analyses of the merger impact alongside traditional analyses of market concentration. These matters are listed in Table 2 and discussed in more detail below. These cases are an indication that courts consider direct analyses of competitive effects in some instances. It is important to note, however, that only two of these matters relied on complex economic modeling of likely competitive effects (in both instances merger simulations). In the remaining cases, the courts looked at natural experiments or actual observed price increases post-transaction. This indicates that, although direct analysis of competitive effects does play some role in litigated merger cases, economic modeling of unilateral effects is still not common in courts. Moreover, it is notable that in all of these cases the courts still dedicated significant attention to

8 However, two of these six matters were litigated after the transaction in question had already gone into effect, which likely made a discussion of direct effects hard to circumvent, given that these effects were already observed rather than predicted.

market definition and market shares, which could indicate a reluctance by the courts to accept the stated position of the Agencies that the evaluation of unilateral competitive effects need not rely on market definition and associated concentration measures.[9]

Table 2

<table>
<tr><th colspan="10">2005-2014 Merger Transactions Litigated in Federal Court by the US Antitrust Agencies Direct Effects Impact Court Opinion</th></tr>
<tr><th rowspan="2">FY when Litigation was Initiated</th><th rowspan="2">Agency</th><th rowspan="2">Transaction in Effect before Litigation</th><th rowspan="2">Transaction Parties</th><th rowspan="2">Litigation Outcome Favorable to:</th><th rowspan="2">Was Market Definition/ Concentration Key in the Court's Opinion?</th><th colspan="2">Was a Discussion of Direct Effects Considered by the Court</th><th rowspan="2">Where Direct Effects Key to the Agency Case?</th></tr>
<tr><th>Theoretical</th><th>Empirical</th></tr>
<tr><td>2013</td><td>FTC</td><td>No</td><td>St. Luke's Health System/ Saltzer Medical Group</td><td>Agency</td><td rowspan="6">Yes, but direct effects also play a role.</td><td rowspan="6">Yes</td><td rowspan="6">Yes</td><td rowspan="6">Yes</td></tr>
<tr><td>2011</td><td>FTC</td><td>No</td><td>ProMedica Health System Inc /St. Lukes Hospital</td><td>Agency</td></tr>
<tr><td>2009</td><td>FFTC</td><td>No</td><td>CCC Information Services Inc./ Mitchell International Inc.</td><td>Agency</td></tr>
<tr><td>2009</td><td>FFTC</td><td>Yes</td><td>Ovation Pharmaceuticals /NeoProfen</td><td>Transaction Parties</td></tr>
<tr><td>2007</td><td>DOJ</td><td>Yes</td><td>Daily Gazette Company /Media News Group, Inc..</td><td>Agency</td></tr>
<tr><td>2007</td><td>FTC</td><td>No</td><td>Paul L. Foster, Western Refining, Inc./Giant Industries, Inc.</td><td>Transaction Parties</td></tr>
</table>

9 *See, e.g.*, Merger Guidelines, *supra* note 1 § 6.

Interestingly, the final court opinion in the 2007 oil refinery acquisition of Giant Industries by Western Refining is perhaps the opinion that most closely reflects the prescriptions of the 2010 Horizontal Merger Guidelines, dedicating a notable portion of its discussion to direct analyses of unilateral competitive effects. In particular, the court considered two natural experiments that predicted the competitive effects of the acquisition and also discussed customers' and suppliers' abilities to discipline a unilateral reduction in output post-transaction.[10] The court also reviewed the results of a merger simulation prepared by the FTC's economists, but ultimately denied the FTC's request for a preliminary injunction.[11] Even in discussing the FTC's *prima facie* case of market concentration, the court made a reference to direct analysis of the likely competitive effects of the transaction: "While the Court is convinced that the merger will eliminate a rival, Giant and Western do not compete strongly or directly against each other, but in a competitive market that includes a number of suppliers and potential suppliers."[12]

Three other transactions in which the courts considered direct analyses of competitive effects ended in judgments in favor of the Agencies. In the 2011 acquisition of St. Luke's by ProMedica and the 2013 acquisition of the Saltzer Medical Group by St. Luke's Hospital, the courts relied heavily on both market definition/concentration and a number of direct analyses of competitive effects. In the ProMedica/St. Luke's matter, the court considered surveys on patient preferences, company reports discussing share shifts between the hospitals, and considerations of the transaction's effects on non-price competition, before ordering the divestiture of St. Luke's assets.[13] In the St. Luke's/Saltzer transaction, the court evaluated the parties' negotiating leverage with payers, the effects of similar prior transactions on patient referral trends, and the patient preferences in choosing between the two hospitals before permanently enjoining the deal.[14] Unilateral effects analysis also played a role in the court's decision regarding the 2009 acquisition of CCC Information Services by Mitchell International, where the court considered (though ultimately found unreliable) a merger simulation that predicted the transaction's price effects, along with two different bidding models prepared by the FTC's economic expert.[15] The court ordered a preliminary injunction against the deal, which was subsequently abandoned by the parties.[16]

The other two transactions in Table 2 involved retrospective analyses of the actual effects of consummated mergers. In the joint operating agreement ("JOA") of two local newspapers in Charleston, West Virginia, the DOJ issued a competitive impact statement that focused on the actual effects of the transaction and concluded that the JOA reduced competition in the local newspaper market because the Charleston Gazette attempted to close the operations of its competitor.[17] Although the court's final judgment in this matter does not include a discussion of its underlying economic rationale, the ordered remedies separating the

---

10 FTC v. Paul L. Foster, Western Refining, Inc. and Giant Industries, Inc., No. CIV 07-352 JB/ACT, Memorandum Opinion, Findings of Fact, Conclusions of Law, and Order at 65-68, ¶ 359-77 (D.N.M. May 29, 2007), *available at* http://lawprofessors.typepad.com/antitrustprof_blog/files/opinion.pdf.

11 *See id.* at 73-76, 103.

12 *See id.* at 97, ¶ 20.

13 FTC v. ProMedica Health System, Inc., Case No. 3:11 CV 47, Findings of Fact and Conclusions of Law (D.N.D. Ohio Mar. 29, 2011), *available at* https://www.ftc.gov/sites/default/files/documents/cases/2011/03/110329promedicafindings.pdf;Fed. Trade Comm'n, Bureau of Competition, & Dep't of Justice, Antitrust Division, Hart-Scott-Rodino Annual Report: Fiscal Year 2011, at16 (2011), *available at* https://www.ftc.gov/sites/default/files/documents/reports_annual/34th-report-fy2011/2011hsrreport_0.pdf.

14 FTC v. St. Luke's Health System, Ltd., Case No. 1:13-CV-00116-BLW, Findings of Fact and Conclusions of Law (D. Idaho Jan. 24, 2014), *available at* https://www.ftc.gov/system/files/documents/cases/140124stlukesfindings.pdf.

15 FTC v. CCC Holdings Inc., et al., Civil Action No. 08-2043 (RMC), Memorandum Opinion at70-72 (D.D.C. Mar. 18, 2009), *available at* http://www.gpo.gov/fdsys/pkg/USCOURTS-dcd-1_08-cv-02043/pdf/USCOURTS-dcd-1_08-cv-02043-0.pdf.

16 Fed. Trade Comm'n, Bureau of Competition, & Dep't of Justice, Antitrust Division, Hart-Scott-Rodino Annual Report: Fiscal Year 2009, at11-12 (2009), *available at* https://www.ftc.gov/sites/default/files/documents/reports_annual/32st-report-fy-2009/101001hsrreport_0.pdf.

17 United States v. Daily Gazette Company and MediaNews Group, Inc., Civil Action No. 2:07-0329, Competitive Impact Statement at 9 (S.D.W. Va. Jan. 20, 2010), *available at* http://www.justice.gov/file/493261/download.

operations of the two papers are in line with the ones proposed by the plaintiff, indicating the court relied on the DOJ's analyses of the actual competitive effects of the deal.[18] In the 2009 litigation related to Ovation Pharmaceuticals' purchase of the drug NeoProfen, the FTC relied heavily on what they considered to be the adverse price effects from the transaction (alleging large price increases of Ovation's existing drug after the acquisition of NeoProfen).[19] However, the court concluded that the price increases were not related to the NeoProfen transaction.[20] A key factor in the court's decision to dismiss the FTC's complaint was a number of physician interviews that indicated Ovation's own drug Indocin and the acquired drug NeoProfen were in separate relevant product markets.[21]

These six matters indicate some movement towards the consideration of unilateral effect analyses in litigated mergers. Notably, courts considered several different types of analyses, including merger simulation models, customer surveys, and natural experiments. Nonetheless, even in the six matters discussed above, market definition was still important to each of the court opinions.

2. The (Too?) Prevalent Role of Market Definition in Litigation

Although the matters described above indicate that courts sometimes consider direct analysis of competitive effects to be important, all of these matters still relied to varying degrees on indirect analyses of relevant markets and related measures of concentration. In addition, in several other matters during the 10-year period from 2005 to 2014, the courts have put almost no weight on direct analyses of likely competitive effects, opting instead to rely on market definition and market shares to support opinions. In three of these six cases, the focus on market definition appears to have been largely driven by the plaintiffs; in another two matters, the Agencies provided direct analyses of competitive effects, but the court's opinion does not indicate a strong reliance on these analyses; and in the final case, the court and the FTC notably diverge in their methodologies, with the court not even addressing direct analyses of the competitive effects of the transaction in its opinion despite the FTC's efforts to introduce such evidence. Table 3 summarizes these findings.

---

18 *See id.* at 12-18; United States v. Daily Gazette Company and MediaNews Group, Inc, Civil Action No. 2:07-0329, Final Judgement at 5-9 (S.D.W. Va. July 19, 2010), *available at* http://www.justice.gov/file/ 493231/download.

19 FTC v. Ovation Pharmaceuticals, Inc., Civil No. 08-6379 (JNE/JJG), Complaint for Permanent Injunction and Other Equitable Relief, Including Disgorgement of Unlawful Monopoly Profits at 2 (D. Minn. Dec. 16, 2008), *available at* https://www.ftc.gov/sites/default/files/documents/cases/2008/12/081216ovationcmpt.pdf.

20 FTC v. Lundbeck, Inc., Civil No. 08-6379 (JNE/JJG), Findings of Fact, Conclusions of Law, and Order at 12, ¶ 45 (D. Minn. Aug., 31, 2010), *sub nom.* FTC v. Ovation Pharmaceuticals, Inc., Civil No. 08-6379 (JNE/JJG) (D. Minn. Dec. 16, 2008), *available at* https://www.ftc.gov/sites/default/files/documents/cases/2010/08/110919lundbeckfindings.pdf.

21 *See id.* at 26-33.

Table 3

2005-2014 Merger Transactions Litigated in Federal Court by the US Antitrust Agencies Direct Effects Have Limited Impact on Court Opinion								
FY when Litigation was Initiated	**Agency**	**Transaction in Effect before Litigation**	**Transaction Parties**	**Litigation Outcome Favorable to:**	**Was Market Definition/ Concentration Key in the Court's Opinion?**	**Was a Discussion of Direct Effects Considered by the Court**		**Where Direct Effects Key to the Agency Case?**
						Theoretical	**Empirical**	
2013	DOJ	No	Bazaarvoice, Inc./ PowerReviews	Agency	Yes	Yes	Yes	Yes
2011	DOJ	No	H&R Block/ TaxACT	Agency	Yes	Yes	Yes	Yes
2011	FFTC	No	Lab Corp/ Westcliff Medical	Transaction Parties	Yes	No	No	Yes
2012	FFTC	No	OSF Healthcare System / Rockford Health System	Agency	Yes	Yes	No	No
2010	DOJ	No	Dean Foods/ Foremost Farms	Agency	Yes	Yes	No	No
2007	FTC	No	Whole Foods Market, Inc./ Wild Oats Market, Inc.	Transaction Parties (Original Decision) /Agency (Appeal)	Yes	No	No	No

In two of these cases, the DOJ relied heavily on unilateral effect analyses in its complaints. The court considered these analyses, but ultimately focused primarily on market concentration. One of these transactions was the 2011 acquisition of tax software provider TaxACT by competitor H&R Block. In its initial complaint, the DOJ devoted significant attention to the direct competition between the two parties, discussing at length TaxACT's market position as a pricing and innovation maverick that competed directly with H&R Block.[22] The DOJ similarly emphasized the direct competition between the parties when it challenged the 2013 acquisition of PowerReviews by Bazaarvoice (both providers of online review platforms). The DOJ alleged that the two firms were each other's closest competitors, which lead to customers enjoying lower prices and higher discounts.[23] In both matters the court downplayed the

22 United States v. H&R Block, Inc., et al., Case No: 1: 11-cv-00948, Complaint at 10-14 (D.D.C. May 23, 2011), *available at* http://www.justice.gov/file/498231/download.

23 United States v. Bazaarvoice, Inc., Case No. C-13-0133-JSC, Complaint at 9-17 (N.D. Cal. Jan. 10, 2013), *available at* http://www.justice.gov/file/488911/download.

significance of unilateral effects and instead focused on market definition and concentration measures, even though its final decision ultimately aligned with the DOJ's position. In the Bazaarvoice opinion, the court specifically emphasized that focusing on the merger effects is unnecessary since the high market concentration is, in itself, sufficient to prove competitive harm:

> The Court need not enter into this seemingly fertile debate over the primacy of market definition or determine whether, in this case, the government could establish anticompetitive effects without first defining a relevant market. Here the government has proposed a market consisting of R&R platforms for retailers and manufacturers. The Court agrees with that definition. Because the market for R&R platforms is highly concentrated, defining the relevant product market as R&R platforms has major consequences for this action.[24]

The court's opinion in H&R Block also underlined the prominence of market concentration, even though the court chose to also discuss the results of the various competitive effects analyses:

> Since the Court has already found that the preponderance of the evidence shows a reasonable likelihood of coordinated effects, the Court need not reach the issue of unilateral effects. *See id* at 67. The Court will discuss it, however, since there has been substantial argument on this topic and the Court's findings regarding unilateral effects bolster the conclusion that this proposed merger will violate Section 7 of the Clayton Act.[25]

In another three matters, both the courts and the Agencies relied mostly on market definition/market concentration (even though two of these matters also included a theoretical discussion of direct effects). The final judgment for the 2010 acquisition of Foremost Farms by competitor dairy producer Dean Foods does not contain an opinion of the relevant arguments considered by the court, but it follows closely the DOJ's proposed remedy to divest one of Foremost's plants.[26] This indicates that the court likely agreed with the DOJ's main argument that the merger would lead to a concentrated market for milk in certain school districts.[27] Similarly, in the 2012 acquisition of Rockford Health System by rival OSF Healthcare, both the FTC complaint and the final court opinion were predominantly focused on market definition and concentration.[28] The court ultimately issued a preliminary injunction against the deal and the defendants abandoned the transaction.[29]

The third transaction in this category is the widely publicized 2007 acquisition of Wild Oats by competing grocery chain Whole Foods. In this case, the FTC set the stage for a case predominantly focused on market definition, by posing the argument that there is a unique market for premium natural and organic supermarkets ("PNOS"). Both the district court, which ruled against the FTC's request for a preliminary injunction, and the appellate court, which found the FTC's argument convincing and remanded the case

---

24 United States v. Bazaarvoice, Inc., Case No. 13-cv-00133-WHO, Memorandum Opinion – Publicly Redacted Version at 123 (N.D. Cal. Jan. 8, 2014), *available at* http://www.justice.gov/file/488846/download.

25 United States v. H&R Block, Inc., et al., Case No. 11-00948 (BAH), Memorandum Opinion at 68 (D.D.C. Nov. 10, 2011), *available at* http://www.justice.gov/file/498141/download.

26 United States, et al. v. Dean Foods Company, Case No. 10-CV-59, Final Judgement at 3 (E.D. Wis. July 29, 2011), *available at* http://www.justice.gov/file/493536/download; United States, et al. v. Dean Foods Company, Case No. 2:10-cv-00059 (JPS), Competitive Impact Statement at 9-12 (E.D. Wis. Mar. 29, 2011), *available at* http://www.justice.gov/file/ 493556/download.

27 *See id.* at 9.

28 FTC v. OSF Healthcare System and Rockford Health, No. 11-cv-50344, Complaint for Temporary Restraining Order and Permanent Injunction (N.D. Ill. Nov. 18, 2011), *available at* https://www.ftc.gov/sites/default/files/documents/cases/2011/11/111118rockfordcmpt.pdf; FTC v. OSF Healthcare System and Rockford Health, No. 11 C 50344, Memorandum Opinion and Order (N.D. Ill. Apr. 5, 2012), *available at* https://www.ftc.gov/sites/default/files/documents/cases/2012/04/120505rockfordmemo.pd.

29 Fed. Trade Comm'n, Bureau of Competition, & Dep't of Justice, Antitrust Division, Hart-Scott-Rodino Annual Report: Fiscal Year 2012, at 14 (2012), *available at* https://www.ftc.gov/sites/default/files/documents/reports_annual/35th-report-fy2012/130430hsrreport_0.pdf.

back to the district court, followed the agency's lead and focused almost exclusively on the question of market definition. Both courts considered multiple market definition analyses, including a critical diversion study performed by the FTC economists, a critical loss analysis presented by the defendants, evidence of price checking of conventional supermarkets by the defendants and evidence of cross-shopping between customers of PNOS and conventional supermarkets.[30] Interestingly, the court of appeal acknowledged that market definition is not always necessary to prove anticompetitive effects—an opinion cited in a number of subsequent matters focused on unilateral effects—but that the "FTC itself made market definition key"[31] in the Whole Foods matter:

> Although the framework we have developed for a prima facie § 7 case rests on defining a market and showing undue concentration in that market, United States v. Baker Hughes Inc., 908 F.2d 981, 982–83 (D.C. Cir. 1990), this analytical structure does not exhaust the possible ways to prove a § 7 violation on the merits, see, e.g., United States v. El Paso Natural Gas Co., 376 U.S. 651, 660 (1964), much less the ways to demonstrate a likelihood of success on the merits in a preliminary proceeding.[32]

On the other hand, in the 2011 Lab Corp. acquisition of Westcliff Medical Laboratories, it is not clear that the court focused on some of the key issues on competitive effects raised by the FTC. The court's order denying the FTC's request for a preliminary injunction focused exclusively on market shares, finding that expanding the market definition beyond what the FTC proposed would significantly lower market shares.[33] At the same time, the FTC's complaint focused on the closeness of competition between the merging parties, arguing that they are seen as the only two options by a lot of doctors. Moreover, the FTC claimed that Westcliff had been a pricing maverick and an aggressive competitor to Lab Corp., resulting in lower prices for customers.[34] Both of these arguments were geared towards the direct effects of the transaction, but both were excluded from the court's opinion. The court denied the plaintiff's request for a preliminary injunction and the FTC ultimately dropped the matter.

---

30 FTC v. Whole Foods Market, Inc. and Wild Oats Markets, Inc., No. 07-5276, *rev'd*, No. 07-cv-01021, at 14-19 (Cir. D.C. July 29, 2008), *available at*https://www.ftc.gov/sites/default/files/documents/cases/2008/07/080729wholefoodsopinion.pdf.

31 *See id.* at 12.

32 *See id.* at 11.

33 FTC v. Laboratory Corporation of America, et al., Case No. SACV 10-1873 AG (MLGx), Order Denying Permanent Injunction at 11, ¶ 42 (C.D. Cal. Feb. 22, 2011), *available at* https://www.ftc.gov/sites/default/files/documents/cases/2011/02/110222labcorporder.pdf.

34 FTC v. Laboratory Corporation of America, et al., No.10-CV-02053 (RWR), Complaint for Temporary Restraining Order and Permanent Injunction Pursuant to Section 13(b) of the Federal Trade Commission Act (D.D.C. Dec. 3, 2010), *available at* https://www.ftc.gov/sites/default/files/documents/cases/2010/12/101203labcorppicmpt.pdf.

IV. Direct Analyses of Unilateral Competitive Effects

Direct analyses of unilateral competitive effects are of principal importance in merger review. They aim to answer the exact questions that are of interest to antitrust agencies—i.e., whether prices are expected to increase following the merger and by how much.

Traditional market concentration analyses rely on the assumption that higher concentration leads to higher prices in a market and therefore attempt to predict post-merger price increases based on the level of market concentration increases. However, drawing inferences from market concentration alone ignores a number of important factors that could also affect post-merger prices, such as the closeness of competition between the merging parties. Direct analyses of competitive effects attempt to incorporate these additional factors and thus would be expected to provide a more accurate and comprehensive picture of the effects of a transaction, compared to market concentration alone. Therefore, if sufficient information is available for an analysis of the unilateral competitive effects of the transaction, we believe that such an analysis should play a central role in litigated mergers, as it currently does in the pre-litigation review of many horizontal mergers.

Some of the most widely utilized analytical tools in the analysis of unilateral competitive effects, especially in horizontal mergers involving differentiated products, are event studies, estimation of diversion ratios, gross upward pricing pressure indices ("GUPPIs"), and merger simulations. Each of these tools has drawbacks and one is often more practical than the others in certain circumstances.

1. Event Studies

Event studies analyze changes in competitive variables (e.g., prices or margins) caused by past events similar to those in the transaction being evaluated, such as past mergers in the same or a related industry or past entry/exit of competitors. The goal is to attempt to predict the future price effects of the current merger. A standard method for studying the likely impact of previous events on competitive variables is difference-in-differences regression analysis, which compares changes in the variable of interest in markets where the event of interest occurred (treatment markets) to markets not affected by the event (control markets). For example, a difference-in-differences regression might compare the pre- and post-event price differences in treatment markets to those in control markets. Larger price increases in treatment markets than in control markets indicates that the relevant event caused a price increase.

A main challenge when performing event studies is finding events that are relevant to the current transaction. Previous mergers in the same or a closely-related industry are typically the most useful events to study, but such events are not always available. In the absence of previous mergers, analysts can estimate the impact of other changes in market structure, such as entry or exit by competitor firms. However, studies of entry/exit events do not directly address the question of interest, i.e., what will be the likely impact of a merger? The price response to entry/exit is not always a good proxy for the price response to a merger. There is some evidence that between entry and exit events, estimates from entry studies are closer directionally and in magnitude to horizontal mergers than are estimates from exit studies, and thus may be more useful than firm/store exits for predicting the likely competitive effects of a merger.[35]

2. Diversion Ratios and Gross Upward Pricing Pressure

A GUPPI is a measure of a firm's incentives to raise prices after a merger. GUPPIs are based on the diversion ratios between the merging firms—i.e., the percentage of sales that would be diverted from Firm 1 to Firm 2, if Firm 1's prices increase, and vice versa—and the merging firms' price-cost margins. There are a number of different methods for calculating diversion ratios, including econometric estimates of own- and cross-price elasticities, and approximations based on customer surveys. GUPPIs compare, for example, the value of diverted sales from Firm 1 to Firm 2 to the value of lost revenues by Firm 1, following an increase in Firm 1's prices. GUPPIs will always predict a price increase by virtue of their construct, so generally only GUPPIs over a certain threshold—often 5%—raise antitrust concerns.

Although the results from these analyses are generally easy to understand and potentially easy to present in court, these analyses also pose some challenges. This could be the reason why, to our knowledge, a GUPPI analysis has not been relied upon in a litigated merger to date, even though such analyses are frequently considered in pre-litigation review. A significant challenge to estimating GUPPIs is that it is often difficult to find the correct inputs required to reliably estimate the cross-price elasticities between the products of the merging firms and thus the appropriate diversion ratios. Practitioners sometimes use measures of substitution that are unrelated to price such as regressions that relate entry/exit events to product sales or switching studies as proxies for diversion ratios due to a price increase. The reliability of such information as a proxy for price-induced substitution raises concerns about the reliability of GUPPIs as a predictor of unilateral merger effects. Another drawback of GUPPI analyses is that even if GUPPIs are assumed to accurately predict the likelihood of a price increase, in the absence of further assumptions, GUPPIs do not provide information about the magnitude of the price increase or likely consumer harm.[36]

3. Merger Simulations

Merger simulations are a more complex tool in the direct analysis of competitive effects compared to both event studies and diversion/GUPPI analyses. A merger simulation involves the use of models to forecast the demand and supply conditions in a market following a merger in order to estimate the post-merger outcomes. Due to their complexity and the significant information requirements, merger simulations may pose practical challenges. Moreover, because merger simulations generally require several assumptions about, for example, market demand, the nature of competition between firms, and costs, and each assumption is an easy target for criticism, merger simulation models can present significant litigation risk.

---

35 Daniel S. Hosken, Luke M. Olson & Loren K. Smith, *Can Entry or Exit Event Studies Inform Horizontal Merger Analysis? Evidence from Grocery Retailing*, 54 Econ. Inquiry 342 (2015) (hypothesizing that exit events are relatively poor predictors of merger effects because by the time a firm exits it is a relatively insignificant competitor).

36 Michael D. Noel, *Upward Price Pressure, Merger Simulation, and Merger Simulation Light*, CPI Antitrust Chronicle, Mar. 2, 2011, *available at* https://www.competitionpolicyinternational.com/upward-price-pressure-merger-simulation-and-merger-simulation-light/.

V. Conclusions

In the evaluation of horizontal mergers, there is an apparent divergence between the evidence that the Agencies consider to indicate a likelihood of competitive effects and the evidence that informs court decisions. In our experience, compared to the courts, the Agencies place relatively more emphasis on direct analyses of the likely competitive effects of a merger and relatively less weight on market definition and market shares. In contrast, it is clear from the recent court decisions summarized in this note that in some cases the courts seriously consider direct analyses of likely competitive effects, but even in these cases the courts' considerations of direct analyses is almost always buttressed with traditional analyses of relevant markets and concentration. Moreover, in some cases the courts relied almost exclusively on market definition and market shares, even when direct analyses of likely competitive effects were presented.

Courts weigh what they consider to be the best available evidence, and if reliable direct analyses of likely competitive effects are unavailable, it is prudent for the courts to fall back on indirect measures of likely competitive effects such as market shares. However, compelling litigants to perform rigorous market definition when convincing direct evidence of the likely competitive effects of a merger is available can lead to wasteful effort on analyses that are at best redundant and at worst misleading.

The Relevant Market Concept in Antitrust Law

GREGORY J. WERDEN*

gregory.werden@usdoj.gov

Senior Economic Counsel, Antitrust Division, US Department of Justice

Abstract

Contrary to the claims of many economists and some antitrust practitioners, the relevant market concept is not the relic of a bygone era. Increased reliance on economic tools has not supplanted the relevant market, but rather clarified its role. The relevant market is the foundation for all of the modern competitive analysis done in antitrust cases, just as the market concept in economics is the foundation for all models economists use to analyze the competitive process and predict industry performance. The relevant market is the device for separating active competitive forces directly and immediately affecting economic performance (e.g., prices) from forces that are passive or have indirect, delayed, or highly uncertain effects on economic performance. Just as economic analysis, antitrust analysis uses this separation to bring analytic order to real-world chaos.

* The views expressed herein are not purported to reflect those of the US Department of Justice.

The relevant market concept developed in antitrust law long before modern competitive analysis,[1] but it is not the relic of a bygone era. Nor was the relevant market introduced just to aid in the assessment of market power.[2] The relevant market has always been the foundation for competitive analysis that the Supreme Court adumbrated when it associated the relevant market with "the area of effective competition."[3] The relevant market is an important analytic tool for separating active competitive forces directly and immediately affecting economic performance (e.g., prices) from forces that are passive or have indirect, delayed, or highly uncertain effects on economic performance.[4] Both antitrust and economics use this separation to bring analytic order to real-world chaos.

I. Partial Equilibrium, the Relevant Market, and Modern Competitive Analysis

To comprehend the relevant market concept in antitrust law, one must understand both its progenitor—the market concept in economics, and the analysis in which economics employs the market concept—partial equilibrium.[5] Partial-equilibrium analysis examines a narrow sector of the economy, termed "the market," separating it from the rest of the economy. Supply and demand is the most familiar example: The interaction of supply and demand within the market for some good determines the equilibrium price of the good and the quantity traded. Every economic force affecting the good's price or quantity in the short-term is reflected in the supply curve or the demand curve, but each is plotted under the assumption that prices of outside goods are constant. This assumption is the hallmark of partial-equilibrium analysis, and the market concept is the embodiment of this assumption.[6]

It is wrong to think that partial-equilibrium analysis assumes away all interaction between the market and the rest of the economy. Demand slopes downward mainly because price changes cause consumers to substitute between the good in the market and goods outside it. And supply could slope upward, in part, because producers shift mobile resources in and out of the market as prices change. The assumption that distinguishes partial-equilibrium analysis is that the interaction between the market and the rest of the economy goes one way, i.e., there is no feedback into the market from outside it. For example, as consumers substitute to outside goods, the result cannot be to bid up their prices, which then feeds back as a shift in the market demand curve.

---

1 On the development of the relevant market concept, *see* Gregory J. Werden, *The History of Antitrust Market Delineation*, 76 Marquette L. Rev. 123 (1992).

2 *Contra* Louis Kaplow, *Why (Ever) Define Markets?*, 124 Harv. L. Rev. 437, 440 (2010) ("the entire rationale for the market definition process is to enable an inference about market power"); *id.* at 467 ("[T]he *raison d'être* for the market definition enterprise is to provide a basis for inferring market power.").

3 Tampa Elec. Co. v. Nashville Coal Co., 365 U.S. 320, 328 (1961); United States v. E.I. du Pont de Nemours & Co., 353 U.S. 586, 593 (1957).

4 *See* Gregory J. Werden, *Why (Ever) Define Markets? An Answer to Professor Kaplow*, 78 Antitrust L.J. 729, 729, 732, 739, 746 (2013).

5 *See* Gregory J. Werden, *Antitrust Needs the Relevant Market*, *in* 2012 Fordham Competition L. Inst. 235, 250-51 (Barry Hawk ed., 2013). The Supreme Court clerk most responsible for its first statement on the relevant market had only a rudimentary understanding. *See* Frederick M. Rowe, *The Decline of Antitrust and the Delusions of Models: The Faustian Pact of Law and Economics*, 72 Geo. L.J. 1511, 1563-65 (1984).

6 *See* Jean Tirole, The Theory of Industrial Organization 12 (1988) (explaining that "the definition of the market should not be too narrow" but narrow enough to "allow partial-equilibrium analysis" and "a single description of the main interactions among firms").

The relevant market in antitrust law also is a partial-equilibrium construct in which a narrow sector of the economy is separated from the rest. From the outset, the Supreme Court described the relevant market as containing only a narrow range of close substitutes. In its first substantive statement on the relevant market, the Court observed that: "For every product, substitutes exist. But a relevant market cannot meaningfully encompass that infinite range. The circle must be drawn narrowly to exclude any other product to which, within reasonable variations in price, only a limited number of buyers will turn. . . ."[7] In the *Cellophane* decision, a few years later, the Court explained that the "market is composed of products that have reasonable interchangeability for the purposes for which they are produced—price, use and qualities considered."[8]

In modern terms, the relevant market encompasses *only* substitutes close enough (to some focal good around which the market is defined) so that a hypothetical monopolist must control all of them before it would want to raise price significantly.[9] The rationale for this smallest market principle,[10] according to the current Horizontal Merger Guidelines, is that "market shares and concentration . . . in the smallest relevant market satisfying the hypothetical monopolist test" usually best "illuminate the evaluation of competitive effects."[11] The Guidelines, however, do not explain why. In my view, the reason is that the active competitive forces directly and immediately determining the effects of horizontal mergers usually are confined to the smallest market satisfying the hypothetical monopolist test.

Modern competitive analysis is partial-equilibrium analysis, and it holds much constant. A model designed to study short-term price competition, for example, holds constant the array of competing products, customers' preferences over them, and the costs of producing each competing product. To make models of competition tractable, economists greatly limit the number of moving parts, and, by construction, only competitive forces central to the issue under study are allowed to be active within a model. A model designed to study short-term price competition, for example, normally does not allow for competition through cost reduction, entry, new product introduction, product improvement, or product repositioning. All those things must be considered separately.

If a model used to assess competitive effects is incorrectly specified, its predictions could be seriously misleading, so specification tests should be applied,[12] and the relevant market provides a useful specification test. A model used to make competitive effects predictions must assume both some particular interaction among competitors and a specific set of competitors interacting. For example, a model might assume that producers of good *A* interact by non-cooperatively and simultaneously selecting quantities produced. Asking whether the relevant market is limited to good *A* is a critical specification test for this

---

7 Times-Picayune Publ'g Co. v. United States, 345 U.S. 594, 612 n.31 (1953).

8 United States v. E.I. du Pont de Nemours & Co., 351 U.S. 377, 404 (1956).

9 On the hypothetical monopolist test, *see* Gregory J. Werden, *The 1982 Merger Guidelines and the Ascent of the Hypothetical Monopolist Paradigm*, 71 Antitrust L.J. 253 (2003); Gregory J. Werden, *Market Delineation under the Merger Guidelines: A Tenth Anniversary Retrospective*, 38 Antitrust Bull. 517 (1993); Gregory J. Werden, *Market Delineation and the Justice Department's Merger Guidelines*, 1983 Duke L.J. 514 [Werden, Duke L.J.]; Gregory J. Werden, *Market Delineation Algorithms Based on the Hypothetical Monopolist Paradigm*, U.S. Department of Justice, Antitrust Division, EAG Discussion Paper 02-8 (2002), *available at* http://ssrn.com/abstract=327282.

10 The smallest market principle has been articulated in each addition of the Merger Guidelines since 1982. The concept was first expressed by Gregory J. Werden, *The Use and Misuse of Shipments Data in Defining Geographic Markets*, 26 Antitrust Bull. 719, 721 (1981) [hereinafter Werden, Antitrust Bull.]. The term first appeared in Gregory J. Werden, *Is There a Principle for Defining Industries? Comment*, 52 S. Econ. J. 532, 535 (1985) [hereinafter Werden, S. Econ. J.].

11 U.S. Dep't of Justice & Fed. Trade Comm'n, Horizontal Merger Guidelines § 4.1.1 (2010), *available at* http://www.justice.gov/atr/public/guidelines/hmg-2010.pdf. The Horizontal Merger Guidelines clearly indicate that the hypothetical monopolist test is a partial-equilibrium construct. The current version of the key passage states that, in applying the test, "the terms of sale of products outside the candidate market are held constant." *Id.* This assumption is the hallmark of partial-equilibrium analysis, and it makes the hypothetical monopolist's demand curve an ordinary Marshallian demand curve, rather than the residual demand curve some have supposed.

12 *See* Gregory J. Werden, Luke M. Froeb & David T. Scheffman, *A* Daubert *Discipline for Merger Simulation*, Antitrust, Summer 2004, at 89 (explaining that models must fit the facts).

model. If good *B* were a good substitute for good *A*, producers of good *A* and producers of good *B* normally all would be part of a single competitive interaction.[13]

Much like the market concept in supply and demand analysis, the relevant market concept in antitrust identifies the locus of active forces materially affecting price or quantity in the short-term. The relevant market does not encompass products or places merely posing future competitive threats, even if important. The *Microsoft* case was all about threats to Microsoft's operating system monopoly, but the appeals court properly rejected the contention that the relevant market extended beyond Personal Computer operating systems to the middleware sources of threats to the monopoly.[14] Limiting the scope of the relevant market affects how certain competitive forces are accounted for, not whether they are accounted for. It is analytically useful to recognize that certain competitive forces operate from outside the relevant market.

II. The Relevant Market in Coordinated Effects Merger Cases

When the hypothetical monopolist test was adopted by the 1982 Merger Guidelines,[15] horizontal merger enforcement considered only coordinated effects and was largely a numbers game. The relevant market determined market shares, which normally were decisive on whether a horizontal merger was challenged. There is more to coordinated-effects analysis today,[16] yet the importance of the relevant market has not diminished because it serves an essential analytic function. The relevant market in a coordinated effects merger case is the group of products and area likely to be subject to coordination, if it occurs.[17] Delineation of the relevant market is the critically important first step in evaluating both the conduciveness of market conditions to coordination and the impact of the merger on both market structure and competitive dynamics.[18]

13 This would not be true if, for example, good *B* were competitively supplied.

14 United States v. Microsoft Corp., 352 U.S. 34, 53-54 (D.C. Cir. 2001) (en banc).

15 The test first appeared in U.S. Dep't of Justice, Competition in the Coal Industry 26-27 (May 1978) (report of the U.S. Department of Justice pursuant to Section 8 of the Federal Coal Leasing Amendments Act of 1975) (stating that a market, for antitrust purposes, is a group of products and area "within which the sellers of a product could maintain significantly higher prices if they combined to form a . . . hypothetical monopoly"). An article written shortly thereafter asserted that: "A market *for antitrust purposes* is any product or group of products and any geographic area in which collective action by all firms (as [through] collusion or merger) would result in a profit maximizing price that significantly exceeded the competitive price." Werden, Antitrust Bull., *supra* note 10, at 721. The article also asserted that "the relevant market in any particular case is the smallest group of products and geographic area that constitutes a market." *Id.*

16 *See, e.g.*, Kai-Uwe Kühn, *The Coordinated Effects of Mergers*, *in* Handbook of Antitrust Economics 105 (Paolo Buccirossi ed., 2008); Janusz A. Ordover, *Coordinated Effects*, *in* ABA Section of Antitrust Law, 2 Issues in Competition Law and Policy 1359 (W. Dale Collins ed., 2008).

17 *See* Werden, S. Econ. J., *supra* note 10, at 535-36; Werden, Duke L.J., *supra* note 9, at 531-32. Within the endless variation on theories of competitive harm from mergers are the cross-market coordinated effects alleged in the Justice Department's challenge to the merger of US Airways and AMR Corp. (American Airlines). The complaint alleged that the merger would substantially lessen competition in relevant markets consisting of individual routes, and one mechanism was cooperation on fares and capacity reductions across multiple markets. Amended Complaint, United States v. US Airways Group, Inc., No. 1:13-cv-01236 (D.D.C. filed Sept. 5, 2013), *available at* http://www.justice.gov/atr/cases/f300400/300479.pdf.

18 Although the utility of the relevant market in coordinated effects cases is widely agreed, Professor Kaplow disputes the utility of the relevant market in the assessment of coordinated effects. *See* Louis Kaplow, *Market Definition: Impossible and Counterproductive*, 79 Antitrust L.J. 361, 374-75 (2013). He argues that cartels typically involve homogeneous goods, so whatever methods are applied to assess coordinated effects should be applied to a putative market consisting of a single homogeneous good, provided it passes the hypothetical monopolist test. If it fails the test, he would reject the possibility of coordinated effects. Kaplow dismisses the possibility of coordination across close substitute products, even though recent successful merger challenges posited such coordination. *See* United States v. H&R Block, Inc., 833 F. Supp. 2d 36, 77-81 (D.D.C. 2011); FTC v. CCC Holdings Inc., 605 F. Supp. 2d 26, 60-67 (D.D.C. 2009). Kaplow does not indicate how to proceed when the merging firms produce many distinct homogenous goods, e.g., countless steel nuts and bolts. Every such good has excellent substitutes within the same industry, and some may have excellent substitutes from other industries.

A reliable assessment of a proposed merger's coordinated effects requires an initial determination of the coordination's likely scope. The scope of likely coordination is critical because it determines which firms, and hence how many, would have to coordinate, and it significantly affects the coordination's apparent difficulty by determining the number and heterogeneity of products, prices, customers, and locations subject to coordination. A coordinated effects assessment can be reliable only if based on an accurate initial prediction of the likely scope of coordination, and that prediction is the relevant market.

The hypothetical monopolist test and the smallest market principle were geared from the outset to predicting the likely scope of coordination. For expositional purposes, the hypothetical monopolist was equated with a cartel,[19] and for calibration purposes, cartels provided both theoretical underpinnings and empirical benchmarking for the smallest market principle. Theorizing about cartel formation provided a rationale for the principle, and examining the scope of prosecuted cartels provided evidence that the hypothetical monopolist test and the smallest market principle yield appropriate relevant markets.

When initially applied in coordinated effects merger cases, the smallest market principle was supported by two theory-based insights. First, "[a]ll else being equal, collusion is most likely between direct competitors producing identical products at the same location, and collusion becomes less likely as the products become less similar or as they are produced at more distant locations."[20] Second, "the costs of forming and maintaining a cartel are likely to rise sufficiently rapidly as the number of cartel participants is increased that the most likely cartel is the smallest one that would raise price significantly, unless a somewhat larger cartel would raise price substantially more."[21] The smallest market principle was later supported by empirical evidence indicating that it yields relevant markets roughly congruent with the real-world cartels that the Justice Department prosecuted.[22]

---

19 *See* Werden, Duke L.J., *supra* note 9, at 524 n.36 ("[T]he Guidelines assess the likelihood of collusion. . . . The hypothetical monopolist postulated in the Guidelines' definition of a market is simply a mechanism for achieving the result of perfect cartelization."). The 2010 Guidelines distinguish between a hypothetical monopolist and a hypothetical cartel for analytic purposes. They state:

> If the pricing incentives of the firms supplying the products in the candidate market differ substantially from those of the hypothetical monopolist, . . . the Agencies may instead employ the concept of a hypothetical profit-maximizing cartel comprised of the firms (with all their products) that sell the products in the candidate market. This approach is most likely to be appropriate if the merging firms sell products outside the candidate market that significantly affect their pricing incentives for products in the candidate market.

Horizontal Merger Guidelines, *supra* note 11, § 4.1.1 n.4.

20 Werden, Duke L.J., *supra* note 9, at 532.

21 Werden, S. Econ. J., *supra* note 10, at 536.

22 This support derives from combining two comparisons. First, the scopes of cartels charged by the Department were compared with the scopes of corresponding Standard Industrial Classification four-digit industries, which were once widely used as markets in empirical studies. *See* Gregory J. Werden, *The Divergence of SIC Industries from Antitrust Markets: Some Evidence from Price Fixing Cases*, 28 Econ. Letters 193 (1988). Then the scopes of relevant markets alleged in the Department's merger complaints were compared with the scopes of corresponding SIC industries. *See* Russell Pittman & Gregory J. Werden, *The Divergence of SIC Industries from Antitrust Markets: Indications from Justice Department Merger Cases*, 33 Econ. Letters 283 (1990). Combining the comparisons indicated that applying the hypothetical monopolist test with the smallest market principle yielded relevant markets with roughly the same scopes as prosecuted cartels.

III. The Relevant Market in Unilateral Effects Merger Cases

When the US merger enforcement agencies began considering unilateral effects, economists began developing quantitative tools for predicting such effects. The agencies and tool developers initially focused on the competitive setting presented by differentiated consumer products. For these mergers, market shares were viewed as poor predictors of likely unilateral effects,[23] and merger simulation was put forward as a superior alternative to reliance on market shares.[24] But even if merger simulation could supplant reliance on market shares, the relevant market remained useful.

The economic modeling in merger simulation mixes art with science, but science provides clear guidance on which products should be included in a simulation: a simulation model should include all products interacting significantly in the real world in the manner postulated by the model. It might be possible to observe directly how products interact, or to measure interaction econometrically, but a satisfactory alternative is applying the hypothetical monopolist test with the smallest market principle. The resulting relevant market should closely approximate the slate of products interacting significantly because it specifies the exact slate of products a hypothetical monopolist would have to control before it would increase prices significantly.

In merger cases involving differentiated consumer products, the relevant market is useful in additional ways. Simulation predictions are sensitive to the aggregate elasticity of demand for the included products, and applying the hypothetical monopolist test is informative as to that elasticity. That elasticity is estimated when the test is applied quantitatively, and it is bounded from above when the test is applied qualitatively.[25] The relevant market also is useful in presenting simulation results. In addition to presenting a price-increase prediction for each product, it is convenient to present a summary statistic—i.e., the weighted-average price increase for all products in the relevant market.

Differentiated consumer products mergers cause increases in the prices of both competing products combined by the merger and their close substitutes. The price increases of non-merging products in reaction to price increases of the merged firm both directly contribute to the overall price effect of the

---

23 *See, e.g.*, Carl Shapiro, *Mergers with Differentiated Products*, Antitrust, Spring 1996, at 23, 28; Gregory J. Werden & George A. Rozanski, *The Application of Section 7 to Differentiated Products Industries: The Market Delineation Dilemma*, Antitrust, Summer 1994, at 40. For a quantitative analysis of the utility of market shares as predictors of unilateral effects with differentiated consumer products, *see* Gregory J. Werden & Luke M. Froeb, *Simulation as an Alternative to Structural Merger Policy in Differentiated Products Industries*, *in* The Economics of the Antitrust Process 65, 73-78 (Malcolm B. Coate & Andrew N. Kleit eds., 1996).

24 *See, e.g.*, Jerry A. Hausman & Gregory K. Leonard, *Economic Analysis of Differentiated Products Mergers Using Real World Data*, 5 Geo. Mason L. Rev. 321 (1997); Jerry Hausman, Gregory Leonard & J. Douglas Zona, *Competitive Analysis with Differentiated Products*, 34 Annales d'Économie et de Statistique 159 (1994); Gregory J. Werden, *Simulating the Effects of Differentiated Products Mergers: A Practical Alternative to Structural Merger Policy*, 5 Geo. Mason L. Rev. 363 (1997); Gregory J. Werden & Luke M. Froeb, *The Effects of Mergers in Differentiated Products Industries: Logit Demand and Merger Policy*, 10 J.L. Econ. & Org. 407 (1994).

25 The hypothetical monopolist test can be framed in terms of a critical demand elasticity, i.e., the greatest value of the elasticity of demand faced by the hypothetical monopolist for which a given price increase, e.g., 5%, would be imposed. *See* Gregory J. Werden, *Demand Elasticities in Antitrust Analysis*, 66 Antitrust L.J. 363, 387-90 (1998).

merger and induce further increases by the merged firm.[26] Excluding a non-merging product from a simulation is equivalent to assuming its price does not react, so the exclusion is of no consequence if its price would react very little because there is only slight diversion to it from the merging firms' products.

The primary determinants of unilateral price effects from mergers involving differentiated consumer products are the pre-merger price–cost margins of competing products combined by the merger and the diversion ratios between pairs of products combined. Nothing relating to non-merging products, or the relevant market as a whole, is as important. Consequently, information relating only to the merging firms is sufficient for a first-order approximation to a merger simulation. Because reactions of non-merging products are omitted, such an approximation necessarily understates the predictions of a full merger simulation. The understatement is insignificant if no competing products combined by the merger have significant diversion ratios to individual non-merging products.[27]

The relevant market is more important in assessing unilateral effects in other competitive settings in which information relating only to the merging firms is not sufficient for a first-order approximation to a merger simulation. For example, competition in many industries is analyzed as a series of auctions.[28] Often, the analysis posits an English auction, in which bidding proceeds in rounds and all bidders know the current winning bid. As bidding proceeds in an English procurement auction, a bidder drops out when the low bid reaches its cost, and the auction ends when the second-lowest-cost bidder drops out. Consequently, the winning bid is the cost of the second-lowest-cost bidder.[29] A merger affects the winning bid only when the merging firms are two lowest cost bidders, and the effect of the merger is then to increase the winning bid to the cost of the third-lowest-cost bidder. Information relating to just the merging firms could be sufficient to identify which customers would be harmed by a merger, but whether the merger harms those customers significantly is determined by information on non-merging rivals.

An English auction model often is used to analyze unilateral effects when the competitive process entails a separate price determination for each customer or procurement. In such a competitive setting, diversion ratios do not exist.[30] Diversion arises when some customers switch to other products in the face of an across-the-board price increase, but in a competitive setting characterized by English auctions, the price for each customer is perfectly tailored, and every contract is awarded to the supplier with the lowest cost for that procurement. Reliably simulating mergers with an auction model requires calibration using real-world data, and critical

---

26 Merger effects are not unilateral only when non-merging firms play no part in them. What makes an effect "unilateral" is that non-merging competitors react to price changes after a merger just as they did before it. *See* Gregory J. Werden & Luke M. Froeb, *Unilateral Competitive Effects of Horizontal Mergers*, *in* Handbook of Antitrust Economics 43, 45-46 (Paolo Buccirossi ed., 2008); Gregory J. Werden, *Unilateral Competitive Effects of Horizontal Mergers I: Basic Concepts and Models*, *in* ABA Section of Antitrust Law, 2 Issues in Competition Law and Policy 1319, 1321-22 (W. Dale Collins ed., 2008).

27 Quantitative tools other than simulation are used to assess unilateral effects with differentiated products. *See* Gregory J. Werden & Luke M. Froeb, *Choosing among Tools for Assessing Unilateral Merger Effects*, 7 Eur. Competition J. 155 (2011). Upward Pricing Pressure ("UPP") is a first-order approximation ignoring the reactions of non-merging products. *See id.* at 161-62; Joseph Farrell & Carl Shapiro, *Antitrust Evaluation of Horizontal Mergers: An Economic Alternative to Market Definition,* 10(1) B.E. J. Theoretical Econ. (Policies & Persp.) art. 9 (2010), *available at* http://faculty.haas.berkeley.edu/shapiro/alternative.pdf. Compensating Marginal Cost Reductions ("CMCRs") are the reductions in marginal costs from merger synergies exactly offsetting the merged firm's incentive to raise prices. Reactions of non-merging products' prices do not affect the CMCRs because the merged firm does not change its prices when its marginal costs are reduced by the amount of the CMCRs. *See* Werden & Froeb, *supra*, at 159-60; Gregory J. Werden, *A Robust Test for Consumer Welfare Enhancing Mergers among Sellers of Differentiated Products*, 44 J. Indus. Econ. 409 (1996).

28 The enforcement agencies have often analyzed competition using an auction model. When the agencies presented 23 case studies of unilateral effects analysis, six were analyzed as auctions. *See* U.S. Dep't of Justice & Fed. Trade Comm'n, Commentary on the Horizontal Merger Guidelines 25-36 (2006), *available at* http://www.justice.gov/atr/public/guidelines/215247.pdf. On predicting the price effects of mergers in auction settings, *see* Gregory J. Werden & Luke M. Froeb, *Unilateral Competitive Effects of Horizontal Mergers II: Auctions and Bargaining*, *in* ABA Section of Antitrust Law, 2 Issues in Competition Law and Policy 1343, 1344-51 (W. Dale Collins ed., 2008).

29 The result would be the same in a second-price sealed-bid procurement auction, which awards the contract to the low bidder at the price of the second-lowest bid. In such an auction, the optimal strategy for each bidder is to bid its cost.

30 *See* Gregory J. Werden, *Unilateral Effects from Mergers: The* Oracle *Case*, *in* Handbook of Research in Trans-Atlantic Antitrust 1, 7-8 (Philip Marsden ed., 2006).

statistics include the frequency with which each merging firm wins the auction. But such frequencies are undeterminable until a specific class of auctions has been defined, and that class is the relevant market.

Finally, consider unilateral effects with homogeneous producer goods not sold though auctions.[31] This competitive setting sharply contrasts with that of differentiated consumer products with regard to the determinants of unilateral price effects from mergers. With differentiated consumer products, the supply-side of the market plays a minor role, but with homogeneous producer goods, the supply-side plays the lead role. In assessing the merger of two producers of good *A*, accurately accounting for supply by rival producers of *A* is essential. And if customers view good *B* a close substitute for *A*, accurately accounting for supply by producers of *B* is almost as important. Delineating the relevant market for good *A*, thus, is a necessary predicate to assessing the likely unilateral effects of the merger.[32] Omitting *B* from a merger simulation would cause an underestimate of the price effects of the merger, the magnitude of which could be quite substantial.

IV. The Relevant Market in Sherman Act Conduct Cases

The Sherman Act protects the competitive process,[33] and assessing a potential violation of either Section 1 or Section 2 of the Act usually requires identifying the specific competitive process at issue, i.e., delineating the relevant market. Exceptions to this general rule are cases involving conduct, such as cartel activity, invariably corrupting the competitive process, or conduct similar enough to be subject to quick-look analysis. In other Sherman Act cases, any determination of whether the challenged conduct harms the competitive process is apt to be highly unreliable without first delineating the relevant market to identify the particular competitive process at issue.[34]

Harms to the competitive process conventionally are divided into the categories of collusion and exclusion. For collusion cases subject to the rule of reason, the relevant market is apt to be a foundation for the

---

31 Several distinct types of unilateral effects are possible with homogeneous producer goods, and different models are used to assess these different effects. The comments here apply with all of these models.

32 Professor Kaplow mistakenly asserts that the merger can be satisfactorily assessed with a model including only good *A* by applying a formula relating the market average price–cost margin to concentration and demand elasticity. *See* Kaplow, *supra* note 18, at 370. That formula, however, is correct only if producers of good *A* interact with each other in a particular way and do not interact at all with producers of other goods. *See* Gregory J. Werden, *The Relevant Market: Possible and Productive*, Antitrust L.J. Online, April 2014, at 6, http://www.americanbar.org/content/dam/aba/publishing/antitrust_law_journal/at_alj_werden.pdf. Moreover, the formula cannot be used to predict merger price effects even when it is correct. *See* Werden & Froeb, *supra* note 26, at 47; Werden, *supra* note 26, at 1327.

33 *See, e.g.*, Cohlmia v. St. John Med. Ctr., 693 F.3d 1269, 1280 (10th Cir. 2012) ("The primary concern of the antitrust laws is the corruption of the competitive process . . ." (internal quotation omitted)); Cascade Health Solutions v. PeaceHealth, 515 F.3d 883, 902 (9th Cir. 2008) (noting that the Supreme "Court has often reinforced the principle that the antitrust laws' prohibitions focus on protecting the competitive process"); Grappone, Inc. v. Subaru of New England, Inc., 858 F.2d 792, 794 (1st Cir. 1988) (Breyer, J.) ("the antitrust laws exist to protect the competitive process itself"); Morrison v. Murray Biscuit Co., 797 F.2d 1430, 1437 (7th Cir. 1986) (Posner, J.) ("The purpose of antitrust law, at least as articulated in the modern cases, is to protect the competitive process . . .").

34 *See* Donald F. Turner, *The Role of the "Market Concept" in Antitrust Law*, 49 Antitrust L.J. 1145, 1145 (1980) ("The key of antitrust is some economic assessment, and you cannot judge the potential impact of a variety of practices without some sense of what the market is in which that conduct is taking place."). The classic statement of Section 1's rule of reason describes an inquiry likely to be impossible without the relevant market:

> The true test for legality is whether the restraint imposed is such as merely regulates and perhaps thereby promotes competition or whether it is such as may suppress or even destroy competition. To determine that question the court must ordinarily consider the facts peculiar to the business to which the restraint is applied; its condition before and after the restraint was imposed; the nature of the restraint and its effect, actual or probable. The history of the restraint, the evil believed to exist, the reason for adopting the particular remedy, the purpose or end sought to be attained, are all relevant facts.
>
> Bd. of Trade of the City of Chicago v. United States, 246 U.S. 231, 238 (1918).

competitive effects assessment. The potential of a restraint to harm the competitive process is first evaluated by examining its coverage in relation to the relevant market and to the conduciveness of the market's structure to collusion. The impact of a restraint either in fostering collusion, or in promoting a procompetitive objective, is then evaluated by examining how it affects competition in the relevant market.

Consider an exchange of price information, which could facilitate pricing coordination, but would not be condemned in the United States (in sharp contrast to the EU) without carefully examining its impact. Competitive concerns might be dispelled by finding that the exchange involves a just small part of a vast relevant market, or aggregated data across many relevant markets. Concerns also might be dispelled by finding that the relevant market is not structurally conducive to pricing coordination. If neither finding is made, the inquiry turns to how participants in the exchange use the information and the resulting impact on competition. The exchange could be procompetitive if the information is used to monitor and forecast demand, but anticompetitive if it is used to assess compliance with suggested price increases. In each of the foregoing inquiries, the perspective of the relevant market can be invaluable.

In all exclusion cases, it is essential to distinguish harm to a competitor from harm to competition,[35] and distinguishing between the two can be infeasible without the perspective of the relevant market. For example, when a single plaintiff is being foreclosed, the perspective of the relevant market is critical in determining whether its foreclosure is apt to harm the competitive process generally.

Courts typically begin assessing potentially exclusionary conduct under Section 1 by considering the defendant's market share, which requires delineating the relevant market. This step is labeled a market power inquiry, but its purpose is to determine the potential of the conduct to harm competition,[36] and the Supreme Court mandated use of the relevant market in assessing market impact,[37] but not in assessing market power.[38] The proportion of the relevant market subject to a restraint is the best simple screen for its potential to harm competition. A firm with a 50% share of the relevant market is apt to possess market power, but its adoption of a restraint affecting just 10% of its sales almost certainly would not have the potential to harm the competitive process.

Application of the rule of reason under Section 1 is a structured inquiry into a restraint's impact on the competitive process.[39] The "plaintiff bears the initial burden of showing . . . an adverse, anticompetitive

35 *See, e.g.*, NYNEX Corp. v. Discon, Inc., 525 U.S. 128, 135 (1998) (holding that the plaintiff "must allege and prove harm, not just to a single competitor, but to the competitive process, *i.e.*, to competition itself"); Atl. Richfield Co. v. USA Petroleum Co., 495 U.S. 328, 338 (1990) ("The antitrust laws were enacted for the protection of *competition*, not *competitors*." (internal quotations omitted)); Agnew v. NCAA, 683 F.3d 328, 335 (7th Cir. 2012) ("[T]he plaintiff must allege, not only an injury to himself, but an injury to the market as well." (internal quotations omitted)); Broadcom Corp. v. Qualcomm Inc., 501 F.3d 297, 308 (3d Cir. 2007) ("Conduct that merely harms competitors, however, while not harming the competitive process itself, is not anticompetitive.").

36 *See* FTC v. Ind. Fed'n of Dentists, 476 U.S. 447, 460 (1986) ("the purpose of the inquiries into market definition and market power is to determine whether an arrangement has the potential for genuine adverse effects on competition"); *Agnew*, 683 F.3d at 337 ("[A] plaintiff's threshold burden under the Rule of Reason analysis involves the showing of a precise market definition in order to demonstrate that a defendant wields market power, which, by definition, means that the defendant can produce anticompetitive effects.").

37 *See* Tampa Electric Co. v. Nashville Coal Co., 365 U.S. 320, 327 (1961) ("[T]he threatened foreclosure of competition must be in relation to the market affected."); United States v. E. I. du Pont de Nemours & Co., 353 U.S. 586, 593-96 (1957) (declaring that "the relevant market is a necessary predicate to" finding a vertical merger unlawful because "[s]ubstantiality can be determined only in terms of the market affected," and holding the acquisition unlawful because it foreclosed a substantial share of the relevant market).

38 The use of the relevant market in a threshold inquiry into market power originated in the lower courts well after the Supreme Court mandated the use of the relevant market. *See* Mark R. Patterson, *The Market Power Requirement in Antitrust Rule of Reason Cases: A Rhetorical History*, 37 San Diego L. Rev. 1 (2000).

39 *See* NCAA v. Bd. of Regents of the Univ. of Okla., 468 U.S. 85, 104 (1984) (Under the rule of reason, "the criterion to be used in judging the validity of a restraint on trade is its impact on competition."); Nat'l Soc'y of Prof'l Eng'rs v. United States, 435 U.S. 679, 688 (1978) (The rule of reason "focuses directly on the challenged restraint's impact on competitive conditions."); Gregory J. Werden, *Antitrust's Rule of Reason: Only Competition Matters*, 79 Antitrust L.J. 713 (2014).

effect within the relevant . . . market."[40] The plaintiff typically attempts to discharge its burden through a structural analysis that begins with delineating the relevant market. As one court explained, "[i]n analyzing agreements that are not *per se* violations of the antitrust laws, the court is looking to whether the action complained of has the potential for genuine adverse effects on competition, and this analysis usually involves an inquiry into market definition and market power."[41] As an alternative, courts have xpressed openness to direct evidence of anticompetitive effects,[42] bypassing any consideration of the relevant market, but one court has rightly warned that: "Economic analysis is virtually meaningless if it is entirely unmoored from at least a rough definition of a product and geographic market."[43]

Exclusion cases under Section 2 demand much the same market analysis as exclusion cases under Section 1. A major difference, however, is that a firm cannot violate Section 2 without possessing, or threatening to obtain, monopoly power. Economists have tools for detecting the exercise of market power without considering market share, but antitrust law distinguishes between monopoly power and mere market power,[44] and economists have no satisfactory tools for detecting monopoly power.[45] Courts hold that monopoly power requires both a dominant share of the relevant market[46] and barriers providing substantial protection from new competition.[47] The relevant market obviously is required in determining whether a defendant possesses a dominant share, and the relevant market could be just as important in evaluating conditions of entry because such conditions could differ substantially between two close substitute products or locations.

---

40 *In re* Insurance Brokerage Antitrust Litig., 618 F.3d 300, 315 (3d Cir. 2010) (internal quotations omitted). *See also* Ark. Carpenters Health & Welfare Fund v. Bayer AG, 604 F.3d 98, 104 (2d Cir. 2010) ("[T]he plaintiff bears the initial burden of showing that the defendant's conduct had an *actual* adverse effect on competition as a whole in the relevant market." (internal quotations omitted)); Schering-Plough Corp. v. FTC, 402 F.3d 1056, 1065 (11th Cir. 2005) ("The plaintiff bears an initial burden of demonstrating that the alleged agreement produced adverse, anti-competitive effects within" the relevant markets.); Tanaka v. Univ. of S. Cal., 252 F.3d 1059, 1063 (9th Cir. 2001) ("The plaintiff bears the initial burden of showing that the restraint produces significant anticompetitive effects within a relevant market." (internal quotations omitted)).

41 Lie v. St. Joseph Hosp. of Mount Clemens, 964 F.2d 567, 569 (6th Cir. 1992) (internal quotations omitted).

42 *See, e.g.*, FTC v. Ind. Fed'n of Dentists, 476 U.S. 447, 460-61 (1986) ("[P]roof of actual detrimental effects, such as a reduction of output, can obviate the need for an inquiry into market power, which is but a surrogate for detrimental effects." (internal quotations omitted)); Todd v. Exxon Corp., 275 F.3d 191, 206 (2d Cir. 2001) ("If a plaintiff can show that a defendant's conduct exerted an actual adverse effect on competition, this is a strong indicator of market power."); Dickson v. Microsoft Corp., 309 F.3d 193, 219 (4th Cir. 2002) ("While anticompetitive effect is often proven through analysis of the relevant market definition and market power, it can also be proven through *actual* anticompetitive effects."); Toys "R" Us v. FTC, 221 F.3d 928, 937 (7th Cir. 2000) ("One [way to prove market power] is through direct evidence of anticompetitive effects.").

43 Republic Tobacco Co. v. N. Atl. Trading Co., 381 F.3d 717, 737 (7th Cir. 2004).

44 *See* Eastman Kodak Co. v. Image Tech. Servs., Inc., 504 U.S. 451, 481 (1992) ("Monopoly power under § 2 requires, of course, something greater than market power under § 1.").

45 Courts occasionally suggest that monopoly power can be proved directly. *See, e.g.*, Broadcom Corp. v. Qualcomm Inc., 501 F.3d 297, 307 (3d Cir. 2007) ("The existence of monopoly power may be proven through direct evidence of supracompetitive prices and restricted output."). But no court has drawn the roadmap to such proof. Persistent high profits, measured in an economically correct manner, could prove monopoly power, but accounting data do not lend themselves to constructing economically correct measures of profit. *See* George J. Benston, *Accounting Numbers and Economic Values*, 27 Antitrust Bull. 161 (1982); Franklin M. Fisher & John J. McGowan, *On the Misuse of Accounting Rates of Return to Infer Monopoly Profits*, 73 Am. Econ. Rev. 82 (1983); Paul A. Grout & Anna Zalewska, *Profitability Measures*, *in* ABA Section of Antitrust Law, 1 Issues in Competition Law and Policy 373 (W. Dale Collins ed., 2008).

46 *See, e.g.*, Kolon Indus. Inc. v. E.I. DuPont de Nemours & Co., 748 F.3d 160, 174 (4th Cir. 2014) ("Although there is no fixed percentage market share that conclusively resolves whether monopoly power exists, the Supreme Court has never found a party with less than 75% market share to have monopoly power."); Colo. Interstate Gas Co. v. Natural Gas Pipeline Co. of Am., 885 F.2d 683, 694 n.18 (10th Cir. 1989) ("While the Supreme Court has refused to specify a minimum market share necessary to indicate a defendant has monopoly power, lower courts generally require a minimum market share of between 70% and 80%."); Exxon Corp. v. Berwick Bay Real Estate Partners, 748 F.2d 937, 940 (5th Cir. 1984) (per curiam) ("[M]onopolization is rarely found when the defendant's share of the relevant market is below 70%.").

47 *See, e.g.*, United States v. Dentsply Int'l, Inc., 399 F.3d 181, 188-89 (3d Cir. 2005) ("in evaluating monopoly power, it is not market share that counts, but the ability to *maintain* market share" (internal quotations omitted)); United States v. Microsoft Corp., 253 F.3d 34, 82 (D.C. Cir. 2001) (en banc) ("a firm cannot possess monopoly power in a market unless that market is also protected by significant barriers to entry"); *Colo. Interstate Gas*, 885 F.2d at 695-97 (finding a firm lacked monopoly power because its "ability to charge monopoly prices will necessarily be temporary").

V. Conclusion

The relevant market concept has been attacked by practitioners who distain economic models[48] and academics who embrace them without reservation.[49] The former understand neither the utility of partial-equilibrium analysis nor how antitrust productively uses economic models. The latter understand neither the limitations of modeling nor how economic models productively use the relevant market. Antitrust needs the relevant market to separate active competitive forces directly and immediately affecting economic performance from all other competitive forces of potential interest. Economics pioneered this separation over a century ago and employs it today in every model of competition. Modern competitive analysis has not supplanted the relevant market, but rather only clarified and refined its analytic function.

---

48 *E.g.*, Edwin S. Rockefeller, The Antitrust Religion 42-44 (2007); Rowe, *supra* note 5, at 1540-53, 1563-69.

49 *E.g.*, Kaplow, *supra* note 18; John E. Lopatka, *Market Definition?*, 39 Rev. Econ. Org. 69, 86 (2011) ("Proponents of UPP analysis [*see* note 27 *supra*] now argue that the [relevant market] is an impediment to sound analysis—a distraction from what really matters in a particular category of mergers.").

The Merger Guidelines and Market Definition: A Powerful Tool for Merger Analysis*

LAWRENCE J. WHITE

lwhite@stern.nyu.edu

Robert Kavesh Professor of Economics, Stern School of Business, New York University

Abstract

Merger analysis has been one of the crucial components of modern antitrust enforcement in the United States. Since 1982 the "horizontal merger guidelines", which were first developed and promulgated by the US Department of Justice and subsequently adopted by the US Federal Trade Commission (and by other federal agencies that have merger review authority), have provided a robust and powerful analytical framework for defining markets for merger analysis.

---

* This article is an extended version of the presentation that was made by the author at the "Global Antitrust Economics" Conference that was organized by Concurrences Review at the George Mason University School of Law and the Law & Economics Center on May 29, 2015.

I. Introduction

Merger analysis has been one of the crucial components of modern antitrust enforcement in the United States. Because the goal of modern antitrust policy has been to enhance the efficiency of the US economy, and because the unbridled exercise of *market* power generally is antithetical to that efficiency, the definition[1] of *markets* has been central for much of antitrust enforcement.[2]

Since 1982[3] the "horizontal merger guidelines" ("HMGs"), which were first developed and promulgated by the US Department of Justice ("DOJ") and subsequently adopted by the US Federal Trade Commission ("FTC") (and by other federal agencies that have merger review authority), have provided a robust and powerful analytical framework for defining markets for merger analysis.

This essay will provide a brief overview of that market definition paradigm and its strengths and limitations.

II. The Basic Paradigm

The basic idea that underlies the market definition paradigm in the HMGs—which was first enunciated by the DOJ in 1982[4]—is that merger policy should be aimed at preventing mergers that would create or enhance market power (in the absence of sufficiently offsetting efficiencies). Accordingly, the first step should be to establish the boundaries of a "market"—i.e., the collection of sellers[5] that might be able to exercise market power—and then determine whether the proposed merger might allow the merging firms (or the collection of firms more generally in the specified market) to exercise market power as a consequence of the merger.[6]

The "mechanism" for this determination has come to be described as "the hypothetical monopolist" or "SSNIP" test. In conducting this test, the analyst asks: if (starting from current circumstances) all of the firms in a tentatively designated market were to be combined into a single decision-making unit (a hypothetical monopolist), could that combined entity increase its profits by achieving a "small but significant nontransitory increase in price" ("SSNIP")?[7] If yes, then that collection of firms constitutes a relevant market for merger analysis (and the smallest such collection of sellers would usually be selected as the relevant market);[8] if no (because too many buyers would switch away to other sellers), then that

---

1 This sometimes referred to as "delineation."

2 The major exception has been enforcement against price fixing, where the "per se" approach has meant that market definition is largely irrelevant for enforcement (but may be relevant for the demonstration of harm and the consequent recovery of damages).

3 There was an earlier set of HMGs, which were promulgated by the DOJ in 1968. These HMGs did not embody a robust analytical framework for market definition and soon fell out of use for merger analysis purposes.

4 As Werden has pointed out, the basic idea was first developed by Adelman (Morris A. Adelman, *Economic Aspects of the Bethlehem Opinion*, 45 VA. L. REV. 684 (1959)). *See* Gregory J. Werden, *The 1982 Merger Guidelines and the Ascent of the Hypothetical Monopolist Paradigm*, 71 ANTITRUST L.J. 253, 254 (2003). At the time that the market definition paradigm was first developed at the DOJ in early 1982, no one there was aware of Adelman's earlier analysis.

5 Generally, it is the smallest group of such sellers that is the focus of the analysis. If the merger involves two or more firms that appear to be significant buyers, then comparable analyses should be applied to the potential exercise of market power by the buyers.

6 If, as is usually the case, the merging firms are each multi-product firms, then this analysis is necessary for each overlapping product.

7 The HMGs specify that 5% is the magnitude of the SSNIP that the enforcement agencies will usually use in their market definition analysis.

8 Notice that the determination of the relevant market focuses on the identification of sellers—since it is sellers that are the entities that could exercise the market power that antitrust policy cares about. The one exception arises if the sellers can practice significant price discrimination (market segmentation) toward a specific group of buyers; in that instance, that group could also be considered as a relevant market.

collection of sellers would not constitute a relevant market, and the sample of sellers would have to be expanded until the SSNIP criterion is satisfied.[9]

In essence, the SSNIP test guides the analysis toward finding the smallest market that is capable of being monopolized.

Once the relevant market has been delineated, the analysis turns to the subsequent steps for determining whether the proposed merger is likely to create or enhance market power. These steps include: measuring the existing concentration of the sellers in the relevant market; measuring the *pro forma* change in concentration that the merger would cause;[10] making a judgment about the conditions of entry by outside firms into the market, as well as the ease by which smaller firms might expand their outputs; measuring buyer concentration (which would be relevant for a market that involves business-to-business sales); assessing the nature of information availability among the sellers and buyers in the market; assessing the typical pricing or marketing practices by the firms in the market; assessing the degree of complexity in the quality and service dimensions of the product at issue; and assessing the antitrust history of the sellers in the relevant market.

Although the HMGs (and especially the market definition paradigm) were quite controversial at the time of their original introduction in 1982, they have stood the test of time, as they continue to be the basis for modern antitrust enforcement in the United States. And, in an important sense, they have met a "market test" in another important dimension: internationally. Most modern economies have competition laws and enforcement agencies,[11] and many of them have adopted merger policies that follow the basic insights of the HMGs.

III. Extending the Paradigm to Sellers of Differentiated Products

The basic "story" of the HMGs that was just summarized was originally developed in the shadow of traditional oligopoly theory, whereby the exercise of market power occurs because of the jointly coordinated behavior of the "few" sellers in a concentrated market.[12] In modern parlance, this is a theory of the "coordinated effects" of a merger, and it best applies to markets where there is little or no differentiation among the products that are being sold (i.e., commodities or homogeneous products). Although differentiated products could be covered—if there are few enough sellers of differentiated products, these sellers could

9 Any switching away by buyers in response to an increase in price could be toward sellers of the same product that are located in a different geographic area and/or toward sellers of a somewhat different product. The market definition paradigm thus encompasses both the concept of geographic markets as well as product markets.

10 The Herfindahl-Hirschman Index ("HHI")—which is computed by summing the squared market shares of all of the sellers in the relevant market—is generally the basis for measuring seller concentration.

11 As of 2009, the International Competition Network ("ICN")—an international association of competition agencies—had a membership of 104 competition agencies from 92 jurisdictions. *See* Int'l Competition Network, ICN Factsheet and Key Messages (April 2009), http://www.internationalcompetitionnetwork.org/uploads/library/doc608.pdf.

12 It is important to remember that this traditional oligopoly theory of coordinated behavior need not involve explicit communication and collusion. Instead, the coordination could be entirely implicit: Each seller (among a few sellers) realizes that the joint interest of the group is best served by refraining from fiercely competitive behavior and realizes that the other (few) sellers are likely to realize this as well. This type of mutual recognition of joint interests is more likely to happen when the numbers of sellers are fewer, when the barriers to entry are higher and/or the difficulties of expansion by smaller sellers are greater, when it is easier for each seller to monitor the actions of the other sellers, etc. It is no accident that this list of conditions tracks closely the subsequent stages of the HMGs' analysis after the relevant market has been delineated.

coordinate a post-merger price increase (and recall that one of the follow-on criteria involves the complexity of quality and service)—there is an important aspect to differentiated products that is not captured by the coordinated effects analysis: the strength of buyers' preferences among the differentiated products.

That gap was closed in the 1992 revision to the HMGs, which explicitly addressed the following issue:[13] To the extent that there are buyers that currently buy from one of the two merging firms and whose runner-up preference is for the products of the other merging firm, then the competitive check that each firm pre-merger exerted toward the other firm with respect to these customers dissolves, and the profit-maximizing result for the post-merger firm is to raise its prices. This result is, of course, exacerbated if the post-merger firm can identify who these specific first choice/second choice ("trapped") customers are and practice price discrimination by raising prices to them only; but the principle applies more broadly: So long as there are any first choice/second choice customers, the merged firm will be less constrained as a consequence of the merger and will find it worthwhile to raise its prices—at least by a little bit.

It is important to note that this post-merger price effect does not require the cooperation of, or coordination with, any other firms that sell similar products (but see the "repositioning" issue that is discussed in the next paragraph). In this sense, any direct price consequence of the merger involves "unilateral effects" (i.e., the actions only of the merged firm) and not the "coordinated effects" of the original analytical framework contained in the HMGs.

The size of this post-merger price increase will be determined by the relative number of such "trapped" customers and the strength of their preferences for the merging firms' products, as compared with their preferences for the products of other (competing) firms. Further, in the spirit of "entry," to the extent that other firms (that produce and sell somewhat related products) reposition their products so as to make those products more appealing (post-merger) to these (previously) trapped customers, this will temper any post-merger price increase. Finally, merger-resultant efficiencies that reduce the relevant marginal costs will also temper any price increases and could produce price decreases.

Although, as was mentioned above, this type of analysis was explicitly included in the HMGs in 1992, it was the "major" revision to the HMGs in 2010 that caused these "unilateral effects" to be seen as the primary analytical approach for the HMGs.[14] However, the seeds of the 2010 emphasis on unilateral effects were thoroughly planted in 1992 and, in that sense, the 2010 revision to the HMGs was less radical than is sometimes claimed.

With respect to market definition, however, there is one consequence of the unilateral-effects approach that has been under-appreciated: If the unilateral-effects analysis identifies a significant (e.g., at least 5%) price increase that seems likely (at least, prior to any consideration of potential efficiencies) to follow from a merger, then *this finding directly identifies a relevant market*. In essence, this finding indicates—with respect to these two products—that this will be a "two-to-one" merger or a "merger to monopoly." This notion of monopoly may not be quite the same as the market power that a local electric utility could exercise if it was released from the restraints of local rate regulation. Nevertheless, if a 5% increase in price is the criterion, then for merger analysis purposes the merger has created a monopoly.

In this context, the hypothetical monopolist (SSNIP) paradigm is redundant and unneeded, and could be a distraction. If a proposed merger involves firms that sell products that clearly are in the differentiated

---

13 *See, e.g.*, Janusz Ordover & Robert Willig, *Economics and the 1992 Merger Guidelines: A Brief Survey*, 8 REV. INDUS. ORG. 139 (1993).

14 *See, e.g.*, Joseph Farrell & Carl Shapiro, *Antitrust Evaluation of Horizontal Mergers: An Economic Alternative to Market Definition,* 10(1) B.E. J. THEORETICAL ECON. (POLICIES & PERSPS.) art. 9 (2010).

(rather than homogeneous) category, then the analysis ought not to start with the hypothetical monopolist (SSNIP) pursuit. Instead, the likely overlapping products of the two firms should be identified, and then customer preferences should be ascertained (e.g., through surveys and/or through econometric studies that try to capture how customers responded when the relative prices of the two firms' products have varied in the past[15]).

Of course, even if significant unilateral effects are not found, it is possible that a coordinated effects analysis would be worthwhile, and a SSNIP approach would be necessary. But the analysis should start with the focus on the overlapping products and the possibility of first choice/second choice customers, and only subsequently (if needed) should the SSNIP approach be employed.

This unilateral effects approach with respect to the definition of a relevant market—i.e., the finding that the merging parties could (post-merger) raise their prices by at least 5% automatically defines those two products as constituting a relevant market—may seem inconsistent with the summary offered above: that a relevant market (for the purposes of merger analysis) is one that can be monopolized. But, if the enforcement agencies are prepared to define a significant exercise of market power as a (post-merger) price increase of 5%, then a "market" in which this can happen—whether that market has been delineated through a SSNIP process or through the analysis of first choice/second choice customers—is the relevant market for merger analysis.

IV. Monopolization Cases (or Abuse of Dominance)

Market definition is needed in antitrust cases that involve allegations of non-merger behavior that has enhanced the market power of a seller that already has market power. The alleged behavior may involve predatory acts—typically involving price-cutting but can also extend to expansions of capacity—and/or vertical restraints (such as tying or exclusive dealing arrangements) that may raise rivals' costs. In order for these actions to be linked to a motive—e.g., the seller was trying to extend its market power, was trying to ward off entry that would have threatened its market power, and/or was trying to discipline a challenger so as to keep its dominance—the existing market power of the seller must be demonstrated. And, of course, this means that a market (within which the seller has been exercising the market power that has been enhanced/extended/protected, etc.) must be delineated.

Unfortunately, the SSNIP paradigm generally will *not* provide a useful guide for delineating a relevant market in such circumstances. The reason for this is important to grasp: The SSNIP paradigm is a test with respect to a *prospective* hypothetical monopolization of a market, whereas the usual allegation in these monopolization cases is that the defendant already has market power.[16]

15 Such econometric studies are usually the basis for predictions of the price consequences of a differentiated-products merger and are usually described as "merger simulation" analyses.

16 At least part of the reason why this issue continues to plague analysis in this area may well be terminological: Economists often (loosely) describe market power (or monopoly power) as the "power to raise price" above competitive levels. *See, e.g.*, Lawrence J. White, *Market Power and Market Definition in Monopolization Cases*, *in* 2 Issues in Competition Law and Policy 913 (Wayne D. Collins ed., 2008). Unfortunately, this is too loose. Economists' standard "workhorse" monopoly model shows that a monopoly can *maintain* its price (and profits) above competitive levels. The "raise price" part is relevant only to describe the process of transition, whereby a competitive industry might transform itself into a monopoly through merger (and thus the hypothetical monopolist exercise of the HMGs) or the formation of a cartel. The failure to remember this distinction may well be part of the reason why the SSNIP test is proposed for monopolization cases.

Further, the posing of a SSNIP test with respect to an actually functioning enterprise should generally be a useless exercise. All profit-maximizing firms should generally be setting their prices at levels such that further increases in prices would be unprofitable.[17] Thus, asking the SSNIP question—could the XYZ Corporation profitably achieve a small but significant and nontransitory increase in price from its current price level?—should generally yield the answer "No," *regardless of whether the firm is truly embedded in a highly competitive market environment or the firm truly possesses market power.*

The failure to realize the uselessness of this question in this context has come to be described as the "Cellophane fallacy," which stems from the decision in *United States v. E.I. du Pont de Nemours & Co.*, 351 U.S. 377 (1956). In that case, the DOJ alleged that cellophane was a relevant market and that du Pont, as the producer of about 75% of the cellophane in the United States (there was only one other producer), possessed market power. Du Pont, in its defense, claimed that the relevant market was all flexible packaging materials (which included glassine, polyethylene, waxed paper, aluminum foil, brown wrapping paper, etc.), within which du Pont held less than a 20% market share, and that du Pont had to meet the competition that was offered by the firms that produced these other materials and, thus, it did not possess market power.

A US Supreme Court majority (four to three in favor, with two abstentions), as well as the (earlier) federal district court judge, sided with du Pont on this issue. In so doing, the Court neglected to realize that some other basis for the determination of the relevant market was needed: If (somehow) the relevant market really was cellophane, then (of course) du Pont would maintain a sufficiently high price of cellophane so that it was facing (at least some) competition from those other flexible packaging materials. Thus, by using the "facing competition" criterion, the Court would never be able to entertain the possibility that cellophane actually was the relevant market.

Unfortunately, there has been little progress since 1956 to help courts or litigants define relevant markets in these kinds of cases. As was just argued, a SSNIP test generally will not offer any help. The one exception has been pointed out by Werden: If a monopolization case involves a *prospective* action by the defendant (and the plaintiff is, say, asking for an injunction), then—just as for merger analysis where a SSNIP test is useful for delineating a relevant market for judging whether a *proposed* merger may create or enhance market power—a SSNIP test may be useful in delineating a relevant market for judging whether a *proposed* action (by the defendant) may create or enhance market power.[18] Although such instances may exist, they are not common in contrast to the situation where the plaintiff is complaining that past actions (e.g., predatory actions or vertical restraints) have harmed the plaintiff and that the defendant undertook the actions to defend or expand its *existing* market power.

Prior to the early 1980s, evidence on profit rates might have helped in the demonstration of the existence of market power and thus (at least indirectly) helped in the delineation of the relevant market. As was noted above, the standard economic model of monopoly indicates that a monopolist should earn higher profits than would the firms in a competitive industry.[19] However, a potent critique by economists in the early 1980s of the use of a company's accounting profits for judgments about what are normal or

---

17 An exception would be firms (e.g., electricity distribution companies) that are subject to some form of profit-limiting governmental regulation.

18 *See* Gregory J. Werden, *Market Delineation under the Merger Guidelines: Monopoly Cases and Alternative Approaches*, 16 Rev. Indus. Org. 211, 212-13 (2000).

19 Indeed, in their critique of the district court opinion in *du Pont*, Stocking and Mueller point out that du Pont's profits in its cellophane business were substantially higher than its profits in its rayon business, where its market position was roughly comparable to its claim regarding its market position for flexible packaging materials. *See* George W. Stocking & Willard F. Mueller, *The Cellophane Case and the New Competition*, 45 Am. Econ. Rev. 29, 60-62 (1955).

competitive profits and what are above-normal profits (and thus, arguably, an indication of market power) has largely eliminated the use of profits for this type of determination.[20]

Even if profit data are not available or are considered unreliable, price data may be helpful in delineating a relevant market. Suppose that a plaintiff in a monopolization case claims that the relevant market for the sale of "widgets" is local metropolitan areas. Suppose further that good data on the relative prices of widgets and seller concentration and other relevant variables (e.g., the costs of selling widgets in those areas) can be collected across a suitable sample (i.e., a "cross-section" sample) of these metropolitan areas. In that case, statistical (typically, econometric) studies may be able to demonstrate that (controlling for other things) higher widget prices are positively associated with seller concentration in these metro areas—i.e., that widgets that are sold in metro areas constitute a market that can be monopolized. And this finding could then be used to support the plaintiff's claim as to the relevant market (within which the defendant's market share and other relevant market-based data could be used to examine the possibility that the defendant possessed market power and that its actions were intended to extend/defend/enhance that market power).

Such data are sometimes available—e.g., for airline markets, where decades of studies have generally established that city-pairs constitute relevant markets.[21] However, it is far from clear—even in an era of "big data"—whether the example of airline data will prove to be the rule, or the exception, for efforts to delineate markets in monopolization cases.

In sum, with the ruling out of the SSNIP test as a general paradigm for monopolization cases, the general unsuitability of accounting profit data, and the uncertainty as to whether suitable price data may be available, a robust paradigm for market definition that can be used in monopolization cases is badly needed.[22] This remains one of the most important tasks for modern antitrust theorists.

---

20 *See, e.g.*, George J. Benston, *Accounting Numbers and Economic Values*, 27 Antitrust Bull. 161 (1982); Franklin M. Fisher & John J. McGowan, *On the Misuse of Accounting Rates of Return to Infer Monopoly Profits*, 73 Am. Econ. Rev. 82 (March 1983). However, it is this author's belief that it was Microsoft's large profits that it was earning from the sales of its Windows operating system in the 1980s and 1990s that helped convince the District Court for D.C. and the Circuit Court of Appeals for the D.C. Circuit that operating systems for personal computers was a relevant market and that Microsoft possessed market power within that market.

21 For discussions of two monopolization cases that alleged predatory behavior—United States v. AMR Corp., 140 F. Supp. 2d 1141 (D. Kan. 2001) and Spirit Airlines, Inc. v. Nw. Airlines, Inc., 431 F.3d 917 (6th Cir. 2005)—*see* (respectively), Aaron S. Edlin & Joseph Farrell, *The* American Airlines *Case: A Chance to Clarify Predation Policy*, *in* The Antitrust Revolution 502 (John E. Kwoka, Jr. & Lawrence J. White eds., 4th ed. 2004); Kenneth G. Elzinga & David E. Mills, *Predatory Pricing in the Airline Industry:* Spirit Airlines v. Northwest Airlines, *in* The Antitrust Revolution 307 (John E. Kwoka, Jr. & Lawrence J. White eds., 6th ed. 2014).

22 Nelson and White have proposed a paradigm for market definition in monopolization cases that they describe as a SSN*D*P: "Would the preservation of the allegedly foreclosed [or predated upon] competitor or group of competitors have led to a small but significant nontransitory *decrease* in price (SSN*D*P) by the defendant?" *See* Philip B Nelson & Lawrence J. White, *Market Definition and the Identification of Market Power in Monopolization Cases: A Critique and a Proposal* 4 (NYU Working Paper No. EC-03-26, 2003),

http://papers.ssrn.com/sol3/papers.cfm?abstract_id=1292646&download=yes. For further details, *see* White, *supra* note 16. That this proposed paradigm has not been put into wide practice leads one to believe that—at least so far—it has not "passed a market test" and that a suitable paradigm is still needed.

V. Conclusion

The HMGs have clearly met a market test: The original paradigm was introduced in 1982, and (with suitable modifications and updates) the HMGs remain as the tool that is used—by the enforcement agencies, by other litigants, and by the courts—for modern merger analysis in the United States. Further, similar analytical tools have been adopted by enforcement agencies abroad.

Within the HMGs, the market definition paradigm—the hypothetical monopolist and the SSNIP test—has also passed a market test, although this paradigm is best reserved for mergers where coordinated effects are considered the primary route through which a proposed merger might create or enhance market power.

However, the SSNIP test does have its limitations: It is generally unneeded for mergers where unilateral effects are considered the primary route through which a merger might create or enhance market power. And it is generally unsuitable—indeed, it is likely to be dangerously misleading—for market definition in monopolization (or abuse of dominance) cases. It cannot be stated too often that a robust paradigm for market definition is still needed for this latter category of antitrust cases.

Editors' Bios

Douglas H. Ginsburg was appointed to the United States Court of Appeals for the District of Columbia in 1986 by President Ronald Reagan. He served as Chief Judge from 2001 to 2008. In addition to remaining with the Court as senior status circuit judge, Judge Ginsburg is a full-time faculty member at the George Mason University School of Law. Prior to his appointment to the DC Circuit, Judge Ginsburg was a professor of law at Harvard University, served as Assistant Attorney General of the Justice Department's Antitrust Division, and was Administrator of the Office of Information and Regulatory Affairs at the Office of Management and Budget.

Joshua D. Wright is the Director of the Global Antitrust Institute and holds a courtesy appointment in the Department of Economics. On January 1, 2013, the US Senate unanimously confirmed Professor Wright as a member of the Federal Trade Commission (FTC), following his nomination by President Obama to that position. He rejoined George Mason University School of Law as a full-time member of the faculty in Fall 2015. Professor Wright is a leading scholar in antitrust law, economics, intellectual property, and consumer protection, and has published more than 70 articles and book chapters, co-authored a leading antitrust casebook, and edited several book volumes focusing on these issues. Professor Wright also served as Co-Editor of the Supreme Court Economic Review, a Senior Editor of the Antitrust Law Journal,and an Editor of the International Review of Law and Economics. Professor Wright's teaching and interests include Antitrust, Contracts, Law and Economics, the intersection of Intellectual Property and Antitrust, and Quantitative Methods. Wright previously served the Commission in the Bureau of Competition as its inaugural Scholar-in-Residence from 2007 to 2008, where he focused on enforcement matters and competition policy. Wright's return to the FTC as a Commissioner marked his fourth stint at the agency, after having served as an intern in both the Bureau of Economics and Bureau of Competition in 1997 and 1998, respectively. Wright received his JD from UCLA in 2002, his PhD in economics from UCLA in 2003, and graduated with honors from the University of California, San Diego in 1998. He is a member of the California Bar.

Nicolas Charbit, PhD, LLM, was admitted to the Paris Bar in 1994. He had been practicing from 1994 to 2005 in the field of competition law with strong emphasis on cartels and network industries. Nicolas wrote for French and international legal journals and taught these subjects at university and business schools. He has published several books and papers on EC and French competition law. He has completed a PhD thesis at Paris Sorbonne University on antitrust law and the public sector. He is the founding partner of the Institute of Competition Law and has been the Editor of Concurrences Review since 2004.

Elisa Ramundo graduated cum laude from the University of Bologna Law School. She holds an LLM at the University of Chicago Law School. Over the years, Elisa has gained professional experience in European, US, and International antitrust law. She worked at the US FTC (Washington, DC) as an international antitrust consultant, and in a tier-one Italian law firm as an associate in the competition practice (Rome/Milan). She also served as a legal intern at the European Commission (Brussels). Elisa is currently the Managing Editor of Concurrences Review and is based in New York City.

Duy D. Pham obtained his JD from the University of Ottawa, graduating cum laude, and his LLM from the Georgetown University Law Center, graduating with Distinction and on the Dean's List. He was previously a Summer and Articling Student at a top Canadian law firm. He is currently an Associate Editor with Concurrences Review and an International Antitrust and Trade Consultant with the World Bank.

Contributors' Bios

Pierre-Yves Cremieux, Analysis Group Managing Principal, specializes in antitrust, industrial organization, and econometrics. He has consulted to law firms, corporations, and government agencies and has testified in jury and bench trials as well as arbitrations and administrative proceedings on behalf of clients in the United States and abroad. He has worked on some of the largest US cartel and monopolization cases of the last decade on issues ranging from liability to damages and class certification. Dr. Cremieux has published a number of academic articles on antitrust issues including global enforcement, regression analysis in antitrust litigation, and class certification. His research has also been cited in leading media outlets including *The Wall Street Journal and Forbes*. Dr. Cremieux is an adjunct professor at the University of Quebec at Montreal and lectures on global antitrust at the Yale School of Management.

John D. Harkrider has worked on some of the largest and most significant antitrust matters over the last 20 years including Ball's $6.8 billion offer to acquire Rexam, PLC, Thermo Fisher Scientific's $13.6 billion pending acquisition of Life Technologies Corporation, Google's $12.5 billion acquisition of Motorola Mobility, Google's Standard Essential Patent decree, MasterCard's IPO, AT&T's $67 billion acquisition of Bell South and AT&T Wireless' $41 billion acquisition of Cingular. An accomplished litigator, he has litigated four DOJ/FTC merger challenges, two private merger challenges, and was retained by the DOJ in its investigation and suit to prevent WorldCom's acquisition of Sprint, the largest merger ever challenged by the DOJ. He also litigated a number of Sherman One and Two matters in District Courts throughout the United States as well as the Second, Seventh, Ninth, and Tenth Circuits. He has won a number of awards, including in 2013, American Lawyer Litigator of the Week and Global Competition Review Matter of the Year, and in 2012, Global Competition Review Lawyer of the Year and Global Competition Review Merger Control Matter of the Year. He is ranked by Chambers, who has called him "an extremely intelligent attorney with formidable understanding of business and finance" as well as a lawyer who "has the best understanding of not only how to build a case, but also how to break it."

Keith N. Hylton, a William Fairfield Warren Professor of Boston University and Professor of Law at Boston University School of Law, joined the BU Law faculty in 1995 after teaching for six years and receiving tenure at Northwestern University School of Law. He is a prolific scholar who is widely recognized for his work across a broad spectrum of topics in law and economics, including tort law, antitrust, labor law, intellectual property, civil procedure, and empirical legal analysis. He has published four books and more than 100 articles in numerous law and economics journals, and serves as a contributing editor of the *Antitrust Law Journal*, co-editor of *Competition Policy International*, and editor of the Social Science Research Network's *Torts and Products Liability Law Abstracts*. He is a former chair of the Section on Torts and Compensation Systems of the American Association of Law Schools, a former chair of the Section on Antitrust and Economic Regulation of the American Association of Law Schools, a former director of the American Law and Economics Association, a former Secretary of the American Bar Association Labor and Employment Law Section, a former member of the editorial board of the *Journal of Legal Education*, current chair of the Law and Economics section of the American Association of Law Schools, and a current member of the American Law Institute.

Francine Lafontaine is the William Davidson Professor of Business Economics and Public Policy at the Ross School of Business, and Professor, Department of Economics, both at the University of Michigan. She served as Director of the Bureau of Economics at the US Federal Trade Commission from Fall of 2014 to December 2015. She returned to the University in January 2016 to take on the role of Associate Dean for Faculty and Research at the Ross School of Business. Her research focuses on contracting, especially contracts used in distribution, and the study of vertical restraints and vertical integration decisions. She also conducts research on the effect of contracting practices on firm performance, and examines issues surrounding business creation and survival in retail and small-scale service industries. Her research (with various co-authors) has been published in, among others, the *American Economic Journal – Applied*, the *American Economic Journal – Micro*, the *Journal of Industrial Economics*, the *Journal of Law and Economics*, the *Journal of Law, Economics and Organization*, the *Journal of Political Economy*, and the *RAND Journal of Economics*. She co-authored *The Economics of Franchising* with Roger D. Blair, published by Cambridge University Press, and edited *Franchise Contracting and Organization* for Edward Elgar. She was the President of the Industrial Organization Society from 2010 to 2012, having served as its Vice-President from 2008 to 2010. From 1997 until joining the FTC, she was a co-editor at the *Journal of Economics & Management Strategy*. She was also co-editor at the *Journal of Law, Economics, & Organization* from 2006 to 2012, and served as Associate Editor at the *RAND Journal of Economics* from 1997 to 2007. In addition to her PhD in economics from the University of British Columbia in Canada, Prof. Lafontaine holds an honorary Doctorate from the Université de Rennes 1, in Rennes, France. Prof. Lafontaine also has worked as an expert witness in legal disputes and antitrust cases relating to franchising and contracting.

Carlos Mena-Labarthe was appointed Chief Prosecutor (*Autoridad Investigadora*) at the Federal Economic Competition Commission of Mexico (COFECE) in October 2014 for a four year term. He has worked for the Mexican competition authority since 2007. He was the head of the Planning, Institutional Relations and International Affairs Unit where he coordinated the efforts to create the first Strategic Plan and the first Annual Plan of the agency and represented the Commission before Congress for the discussions of a new law in 2014. He was director of cartels and interstate commerce from 2007 to 2008 and from 2008 to September 2013, he was the Director General of the Cartel Investigations Division. Mr. Mena has extensive experience in the fields of regulation and competition law. Prior to joining the Mexican competition authority he worked for national and international law firms in their competition law practice. He was an international Fellow of the Federal Trade Commission of the United States of America. He has also received training in investigations and management of enforcement agencies at the European Commission (DGComp), the Canadian Competition Bureau and the Australian Competition and Consumer Commission. He has written for numerous publications and is the editor and co-author of five books on competition law, regulation and public policy. Mr. Mena holds a Master's Degree in Business Law with honors from the Attorney Bar Association in Madrid, Spain; a Master's Degree in Regulation from the London School of Economics and Political Science with distinction for the best overall performance; and a degree with first-class honors in Law from ITAM.

Maureen K. Ohlhausen was sworn in as a Commissioner of the US Federal Trade Commission on April 4, 2012, to a term that expires in September 2018. Prior to joining the Commission, Ohlhausen was a partner at Wilkinson Barker Knauer, LLP, where she focused on FTC issues, including privacy, data protection, and cybersecurity. Ohlhausen previously served at the Commission for 11 years, most recently as Director of the Office of Policy Planning from 2004 to 2008, where she led the FTC's Internet Access Task Force. She was also Deputy Director of that office. From 1998 to 2001, Ohlhausen was an attorney advisor for former FTC Commissioner Orson Swindle, advising him on competition and consumer protection matters. She started at the FTC General Counsel's Office in 1997. Before coming to the FTC, Ohlhausen spent five years at the US Court of Appeals for the DC Circuit, serving as a law clerk for Judge David B. Sentelle and as a staff attorney. Ohlhausen also clerked for Judge Robert Yock of the US Court of Federal Claims from 1991 to 1992. Ohlhausen graduated with distinction from George Mason University School of Law in 1991 and graduated with honors from the University of Virginia in 1984. Ohlhausen was on the adjunct faculty at George Mason University School of Law, where she taught privacy law and unfair trade practices. She served as a Senior Editor of the Antitrust Law Journal and a member of the American Bar Association Task Force on Competition and Public Policy. She has authored a variety of articles on competition law, privacy, and technology matters.

William H. Page is the Marshall M. Criser Eminent Scholar at the University of Florida Levin College of Law. He has authored over 50 articles and book chapters on antitrust law and economics. He is co-author (with John Lopatka) of *The Microsoft Case: Antitrust, High Technology, and Consumer Welfare* (University of Chicago Press 2007) and is the co-author and editor (with Joseph Bauer and John Lopatka) of *Kintner's Federal Antitrust Law* (Lexis-Nexis). He was a trial attorney with the Antitrust Division of the US Department of Justice and has taught at Boston University and at Mississippi College, where he was the J. Will Young Professor of Law. He received his JD summa cum laude from the University of New Mexico and his LLM from the University of Chicago.

Daniel L. Rubinfeld is Professor of Economics Emeritus at the University of California, Berkeley and Professor of Law at New York University School of Law. He served from June 1997 through December 1998 as Deputy Assistant Attorney General for Antitrust in the US Department of Justice. Professor Rubinfeld is the author of a variety of articles relating to antitrust and competition policy, law and economics, law and statistics, and public economics and of two textbooks, *Microeconomics and Econometric Models and Economic Forecasts*. He has consulted for private parties and for a range of public agencies including the US Federal Trade Commission, the Antitrust Division of the Department of Justice, and the State of California Attorney General's Office. In the past he has been a fellow at the National Bureau of Economic Research ("NBER"), the Center for Advanced Studies in the Behavioral Sciences, and the John Simon Guggenheim Foundation. He received an honorary doctorate from the University of Basel. Professor Rubinfeld teaches seminars in antitrust law and economics and in quantitative methods, and is a member of the American Academy of Arts and Sciences and a research fellow at the NBER.

Loren Smith specializes in the application of economic and econometric tools to antitrust and competition matters. His experience includes the analysis of horizontal and vertical mergers, vertical restraints, pay-for-delay, and exclusionary conduct. Since joining Compass Lexecon in 2013, he has assisted clients with government investigations and private litigation in industries that include retail, healthcare, consumer products, and intermediate goods. Prior to joining Compass Lexecon, Smith worked at the US Federal Trade Commission as a staff economist. While at the FTC, he supported significant settlement negotiations such as SCI's acquisition of the Alderwoods Group in 2006 and major litigation such as FTC v. Watson, co-authored a report to Congress, and provided technical assistance and training to competition agencies in South Africa, Brazil, and Hungary. Smith has taught microeconomics and econometrics at the University of Virginia and Johns Hopkins University, and his research has been published in academic journals that include the *Journal of Applied Econometrics* and the *Journal of Economics and Management Strategy*. Smith received a PhD in economics from the University of Virginia in 2006.

Maria Stoyadinova is a Vice President of Compass Lexecon. She has experience consulting on a number of merger and acquisition cases in the food, retail, medical equipment, and information technology sectors. She has also been involved in a variety of litigation and antitrust matters, including breach of contract, price fixing, and intellectual property disputes in the telecommunications, advanced fibers, office supply, and pharmaceutical industries. Previously, Stoyadinova worked as an Associate at LECG, a Managing Analyst at the Compass Lexecon Los Angeles office and a Consultant in the Poverty Reduction and Economic Management division at the World Bank. Maria holds an MA with honors from the Johns Hopkins School of Advanced International Studies, with concentrations in International Law and International Economics.

Gregory J. Werden has worked in the Antitrust Division of the US Department of Justice since 1977 on a wide array of cases and policy matters. Among the policy matters were enforcement guidelines relating to collaboration among competitors, intellectual property, international operations, and mergers. He assisted in the preparation of over 70 amicus briefs filed with the Supreme Court, and since 1985 worked on all appeals in Department of Justice civil antitrust cases. Werden has also authored more than 150 scholarly publications on antitrust policy and related topics, including approximately 30 on the relevant market and how it is delineated.

Lawrence J. White has been with New York University Leonard N. Stern School of Business for more than 35 years. His primary research areas of interest include financial regulation, antitrust, network industries, international banking, and applied microeconomics. Professor White has published numerous articles in the *Journal of Business*, *Journal of Economic Perspectives*, *Journal of Economic Literature*, *Journal of Political Economy*, *American Economic Review*, *Review of Economics and Statistics*, *Quarterly Journal of Economics*, and other leading journals in economics, finance, and law. He is the author of *The S&L Debacle: Public Policy Lessons for Bank and Thrift Regulation*, among other books, and he is the co-editor (with John Kwoka) of the 6th edition of *The Antitrust Revolution*. He contributed chapters to both of the NYU Stern books on the financial crisis—*Restoring Financial Stability and Regulating Wall Street*. He is the co-author (with Stern's Viral Acharya, Matthew Richardson, and Stijn Van Nieuwerburgh) of *Guaranteed to Fail: Fannie Mae, Freddie Mac, and the Debacle of Mortgage Finance*.

Concurrences Review

Concurrences is a print and online quarterly peer reviewed journal dedicated to EU and national competitions laws. It has been launched in 2004 as the flagship of the Institute of Competition Law in order to provide a forum for academics, practitioners and enforcers. The Institute's influence and expertise has garnered interviews with such figures as Christine Lagarde, Bill Kovacic, François Hollande and Margarethe Vestager.

CONTENTS

More than 15,000 articles, print and/or online. Quarterly issues provide current coverage with contributions from the EU or national or foreign countries thanks to more than 1,200 authors in Europe and abroad. Approximately 25 % of the contributions are published in English, 75 % in French, as the official language of the General Court of justice of the EU; all contributions have English abstracts.

FORMAT

In order to balance academic contributions with opinions or legal practice notes, Concurrences provides its insight and analysis in a number of formats:

- Forewords: Opinions by leading academics or enforcers
- Interviews: Interviews of antitrust experts
- On-Topics: 4 to 6 short papers on hot issues
- Law & Economics: Short papers written by economists for a legal audience
- Articles: Long academic papers
- Case Summaries: Case commentary on EU and French case law
- Legal Practice: Short papers for in-house counsels
- International: Medium size papers on international policies
- Books Review: Summaries of recent antitrust books
- Articles Review: Summaries of leading articles published in 45 antitrust journals

BOARDS

The Scientific Committee is headed by Laurence Idot, Professor at Panthéon Assas University. The International Committee is headed by Frederic Jenny, OECD Competition Comitteee Chairman. Boards members include Bruno Lasserre, Mario Monti, Howard Shelanski, Richard Whish, Wouter Wils, etc.

ONLINE VERSION

Concurrences website provides all articles published since its inception, in addition to selected articles published online only in the electronic supplement.

WRITE FOR CONCURRENCES

Concurrences welcome spontaneous contributions. Except in rare circumstances, the journal accepts only unpublished articles, whatever the form and nature of the contribution. The Editorial Board checks the form of the proposals, and then submits these to the Scientific Committee. Selection of the papers is conditional to a peer review by at least two members of the Committee. Within a month, the Committee assesses whether the draft article can be published and notifies the author.

e-Competitions
Antitrust Case Laws e-Bulletin

e-Competitions Bulletin

CASE LAW DATABASE

e-Competitions is the only online resource that provides consistent coverage of antitrust cases from 55 jurisdictions, organized into a searchable database structure. e-Competitions concentrates on cases summaries taking into account that in the context of a continuing growing number of sources there is a need for factual information, i.e., case law.

- 12,000 case summaries
- 2,600 authors
- 55 countries covered
- 24,000 subscribers

SOPHISTICATED EDITORIAL AND IT ENRICHMENT

e-Competitions is structured as a database. The editors make a sophisticated technical and legal work on all articles by tagging these with key words, drafting abstracts and writing html code to increase Google ranking. There is a team of antitrust lawyers – PhD and judges clerks - and a team of IT experts. e-Competitions makes comparative law possible. Thanks to this expert editorial work, it is possible to search and compare cases.

PRESTIGIOUS BOARDS

e-Competitions draws upon highly distinguished editors, all leading experts in national or international antitrust. Advisory Board Members include: Sir Christopher Bellamy, Ioanis Lianos (UCL), Eleanor Fox (NYU), Damien Géradin (Tilburg University), Barry Hawk (Fordham University) Fred Jenny (OECD), Jacqueline Riffault-Silk (Cour de cassation), Wouter Wils (DG COMP), etc.

LEADING PARTNERS

- Association of European Competition Law Judges: The AECLJ is a forum for judges of national Courts specializing in antitrust case law. Members timely feed e-Competitions with just released cases.
- Academics partners: Antitrust research centres from leading universities write regularly in e-Competitions: University College London, King's College London, Queen Mary University, etc.
- Law firms: Global law firms and antitrust niche firms write detailed cases summaries specifically for e-Competitions: Allen & Overy, DLA Piper, Jones Day, Norton Rose Fulbright, Skadden Arps, White & Case, etc.

The Institute of Competition Law

The Institute of Competition Law is a publishing company, founded in 2004 by Dr. Nicolas Charbit, based in Paris and New-York. The Institute cultivates scholarship and discussion about antitrust issues though publications and conferences. Each publication and event is supervised by editorial boards and scientific or steering committees to ensure independence, objectivity, and academic rigor. Thanks to this management, the Institute has become one of the few think tanks in Europe to have significant influence on antitrust policies.

AIM

The Institute focuses government, business and academic attention on a broad range of subjects which concern competition laws, regulations and related economics.

BOARDS

To maintain its unique focus, the Institute relies upon highly distinguished editors, all leading experts in national or international antitrust: Bill Kovacic, Mario Monti, Eleanor Fox, Barry Hawk, Laurence Idot, Fred Jenny, etc.

AUTHORS

3,800 authors, from 55 jurisdictions.

PARTNERS

- Universities: University College London, King's College London, Queen Mary University, Paris Sorbonne Panthéon-Assas, etc.
- Law firms: Allen & Overy, Cleary Gottlieb Steen & Hamilton, DLA Piper, Hogan Lovells, Jones Day, Norton Rose Fulbright, Skadden Arps, White & Case, etc.

EVENTS

More than 250 events since 2004 in Brussels, London, New York, Paris, Singapour and Washington, DC.

ONLINE VERSION

Concurrences website provides all articles published since its inception.

PUBLICATIONS

The Institute publishes Concurrences Journal, a print and online quarterly peer-reviewed journal dedicated to EU and national competitions laws. e-Competitions is a bi-monthly antitrust news bulletin covering 55 countries. The e-Competitions database contains over 12,000 case summaries from 2,600 authors.

www.ingramcontent.com/pod-product-compliance
Lightning Source LLC
LaVergne TN
LVHW072155150926
848178LV00011B/133